PRAHA PRAGUE PRAHA

Artěl Style

© 2007 by Karen Feldman
All rights reserved

Artěl Books
Prague – New York
www.artelstyle.com

PUBLISHER
Karen Feldman

EDITOR
Rob McQuilkin

GRAPHIC DESIGN
Beverly Joel, pulp, ink.

COPYEDITOR, ENGLISH &
INDEX
Scott Ross

COPYEDITOR, CZECH
Honza Dvořák

CARTOGRAPHER
Copyright © Touring Editore
srl, Milano.
All rights reserved

CARTOGRAPHER TRAM MAP
Robin Woods

HIPSTER GUIDE
Sarah Morris

FACT CHECKING
Sylvie Dejmková

TEL
+420 271 732 161
EMAIL
info@artelstyle.com

Printed in the Czech Republic

First Edition: May 2007
ISBN 978-0-9792-8560-8

First Edition

SPECIAL THANKS
Rob McQuilkin, William B.
Russell Jr., Kristýna Fialová,
Honza Dvořák, Daniela Beer,
Simona Pekárková, Magda
Hadačová, Sarah Morris,
Hilary St. Jonn, Adrian Barek,
and Scott Ross.

PHOTO CAPTIONS & CREDITS
Cover (background, top): Old
Town Square, c. 1930;
(background, bottom):
Charles Bridge, c. 1955;
(bottom): Porcelain Wellies
with Czech Blue Onion Motif,
photo by David A. Land,
2006

p. 4: Towers of Charles Bridge,
c. 1940

p. 22: Baroque arches by Týn,
c. 1940

p. 38–39: Czechoslovakian
WW II Commemorative
Painting, 1945

p. 40: Charles Bridge, c. 1955

p. 66: Toy store window in
Nové Město, c. 1962; (Source:
ČTK / Czech News Agency)

p. 130: State Organized
Hairdressing Show, Lucerna
Palace, 1966 (Source: ČTK /
Czech News Agency)

p. 160: The Pride of Žižkov –
Complete with Climbing
Faceless Babies

p. 184: Metro Escalator,
Muzeum Station, 1980 (photo
by Jaroslav Vebr)

Back cover: Škoda Felicia
Convertible at Karlštejn
Castle: 1959 (Source: Archive
of the History of the Škoda
Auto Company)

TABLE OF CONTENTS

Introduction

In October of 1994, I moved from San Francisco to Prague to oversee production at a startup shampoo company owned by an American— a position I was 100% unqualified for, other than basically being a trustworthy person. This was the start of my love affair with Prague. Four years later, I founded my own luxury crystal company, Artěl Glass. I've been in Prague ever since, and I now wholeheartedly think of this foreign capital as home. My decision to move here permanently was a most unexpected twist in my life, as I'd originally planned to stay for only a year.

Over the nearly 13 years that I've lived in Prague, the flow of visitors has been constant. Many have been people I know; others, friends of friends; and more than a handful have been people who simply managed to get my e-mail address through the very vaguest of connections. Each inquiry, however, brought the same request: a list of my personal must-see-and-do suggestions for their visit to Prague. Each time I answered an inquiry, I'd add some new information to a file I kept containing an ever-expanding list of shops, restaurants and often-overlooked sights, which I would send as an email attachment to my correspondent.

Look, everyone has a certain skill set; apparently, mine includes locating, and spending money on, fabulous finds that always seem to be worthy of purchase. Few things give me more pleasure than finding the perfect little something, be it a small trinket that I know someone will absolutely love, or an item that has been on my own 'must find' list for months. Needless to say, it's always broken my heart to hear those famous words, "there's nothing to buy in Prague," because I can assure you, based on personal experience (and the often sadly precarious balance of my checking account), this statement is absolutely *not true*. One of the primary purposes of this book, then, is to show you how to spend your money shopping in Prague, and I hasten to add that the bulk of these recommendations will be for Czech-made products.

Another one of my skills is gathering and sharing useful information, and over time I began to ponder the idea of wrapping up all of my Prague recommendations into a book that might fill a much-needed niche in the existing tour book market. As you can see, that's exactly what I ended up doing. You'll also notice that many of the photographs and illustrations included are vintage; this is proof of two things: 1. my love of "fabulous finds" and 2. some things never change— one of them, happily enough, being Prague's wonderful architecture.

This book is *not* intended as a comprehensive guide to Prague. Rather, I hope you'll find it a fun complement to the stodgier (and perhaps less materialistic) guides out there as you plan your visit to Prague.

It is inevitable that there will be oversights, for Prague is an ever-evolving city, and I will be more than receptive to comments and feedback that will help this guide stay up-to-date. Indeed, I've included an "Are You Satisfied?" form at the back of the book that can be submitted either by post or by visiting our website. I thank you in advance for taking the time to fill out and submit this form, as I will personally read every form that is sent in. Anyone whose suggestion is incorporated into our next edition will receive an updated copy of the book for free (so don't forget to leave your mailing address!).

Just To Clarify...

I personally visited *all* the shops, hotels (where I stayed for at least one night), restaurants, cafes, and sights in this book (OK, minus the helicopter and hot air balloon rides, which I just found out about recently). That is, every entry in this book is something I personally recommend, based on my own experience.

I did *not* receive any discounts, payments, or kickbacks in exchange for inclusion or a positive review in this book. Call me naïve, but I thought this was the norm until I started writing this book and began receiving offers and inquiries from various proprietors about how much I wanted them to pay. I turned all of them down in order to maintain objectivity, and I think it's important to share this fact with my readers.

BEFORE YOU GO

When To Go

Spring and autumn are my two favorite times of year in the Czech Republic. So, if at all possible, try to plan your trip for April/May or September/October. During the spring, the weather is ideal and the countryside is bursting with fruit-tree and chestnut blossoms, as well as amazing yellow fields of rapeseed. The autumn brings ideal temperatures along with the changing leaves. Summer, on the other hand, can be oppressively hot, which is especially unpleasant since most of the city does not have air-conditioning. Perhaps worse is the endless sea of other summer tourists. And while a snow-dusted Prague can be extremely charming if you're lucky enough to catch it, the days of winter are terribly short (with darkness falling around 4 pm), so there's not too much bang for your sightseeing buck...

National Holidays

January 1: New Year's Day: Anniversary of the establishment of the Czech Republic in 1993.

March/April—Easter Monday (Yes, Monday!): In the Czech Republic, Easter is celebrated on Monday, not on Sunday, as in other countries' traditions.

May 1: Labor Day

May 8: Liberation Day (Commemorating Prague's liberation from German occupation in May of 1945).

July 5: Cyril and Methodius Day

July 6: Master Jan Hus Day (A famous religious reformer whose teaching helped shape the Protestant Reformation).

September 28: Saint's Day of St. Wenceslas

October 28: Establishment of the First Republic of Czechoslovakia in 1918

November 17: Commemorating the Velvet Revolution of November 1989

December 24: Christmas Eve

December 25: Christmas

December 26: St. Stephen's Day

CHARLES BRIDGE IN WINTER, C. 1910–1920

Time Zone

Prague is on Central European Time, one hour ahead of GMT (Greenwich Mean Time)

London:	1 hour behind
New York:	6 hours behind
Los Angeles:	9 hours behind
Hong Kong:	7 hours ahead
Sydney:	8 hours ahead

What To Take

1. A copy of your passport!
Once you're here, leave your passport in a safe place within your hotel room. Never carry your passport around town; it's simply unnecessary, and the risk far outweighs the need.

2. Any Necessary Visa!
Be certain to check your country's particular travel requirements for visiting the Czech Republic well in advance of your departure. Countries within the European Union vary on requirements. Please do not assume that if you're fine to travel in Germany the same will necessarily hold true in the Czech Republic, or you may find yourself being turned away.

3. Electrical Adapters!
Should you bring a laptop computer or other appliances, you will need an adapter. The power supply in the Czech Republic is 220 volts and the sockets require a two-pin plug.

4. A small travel umbrella that can be carried around comfortably on a daily basis.

5. Comfortable walking shoes are also essential; cobblestones can be killers if you're not used to them!

One Last Suggestion:
Scan your Passport & Driver's License. Before you leave, scan a copy of your passport and driver's license and send the scans in an attachment to an email address you can access from anywhere. This way, should any unfortunate incidents occur—God forbid—you'll have something to work with.

Money

The currency in the Czech Republic is the Czech crown (koruna česká) and you will see this abbreviated as either Kč or CZK. For the purposes of this book, we will use the latter (CZK).

Notes are available in the following denominations: 50, 100, 200, 500, 1000, 2000, and 5000.

Coins are available in the following denominations: 1, 2, 5, 10, 20, and 50.

There are 100 Heller in 1 CZK; currently, only 50 Heller coins are available.

EXCHANGE RATE
At the time of writing (January 2007), the exchange rate was as follows:

28 CZK to €1
22 CZK to $1

Although the Czech Republic is a member of the European Union, it is not yet using Euros and probably won't be until 2012. Some stores, hotels and restaurants will accept Euros, but this is not at all the norm. The currency of everyday use remains the Czech crown.

BEFORE YOU GO
If you have an ATM card, there is really no need to exchange money before you arrive. However, if you'll feel safer having some of the local currency on hand, get about 2,000 CZK, as this will certainly cover all of your initial expenses when you arrive.

CREDIT CARDS AND DEBIT CARDS
Credit cards and debit

Everyday Items and How Much They Cost in Prague

ITEM	PRICE IN CZK	PRICE IN USD
Latte at Coffee Heaven	49 CZK	$2.22
Bottle of Coke	11 CZK	$0.50
Bottle of Mineral Water	11 CZK	$0.50
Beer .5 Liters	20 CZK	$0.90
The International Herald Tribune	100 CZK	$4.54
Public Transport Ticket	20 CZK	$0.90
Movie Ticket	159 CZK	$7.22
1 Liter of Gas	31 CZK	$1.40
1 Gallon of Gas	117 CZK	$5.33
McDonald's Cheeseburger	20 CZK	$0.90
Pint of Häagen-Dazs	149 CZK	$6.77
Snickers	11 CZK	$0.50

cards are widely accepted in Prague, so many of your expenses can be handled this way.

MasterCard and Visa are the most widely accepted cards, so be sure to have at least one of these if you plan to use credit cards as a method of payment.

ATM MACHINES
Known in the Czech Republic as *Bankomats*, ATMs are available throughout the city with an English language option, and you should have little difficulty using them for cash withdrawal.

CURRENCY EXCHANGE
Throughout Prague there are numerous options for the exchange of currencies. However, not all of them are wise choices.

Banks: Your best bet is an actual bank; Komerční banka at Na Příkopě 33 in Staré Město offers some of the lowest rates.

Hotels: Your hotel will most likely offer currency exchange, but rates will almost certainly be less than favorable.

Bureaux de Change: These operations are to be avoided. Though the rates they quote might seem fine, I assure you they will get you in some way, usually with commission rates that are exceptionally high.

Offers from random individuals on the street: Pay no attention to such people, as they are certainly up to no good. Just walk away briskly and refuse to engage in conversation.

Tele-Communications

MOBILE (CELL) PHONES
If you can't live without your cell phone, it might make sense to purchase one in the Czech Republic when you arrive. This is cheaper and easier than renting one from abroad. There are three main providers in the Czech Republic and Vodafone, for now, is the cheapest. You will need to purchase a phone at full price; (prices start at 1,250 CZK) and a SIM card including a number and credit for 200 CZK, 500 CZK or 1,000 CZK. You will be connected, with credit, for $65. The same phone can be used when you travel to other European countries; simply purchase a new local SIM card providing you with a local number and credit.

THE THREE LOCAL PROVIDERS
Vodafone
www.vodafone.cz

T-Mobile
www.t-mobile.cz

O2
www.o2.com

IMPORTANT TELEPHONE NUMBERS
Czech Country Code +420
Emergency 112
Ambulance 155
General Information 2444
Emergency Road Service 1230, 1240

POSTCARD SENT BY A CZECH PRISONER TO HIS LOVER IN PRAGUE, C. 1931

Pickpocketing And Crime

Its official: according to insurers in London, the Czech Republic, while basically an incredibly safe city to walk around in, has the highest number of claims from travelers who have been pick-pocketed.

Where do you need to be especially vigilant? Just about anywhere, to be perfectly honest—in trams, in the metro, on the Charles Bridge, in the gift shop at the Jewish museum, or even at that really sweet café. Should luck not be on your side, I've listed several police stations in Prague 1 and 2 (see p. 186), which will come in handy.

CZECHOSLOVAKIAN NATIONAL COAT OF ARMS, C. 1948

I Was Pick-Pocketed! Is It Worth My Time to File a Police Report?

If you want to file an insurance claim, or if a stolen item was purchased in the last 90 days with a credit card that offers a buyer's protection service, then it will probably be necessary for you to obtain a police report.

If you don't plan on filing a claim, don't bother going to the police; it's a waste of time and energy, as I can assure you they will *not* recover your belongings. As pick-pocketing is so prevalent in Prague, it can often take two or three hours to file a report. NOTE: If a stolen item was purchased with American Express, you should call first to see if a police report is necessary; they often waive this requirement.

Betcha Didn't Know

1. In 1823, fingerprints were first recognized as a form of identification by Jan Evangelista Purkyně, a Czech.

2. In 1841, the sugar cube was invented in the Czech Republic by Jakub Kryštof Rad.

3. In 1892, Daniel Swarovski, a Czech, invented a unique electrical device for machine-cut faceted beads and stones resembling precious gems, resulting in extremely sharp edges on each facet and causing a rainbow refraction and optical purity, which revolutionized the costume jewelry industry.

4. In 1907, classification of human blood into four groups (A, B, AB & O) was initiated by Jan

IVANA TRUMP, CZECH NATIVE, C. 1990
(source: WWW.CZSK.NET/ SVET/CLANKY/OSOBNOSTI/ TRUMPOVA.HTML)

Janský, a Czech.

5. In 1913, Baťa Shoes, the largest shoe manufacturer in the world, was started in the Czech Republic by Tomáš Baťa. As of 1985, it manufactured shoes in 61 countries, operated 92 plants and 6000 retail stores, and sold through 100,000 merchants in 115 countries. The

company makes a million pairs of shoes a day. If you want to visit the Baťa museum, however, you'll have to go to Canada, as the founder emigrated there before WWII.

6. Until WWII, Czechs drove on the left side of the street, just as in Great Britain. When Hitler invaded in 1939 he changed it to the right side. After the war ended, the Czechs never bothered to change it back again. As a result, if you go to the National Technical Museum you'll see several cars with steering wheels on the right versus the left hand side.

7. In 1949, Ivana Trump (maiden name Zelníčková) was born in the industrial town of Zlín. As an alternate member of the Czechoslovakian Olympic ski

LOOK, HE'S ON THE WRONG SIDE!
(TATRA 77 ADVERTISEMENT, C. 1930)

POHLED Z 21.BUDOVY NA ČÁST NÁMĚSTÍ PRÁCE - ZAČÁTEK 40.LET

ZLÍN, IVANA TRUMP'S HOMETOWN, C. 1940

(until 1971). They have since become highly collectible, and an annual rally is held in Hradec Králové, the manufacturer's hometown.

9. In 1961, the first modern gel-based contact lenses were invented by Otto Wichterle, a Czech, on a homemade apparatus using a child's building set.

10. In 1966, the plastic explosive Semtex was invented by Stanislav Brebera, a Czech.

11. In 2006, Czechs had the largest per capita beer consumption in the world, at 163.5 liters annually. The average Czech beer is .5 liters, so this equals 327 beers per person each year!

team in 1968, she defected to America and went on to marry "The Donald."

8. In 1953, Velorex, a Czech manufacturer, introduced a crazy little car that has been referred to as a "Flying Tent" due to the vinyl that was stretched over its cage structure. The Velorex has 3 wheels, 4 gears and an engine that can run backwards! This means you don't have a conventional reverse gear, but the handy option of 4 reverse speeds. Invalids received subsidies to buy these primitive but well-liked cars, which enjoyed a very long production run

VELOREX RALLY, C. 1965

GETTING AROUND

Getting To Prague

BY AIR

Prague's Airport, Ruzyně, is 19km (12 miles) northwest of the city center. There are two terminals, so if someone is meeting you at the airport, be certain to specify *which* terminal you will be arriving at.

The good news is that the airport is small, efficient and new. There are few airports in which you can land, go through passport control, collect your baggage and go through customs control in 30 minutes or less; happily, Prague is one of them. Both passport control and customs clearance are very informal, so you should ease through both without any problem. The only time I've ever been stopped at customs I was carrying large boxes, and even then it was easy to talk my way through it. If they do stop you they will request to see your passport.

The easiest and quickest way to get into town is by taxi. There are two firms at the airport that provide taxis: Airport Taxi (white cars) and Taxi AAA (yellow cars). I prefer Taxi AAA. Either firm should be able to quote you an approximate price in advance. A taxi ride to the center should be no more than 500 CZK, and an absolute maximum of 600 CZK. I live beyond the center in Vinohrady, and it's usually 550 CZK to my neighborhood, so yours should be less.

STATUE OF ST. WENCESLAS, OVERLOOKING WENCESLAS SQUARE

CZECH AIRLINES, C. 1955
(PHOTO COURTESY OF CZECH AIRLINES)

■ ■ ■ ■ ■ ■ ■ ■ ■ ■ ■ ■ ■ ■
ČEDOK
Na Příkopě 18, Prague 1,
Nové Město
www.cedok.cz
TEL 224 197 699 information,
224 447 106 reservations
HOURS Mon–Fri: 09:00–
19:00; Sat & Sun: 09:00–
14:00
METRO Můstek ● ●
TRAM 5, 8, 14 to Náměstí
Republiky

Two International Train Stations

■ ■ ■ ■ ■ ■ ■ ■ ■ ■ ■ ■ ■ ■
Hlavní nádraží–Main Station
Wilsonova 8, Prague 2,
Nové Město
METRO Hlavní nádraží ●
TRAM 5, 9, 26, to Hlavní
nádraží

■ ■ ■ ■ ■ ■ ■ ■ ■ ■ ■ ■ ■ ■
Nádraží Holešovice
39 Vrbenského, Prague 7,
Holešovice
METRO Nádraží Holešovice ●
TRAM 12, 25 to Nádraží
Holešovice

If you need local currency, there will be three *bankomats* (ATMs) after you have exited the sliding glass doors just beyond customs control. You will see them to your left (KB, Česká spořitelna, and ČSOB; any of which are fine to utilize).

BY TRAIN

Neither of Prague's main train stations is charming, welcoming, or easy. If you do plan to arrive by train, I would *highly* recommend that you have someone from your hotel meet you at the station for direct transfer.

On the upside, trains do run on time, are comfortable, and often provide a cheaper option than flying when traveling to nearby cities such as Berlin, Dresden, Munich or Vienna.

For longer trips to cities such as Budapest and Krakow that usually call for overnight trains, I recommend that you fly. ČSA (Czech Airlines) has daily flights to both cities. Overnight trains tend to arrive at an ungodly hour in the morning, and you're unlikely to score a good night's sleep, as the train starts and stops throughout the night with frequent passport checking. In short, it simply is not worth the money saved unless you happen to love trains, have a lot of time on your hands, or find yourself on a tight budget.

COUNTRY	CITY	JOURNEY TIME	TRAINS DAILY
Austria	Vienna	4.5 hours	7
Germany	Berlin	5 hours	7
	Dresden	2.5 hours	9
	Frankfurt	10 hours	1
	Hamburg	7.5 hours	4
	Munich	6 hours	3
	Nuremberg	5 hours	3
Hungary	Budapest	9 hours	2
Poland	Krakow	9 hours	2
	Warsaw	10 hours	2
Slovakia	Bratislava	5 hours	8

The easiest place in Prague to purchase train tickets and inquire about options is at the former state-run travel agency (and still the biggest one), ČEDOK.

■ ■ ■ ■ ■ ■ ■ ■ ■ ■ ■ ■ ■ ■
Information line for all rail travel–24 hours
TEL 221 111 122
English Spoken

EDUCATIONAL POSTER: *SAFETY IN THE STREETS* (PRAGUE, C. 1939)

Getting Around Prague

Prague is a very small city, and to be honest the most charming way to get around is on foot. Don't be fooled by all the metro stops, they are actually extremely close together. However, as you'll be doing *lots* of walking in Prague, there are definitely times when you'll want to utilize public transport (especially when going up the hill to the Prague Castle), and luckily, Prague has an excellent public transport system. As in New York City, it's the easiest, quickest and least expensive way to get around town. The system includes the metro, trams, buses, and even a funicular. Unless you go to the zoo or Troja Chateau (both of which involve a bus) you'll probably only utilize the metro and trams during your visit.

The systems are extremely simple, and with a bit of common sense you should not experience any problems.

NOTE: I've included the names of the nearest metro and/or tram-stop for every listing in this book to make finding your destination as simple as possible.

If you do plan to use public transport during your visit, I highly recommend that you get a Travel Pass, as it will save you lots of time fiddling with single tickets or seeking them out.

Tickets

SINGLE TICKETS
14 CZK: single journey up to 20 minutes or 5 stops on the metro (no transfer)
20 CZK: travel on whole system up to 75 minutes or 90 minutes at night, including transfers

TRAVEL PASSES
24hr ...... 120 CZK
3 day ...... 220 CZK
7 day ...... 280 CZK
15 day ..... 320 CZK

Where to purchase single tickets and a day pass
Single tickets or a one day pass can be purchased from machines at all metro stations and some tram stops, *tabáks* (tobacco/newsstands throughout the city), hotels, information centers and windows at some metro stations.

Where to purchase travel passes longer than 1 day
These can only be purchased from windows

at metro stations or information offices; I find it easiest to pick them up at the Muzeum metro stop, which is open daily. Můstek metro stop is another good option, but this is open on weekdays only.

NOTE: Your name and date of birth must be written on the back of the pass.

Muzeum

HOURS Daily 07:00–21:00
TEL 222 623 777
Beneath McDonald's entrance

Můstek

HOURS Mon–Fri 07:00–18:00
TEL 222 646 350
Beneath Jungmannova entrance

VALIDATING TICKETS

Tickets are only valid once you have inserted them in the yellow validating machines visible as you pass into the metro or board a tram. Be sure to insert them face up in the direction the arrow is printed. These machines will then stamp your ticket with the date and time. For both single tickets and travel passes, you will only need to do this the very first time you use it. After that, simply keep it with you in case you're asked to show it.

For the metro, the machines will be on the platform immediately before you descend the escalator.

On trams and buses, the machines will be located close to the doors, and, should you be carrying a fresh ticket or pass, you will validate it once you're already on.

Public transport in Prague is based on a trust system, but from time to time, especially at metro stops like Můstek or Malostranská or on the 22 or 23 trams, plain-clothes inspectors with metal badges in hand will ask to see your validated ticket. If you fail to show one, you will be required to pay a fine (currently 400 CZK). If you refuse to pay this fine, the police will be called, and if you don't have money they will bring you to a *bankomat* so you can withdraw the cash to make the payment.

Metro

Hours: 05:00–24:00
Departures: During rush-hour, every 2 to 4 minutes; during off-peak-hours, every 4 to 10 minutes.

The Prague metro opened in 1975, and is made up of three lines designated by letters and colors:

Line A: Green
(Depo Hostivař – Dejvická)
Line B: Yellow
(Černý Most – Zličín)
Line C: Red
(Ládví – Háje)

Colors are far more memorable than letters, so moving forward I'll simply refer to them as the Green ●, Yellow ○ or Red ● lines.

Transfers are possible at three stations:
Muzeum: Green + Red Lines
Můstek: Green + Yellow Lines
Florenc: Yellow + Red Lines

Metro Stations are indicated by the following logo:

After you've decided where you want to travel and what color line you need to use to get there, you'll descend what is often a very steep and quick escalator to the platform, which will have two sides. You will need to determine which side of the platform is correct for your end destination. Signage clearly marks the station you're at, and by determining whether the stop you want to go to is to the right or left of the current station, you can establish which side to stand on.

PRAGUE METRO – LENINOVA, NOW DEJVICKÁ, C. 1974
(SOURCE: ARCHIVE DP)

MALÁ STRANA, C. 1971

Trams

Hours: 04:30–24:00
Night trams: 24:00–04:30

Part of Prague since 1900, trams are still the backbone of the public transport system. Not only are they incredibly efficient (they cover every nook and cranny of the city), they also give visitors the opportunity to sightsee along the way. The 22 and 23 tramlines are famous for the sights and vistas along their route, and if you take either of these to the Prague Castle, try to get a seat on the right side so you can enjoy the panoramic view of Prague on your way up the hill.

Although you'll see plenty of new trams, the bulk of Prague's fleet (thank goodness) dates back to a design that was introduced in 1961 and manufactured through 1973. Their wonderfully rounded design is now iconic, and a favorite feature may be the fiberglass seats mounted directly on heaters, a big plus during the blistering cold winter months. No trip to Prague would be complete without taking at least one ride on these classic (and sadly, soon to be extinct) tramcars.

Which side should I be on?
Simply knowing what number tram you need to take is *not* enough; you must know which direction you need to go in as well, as every tram stop will have two directions to choose from. To determine which side you should be on, you will need to look at the tram route list posted just under the sign showing which tram numbers are available at a given stop.

• The sign will list all the stops that the tram will make.
• The stop you're at will be highlighted.
• If the stop you want to go to is below the highlighted stop, you're on the correct side.
• If the stop you want to go to is above the highlighted stop, you're on the wrong side and must change.

To the left of your listed stop there will be a number signifying how many minutes it will take you to reach your destination. Shockingly, this information is almost always dead on. Don't ask me how they do this...

How long do I need to wait for my tram?
Once you have found your tram and the right direction, you can check the timetables, which are divided into weekdays and weekends, to see when the next tram will come. As noted above, this information is remarkably accurate.

Facts about the metro and tram:
• You are expected to offer your seat to pregnant women or the elderly.
• Children under 6 ride for free.

16

- Pets require a ticket unless they are in a bag.
- Luggage, if large, requires a 10 CZK ticket.

Taxis

Prague has a terrible reputation for surly taxi drivers grossly over-charging foreigners. If you hail a taxi or pick one up at a taxi stand, that reputation will be proven 100% accurate. A word to the wise: **DO NOT HAIL A TAXI!** It is more than likely *not* to go well. Instead, you should call a taxi—the firms listed below speak English and are trustworthy:

AAA Taxi
TEL 221 102 211, 729 331 133

City Taxi
TEL 233 103 310

If you're at a restaurant, by all means ask them to call you a taxi; they will not be put off by the request.

If you don't have a phone and desperately need to take a taxi, make sure to agree on a price before entering the taxi. If you're in the center of town (Prague 1 or 2) and going to another location within this area, the cost should *not* exceed 200 CZK.

FREQUENTLY ASKED QUESTIONS

Is there any reason why I should not fly ČSA (Czech Airlines)?
NO! ČSA is great. If at all possible I always try to fly ČSA, as their on-time performance is excellent and my bags have never been lost or delayed. They are also the only carrier to fly directly from the U.S. to Prague; it's a co-share with Delta but the airplane will be ČSA. The downside of this flight is that coach seating is *very* tight and the in-flight entertainment is not up-to-par with the other major carriers.

How much should I tip taxi drivers?
10%

How much should I tip at restaurants?
10%

Can I drink the water?
Yes, and you'll be absolutely fine, as was officially confirmed for me on a recent visit to the Prague Water Works. That said, you will not be able to order tap water at a restaurant. So try my two local favorites: Mattoni (I find it superior to both Perrier and San Pellegrino, hands down) or Bonaqua. In most grocery stores you will also find Aquila, another favorite of mine. But be sure to clarify whether you want it with bubbles or not, as flat water is not the norm. Should you purchase water in a store, you will need to be familiar with the following terms:
Perlivá: Sparkling; cap usually red
Neperlivá: Still; cap usually blue
Jemně perlivá: Medium Sparkling (my personal favorite); cap usually green

Can I negotiate prices in stores?
In antique stores absolutely, and I encourage you to try. In general you can expect to get about 10% off the marked price.

However, For general merchandise, is it not normal to bargain for or negotiate for a better price—even the price of a new car. I found this out in 2000 when I went to purchase my first car in the Czech Republic. I brought my office manager to help me negotiate. As I planned to pay for the car in cash, I figured we would be able to get a sizable discount. It became immediately apparent, however, that both the salesman and my office manager were flabbergasted at my request. Only after the fact did I learn that my behavior was not at all kosher. Still, as it was clear that I was not leaving without getting a discount, the poor salesman finally gave in, and in the end we managed to save about 7% off of the base price.

What is the local tax rate?
- Value Added Tax (VAT): 19%
- Corporate Tax: 24%
- Personal Tax: 12%–32%, depending on your salary
- Mandatory social and health insurance payments are based on an employee's gross salary; both the employer and employee contribute.
- Employer contributes social tax of 26% and health insurance of 9%
- Employee contributes social tax of 8% and health insurance of 4.5%

Is it worth it to go to see the Jewish cemetery?
I recommend you seek out an alternative way to view it, say, from the bathroom at the Decorative Arts Museum, which happens to border the cemetery and boasts the best view in town. ADDRESS: 17 listopadu 2, Staré Město, Prague 1

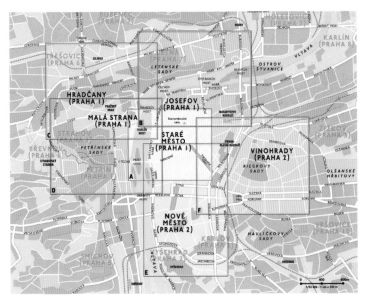

PRAGUE OVERVIEW

What are the various sections of town I am likely to visit?

MALÁ STRANA

Lesser Town—Located just below the castle, this is the oldest part of the city. Quaint, charming and historic, it's packed with Baroque and Renaissance architecture. Lots of hotels, restaurants, small shops and very expensive real estate (mostly inhabited by expats) fill this quarter, so there are very few businesses based here.

HRADČANY

Castle District—An outgrowth of Malá Strana, this is the crown jewel of Prague. The Prague Castle (Pražský hrad) presides over the neighborhood, along with several smaller palaces (most of them now

serving as museums) and beautiful gardens.

STARÉ MĚSTO

Old Town—This is the pulse of the city center: business, shopping, depart-ment stores, restaurants, expensive real estate, and where Czechs gather when a hockey championship is won.

JOSEFOV

The Jewish Quarter—This part of Old Town is where you'll find most of the Jewish sights as well as magnificent turn-of-the-century Art Nouveau buildings. These serve as apartments for rich Czechs and expats, as well as a few lucky Czechs who have lived there since communism and enjoy rent control. One family I know lives in a 110 sq. meter (1184 sq. ft.)

apartment on Pařížská (the fanciest street in town) and pays a mere 3,550 CZK ($161) for rent, not counting 3,600 CZK ($164) per month in utilities (it's such *a trial* having to heat a place with four-meter [13 ft.] ceilings).

NOVÉ MĚSTO

New Town—This section of town borders Old Town but is definitely a bit grittier and less touristy. The real estate is generally more affordable here, and you'll find lots of businesses, restaurants, and shops.

VINOHRADY

Vineyard District—A residential and business district, bordering Nové Město. Both Czechs and expats choose this area to live in, as it's much more "real" than downtown with a neighborhood feel, yet you're only one or two metro stops from the city center. The buildings are primarily Art Nouveau (although less glamorous than downtown) and Functionalist.

What is the difference between the blue and red numbers on the buildings, and which one should I reference to find an address?
The numbering system dates back to 1805:
Blue numbers are for street addresses. These are the numbers you care about. The lowest numbers are always closer to the river, a fact I only recently learned. **Red numbers** are used by the cadastre office (land registry) in each district in Prague. Each building

or house has a specific number in its district.

How much do you pay for your apartment? How big is it?
I pay $577 (12,700 CZK) a month for a very comfortable 1-bedroom apartment that is 75 sq. meters (807 sq. ft.). My rent represents what a Czech would pay versus what a foreigner generally would. A real bargain in comparison with New York City or London rents, but it's important to remember that the average salary in the Czech Republic is only $591 (13,000 CZK) a month; in other words, in proportion to salaries, rents are actually very high in Prague. This is somewhat resolved

by rent control. For example, I am the only foreigner in my building; all of the other tenants have been there since before the fall of communism, and their rent for the same size apartment is approximately $155 (3,410 CZK) per month. Currently, this is a big issue between landlords and government. It's almost impossible to make capital improvements (desperately needed after 50 years of neglect) when the income from rent does not even begin to cover the apartment itself, let alone the building.

Is it difficult to invest in real estate?
No, but as a foreigner you must have a business entity in the Czech Republic and submit an annual tax return. To set up such a business is not difficult and many firms have shell-companies already established to make the process very quick. The same firms offer annual management of the business entity (including tax returns) for a fee.

Investing in real estate in Prague has recently become rather chic; the most popular opportunities tend to be renovated apartments in Prague 1 and 2 that can be rented out. People actually buy them in bulk; I heard of one gentleman who bought 25 apartments in one day.

Another bonus is that property tax is basically nonexistent. For my country house in Southern Bohemia the annual tax is $10 (225 CZK). It surely costs the tax office more than that just to process the payment! This is a

BUILDING NUMBERS (BLUE VS. RED), KOŽNÁ STREET, 1910

huge advantage once you're an owner, but it also means that properties don't change hands often. If you purchase an apartment in a building that is not completely renovated, your neighbor's apartment is likely in total disrepair. While they may be unable to afford renovations, they also have little motivation to move or sell the apartment since it only costs them $10 annually to own. I was looking at houses in one neighborhood and none—that's right, not a single one—had changed hands since before WWII. Needless to say, I would not describe Prague as a buyer's market.

Nonetheless, if you're interested in such an investment, contact: Jason Cahill (jca@orco.cz) of Orco, www.orcogroup. com; they are one of the biggest firms in Prague offering new and renovated properties.

Where do all the Czechs disappear to on spring and summer weekends when the city seems so empty?
Virtually every Praguer has a country house (whether a modest *chata* or a more substantial *chalupa*), where they escape on spring and summer weekends. It was one of the few things under communism that the government was not interested in controlling. East Hampton it is *not*! However, there are advantages: roosters wake you in the morning, fresh farm eggs from the chicken coop across the way, apple and cherry blossoms each spring with a bounty of fruit

soon to follow, and *most* importantly, one of the most picturesque and unspoiled countrysides I've ever seen.

How did people get jobs under communism? And were they able to change those jobs or firms if they were not happy? Did people get fired? Did everyone earn the same amount?
There was 0% unemployment under communism, so getting a job was not a big accomplishment. At that time all high schools were specialized for some particular trade: Carpentry, glass making, or running a hotel, for example. Part of the course work included on-the-job training at a firm or organization, and after graduation, it was typical that one would work for that same firm.

Firing, as such, did not exist. This perhaps is not surprising, given that the goal was 100% employment. However, it was possible to be put in a lower position with less pay. There were only two reasons someone would ever be let go: for political reasons or if they were stealing "too much" (everyone stole). My co-worker Kristýna noted, "I don't think anyone bought a single brick; *everyone* stole under communism. If you look at people's *chatas* (country houses) you can tell where they were working at each point in their building process—the railways, say, or the glass industry—just based on the various materials utilized in the construction."

Job-hopping was not possible, so if you were

unhappy you were basically out of luck.

Salaries were not equal, but the differential was not based on talent or efficiency. Rather, salary differentials were dependent primarily on two things:
• If someone was a member of the communist party, they could be paid over double what a non-member in the same position would be paid. For example: 2,800 CZK vs. 1,100 CZK.
• True laborers, such as coal miners, were among the highest paid, which makes sense if you consider the philosophy behind communism.

What is that needle-like structure sticking up in the sky above Prague?
Among locals, the Žižkov TV Tower is the city's most hated building. Though not put into use until after the Velvet Revolution, it was intended, according to local lore, to jam foreign radio signals. At 216 meters (709 ft.) it's the tallest building in Prague. The communist regime unabashedly cleared away an old Jewish cemetery to make room for the structure, but was kind enough to leave a little swatch as a reminder of what used to be there. Perhaps this has something to do with the bronze statues of babies crawling up the tower. These were made by local artist David Černý, the same artist who did the upside-down horse in the Lucerna arcade, as if to mock a statelier (and more self-satisfied) notion of Czech national history.

I Only Have One Day In Prague, So What Should I Do?!

Start early!

• Have breakfast at **Café Savoy** (see p. 143).

Take tram numbers 22 or 23 to the **Prague Castle** area; sit on the right side to get a great view of the city when the tram goes up the hill to the castle. Get off at Pohořelec.

• Go see the ceiling fresco at **Strahov Monastery Library** this is simply amazing.

• Stroll around **Prague Castle**. Definitely pop into **St. Vitus Cathedral** (see p. 47).

• Have lunch at the **Lobkowicz Café** (see p. 154).

• Go view the collection at **Lobkowicz Palace** (see p. 46).

• Follow the steep **Old Prague Castle Stairs** down to the metro (see photo above).

• Take the **metro** from Malostranská to Staroměstska—you can certainly walk, but the metro is very cool...

• Head to the **Jewish Quarter** (see p. 43/Map A)—Check out the Spanish Synagogue in particular.

• Take a break on Pařížská—Ice cream at **Cremeria Milano** or a coffee at **Coffee Heaven** is certain to hit the spot (see p. 152).

• Check the time at the **Clock tower** in Old Town Square—For a fantastic view of Old Town, visit this clock tower and take the glass elevator to the lookout (see p. 64).

• Walk down **Celetná** to **Obecní dům** (the Municipal House)—Once inside Obecní dům, be certain to look at all the public spaces, including the pub and bar in the basement (see p. 54).

THE OLD PRAGUE CASTLE STAIRS, C. 1920

• Have a drink at **Grand Café Orient**—An exquisitely restored Cubist café that originally opened in 1912. The ambience will exceed the quality of the drink (see p. 153).

• Dinner at **Coda** in the Aria Hotel—If it's warm enough to eat outside, Coda, in the heart of Malá Strana, has a sublime view from their roof top terrace (see p. 143).

• Alternatively, dine at **Kampa Park**—Located on the bank of the Vltava, overlooking the river and illuminated arches of Charles Bridge, Kampa Park offers one of the most romantic and unique dinner venues in town (see p. 145).

• After dinner—Stroll over the **Charles Bridge** (see photo on left); no visit to Prague is complete without it. My favorite time is always at night when the city is lit up and the bridge is less crowded.

Go home; you must be exhausted!

CHARLES BRIDGE (KARLŮV MOST), C. 1955

Hotels

Hotels By Area

MALÁ STRANA
MALOSTRANSKÉ NÁMĚSTÍ
Aria Hotel 1 A
Tržiště 9, p. 26

**Mandarin Oriental
Prague 2** A
Nebovidská 1, p. 31

STARÉ MĚSTO
OLD TOWN SQUARE & JEWISH QUARTER
Four Seasons Prague 3 C
Veleslavínova 2A, p. 28

Hotel Josef 4 B
Rybná 20, p. 29

Maximilian 5 B
Haštalská 14, p. 32

Pachtuv Palace 6 C
Karolíny Světlé 34, p. 33

NOVÉ MĚSTO
The ICON Hotel 7 C
V Jámě 6, p. 30

FURTHER AFIELD
VINOHRADY
Le Palais *
U Zvonařky 1, p. 34

*location not visible on
featured maps

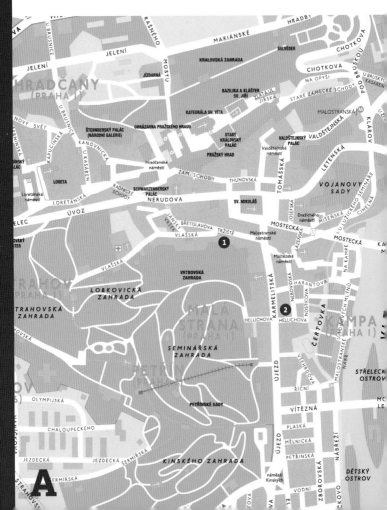

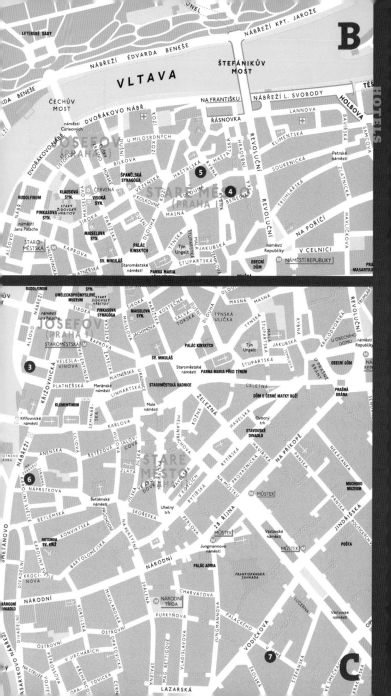

There is no one hotel that I consider the "must stay" location in Prague; what I *can* tell you is that *each* hotel listed is a place I have stayed myself—some for the purposes of this book, and others simply as a means of escaping my apartment and my cats (to whom I'm allergic) for a night of peaceful sleep—and I would recommend all of them to friends without hesitation.

First, for Those Not on Any Kind of Budget, Here Are Four Hotel Rooms That Are Sure to Satisfy:

One Night and It Must be Perfect
(Spectacular View From a Spectacular Room)
Four Seasons Hotel – Room 701 (see p. 28).

Can I Stay Forever? (Spectacular View from the Best Private Terrace in Town)
Mandarin Oriental – Presidential Suite (see p. 31).

Summer – (Five Windows Overlooking the Most Beautiful Baroque Garden in Prague)
Aria Hotel – The Dvořák Suite (see below).

Cozy Winter Retreat – (Fireplace in Your Room, NOTHING Is More Cozy than That)
Le Palais – The Marold Suite (see p. 34).

And Second, for Those on a "Slight" Budget, but Still Hoping for Perfection:

Oh-So-Prague and Romantic Too – (A Perfect Location and Fabulous View)
Pachtuv Palace – The Smetana Suite room 209 (see p. 33).

Just To Clarify, I Did Not Pay for All of My Hotel Visits

In the introduction and above, I noted that I personally stayed at all of the hotels I've chosen to recommend. At each hotel, I did offer to pay for my visit; however, when I mentioned that I was working on this book, some proprietors insisted that my stay be "comped" (i.e., no charge), while others accepted my money happily. The good news for my readers is that in each case where the hotel's Public Relations director or General Manager knew why I was there, the staff never seemed aware of who I was or the purpose of my visit. In other words, in each hotel, I was definitely left with the impression (for better or worse) that I was treated just like any other guest would be.

Hotels are listed alphabetically. Room prices are subject to availability, of course, and do not include a VAT (value added tax) of 5%, unless stated otherwise. All hotels listed feature DVD players in every room.

NOTE: For all hotel listings, I've included what I like to call the "Bed and Linen Factor," wherein I list one of three classifications:
• So nice you want to steal the sheets
•Lovely—almost as nice as my own bed
•Perfectly adequate

As I use my own bed as a point of reference, I thought it would be useful to let you know what I sleep in at home: 400 thread-count custom-made bedding with embroidery. My pillow and duvet are goose-down and made locally. It's the 400 thread-count that is key to my bedding happiness, as my sheets are silky and buttery to the touch. Needless to say I can't wait to get into them every evening!

▪ ▪ ▪ ▪ ▪ ▪ ▪ ▪ ▪ ▪ ▪ ▪ ▪
Aria Hotel
Tržiště 9, Prague 1, Malá Strana
www.aria.cz
TEL 225 334 111
METRO Malostranská ●
TRAM 12, 20, 22, 23 to Malostranské náměstí

Blessed with a brilliant location in the heart of Malá Strana, the Aria Hotel

VRTBOVSKÁ GARDEN, MALÁ STRANA (PHOTO COURTESY OF ARIA HOTEL)

overlooks Vrtbovská, a fantastic Baroque garden. Absolutely request a room overlooking the garden! The hotel can also arrange for rental of the garden and can assist with catering, be it a romantic dinner for two or a wedding for 200. The hotel is top-notch, and it's clear that the Slovak owner cut *no* corners. The lobby even has several prints and sculptures from his personal art collection. The appealing rooms are modern in décor, with a color palate that varies from floor to floor. The hotel is dedicated to several musical genres—jazz, opera, classical and contemporary—and each of the 52 rooms celebrates an individual artist or group who was of particular influence to their genre.

DESIGN
Contemporary with accents of Art Deco

STATS
Rooms: 52 rooms, including 6 with garden views
Rates: Start at €205 Low Season / €355 High Season, including breakfast
Check-in: 15:00
Checkout: 13:00
Gym: Small but suitable, including a view of the garden! Turkish steam baths in locker rooms. Massages available.
Internet: In-room flat-screen computer with high-speed internet access. Wi-Fi in lobby; your own laptop required. All services are free of charge.
Nightly turndown service
Bed and Linen Factor: Lovely—almost as nice as my own bed.

Bath Products: Molton Brown
Daily Newspaper: Wide selection available in Winter Garden
Pets: Not Allowed
Parking: No Charge
Library: 3000 CDs and 400 DVDs available for use by guests

RECOMMENDATIONS & EXTRAS
Room 411: The Mozart Suite has five windows facing the garden and an extra bedroom with twin beds, perfect for a family of four. The living room is large and has a kitchenette, which could prove very handy. If this room is not available but you'd still like a two-bedroom suite, the Beethoven is the other interesting option. It has a very homey feel (including a kitchenette), though the

living room is smaller and the view of the garden is less interesting, as it is one floor below the Mozart Suite.

Room 313: The Tchaikovsky Room has two windows facing the garden. The room isn't huge, but it is *very* romantic and has one *enormous* benefit: it's the only room in the hotel from which you can sneak out the window at night and take a romantic stroll in the fabulous gardens. Shhh… don't tell them it was me who told you!

Room 309: The Dvořák Suite includes one bedroom and a wonderful view of the bottom-most section of the garden, which happens to be the most beautiful.

Room 412: Nestled in the attic of the Aria Hotel, the Billie Holiday Suite would be *perfect* as a bachelor pad for a movie star in Prague on a long-term project. The living room is vast, including two sofas, a huge flat-screen TV, a small dining table and a kitchenette. The bedroom is in the back, and the suite even offers a study with its own sofa and TV. Needless to say, there is *plenty* of space. Although the suite does offer views to the garden, the small dormers make that view a much less important part of the experience, relative to comfort and privacy.

EATING IN

Breakfast: 07:00–11:00
Served in the winter garden, which is lovely; buffet plus an extensive à la carte menu at no additional fee.

Dinner & Lunch: 11:00–23:00
Coda, the Aria Hotel's restaurant, is a perfect retreat for lunch, dinner or a simple mid-day coffee break (see p. 143).

Request: The table for four located in the back room with the banquet facing the lobby.

Room Service: 24 hours

STAYING IN

Private Screening Room: The room seats up to 40 people, and is rumored to feature the same electronic equipment Steven Spielberg has in his home. Hotel guests are welcome to use it when it's not booked.

"The Music Box": A private entertainment room with a plasma-screen and super-comfy sectional sofa. Perfect for kids; set them up with a video while you enjoy dinner, or for a rainy day activity.

ALSO WORTH NOTING

The suites, for example the Mozart and Billie Holiday, are a "bargain" in relation to comparable suites at the Four Seasons and Mandarin Oriental.

The Jazz Floor is in the attic, so if you don't like slanted ceilings avoid it.

Ivana Stehlíková, the hotel's music director, is rumored to be the "go to girl" for impossible-to-get tickets in town.

■ ■ ■ ■ ■ ■ ■ ■ ■ ■ ■ ■ ■ ■
Four Seasons Prague
Veleslavínova 2a, Prague 1, Staré Město
www.fourseasons.com/prague
TEL 221 427 000
METRO Staroměstská ●
TRAM 17, 18 to Staroměstská

The riverside location at the Four Seasons simply cannot be beat—nor can the service. No request is too big, too small, or too obscure for them, so if you're dying to, say, take a helicopter ride over Prague, they will not let you down. The flowers in each room are lovely, the bathrooms are big, and the "cheap" rooms are actually quite spacious. They have also received endless compliments for deliciously comfortable beds and linens to match. If you love a safe bet, put your chips on the Four Seasons; needless to say, every time my mother advises me that a new friend of hers is visiting Prague, inevitably and without fail, this is where they stay.

DESIGN
Baroque building with neutral interior and use of color

STATS
Rooms: 162 rooms including 16 with river views, 6 Renaissance Deluxe rooms and 1 Presidential Suite.
Rates: Start at €225 Low Season / €375 High Season, including breakfast Rates without breakfast also possible, though oddly in low season they are *more* expensive!
Check-in: 15:00
Checkout: 12:00
Gym: Small but well equipped. Each station has its own TV and headphones. A very nice environment to work out in, but often overcrowded. Massages, manicures and pedicures are also available.
Internet: In-room high-speed internet (laptop required), Wi-Fi in lobby, and two computers in business center. Fees apply to all options.
Nightly turndown service
Bed and Linen Factor: So nice you want to steal the sheets

Bath Products: L'Occitane
Daily Newspaper: *The International Herald Tribune* or *Wall Street Journal* delivered to your room
Pets: No Charge (small only)
Parking: €32 per day
Jogging map available

RECOMMENDATIONS & EXTRAS

Room 701: Premier suite with Prague Castle view: I immediately fell for this room, both the oak-paneled living room (which is massive and even includes a dining room table) and the bedroom offer expansive and unobstructed views of the Prague Castle; you can look directly at the castle while lying in bed! Better yet, you can see the reflection of the castle in the bathroom mirror while lying in the tub for a soak. This is the pied-à-terre *everyone* who stays there will *wish* they owned! It speaks perfectly of the magic of Prague. Not only will you not need to leave your room, you won't *want* to!

NOTE: The suite includes a small kitchenette off the living room and a second bedroom is possible.

Room 431: A one bedroom suite with Prague Castle view: A wonderful backup if 701 is simply too expensive (or not available), as it's about half the price. This suite features floor-to-ceiling windows offering a fabulous view of the Prague Castle across the river. The décor is very romantic with a very fresh use of colors. I'm confident that you will not be disappointed.

Rooms 510 & 514: Renaissance deluxe rooms: Both

with soaring ceilings creating an atmosphere true to Prague's architectural and decorative grandeur. Although there are six of these rooms throughout the hotel, these two are absolutely the best.

EATING IN
Breakfast: 06:30–11:00
À la carte, if not included in room rate.
Dinner & Lunch: 11:30–24:00
Allegro, the Four Seasons Hotel restaurant will not let even the most discerning gourmand down, but the bill will be as princely as the food (see p. 141).
Request: Anything with a river view, by window or railing; the terrace is lovely if the weather is good.
Room Service: 24 hours

STAYING IN
Allegro Bar: 11:00–01:30
Summer Terrace: 11:30–22:00
A perfect mid-day retreat from the bustle of touristy Prague. Perfect for lunch or even just an afternoon coffee or ice cream. With a cool summer breeze coming in off the river, this is the perfect way to re-energize before heading out to your next activity.

ALSO WORTH NOTING
In the spring of 2007, the Four Seasons Hotel will begin a remodeling project of all guestrooms and public areas. The objective is to add style and decoration, inspired by the Austro-Hungarian Empire, to create the Prague atmosphere within its walls. The details will include Bohemian crystal chandeliers, hand-painted stenciling, ceiling moldings and Biedermeier-style furniture.

■ ■ ■ ■ ■ ■ ■ ■ ■ ■ ■ ■ ■ ■
Hotel Josef
Rybná 20, Prague 1,
Staré Město
www.hoteljosef.com
TEL 221 700 111
METRO Náměstí Republiky
TRAM 5, 8, 14 to Dlouhá třída

The Hotel Josef is definitely a boutique hotel for the hip, and while I would not describe either myself or my own aesthetic as especially hip, I had a great stay that far exceeded my expectations. The service was excellent, and the bed, sheets, heated bathroom floor and amenities were all far more deluxe than I'd expected. Its close proximity to both Old Town Square and Obecní dům is a definite plus as well. I personally often use it when clients visit, as the location is great and rates are less expensive than many of the other hotels I've listed. However this hotel is definitely *not* for everyone, as the very contemporary décor is simply not neutral enough to agree with everyone's personal aesthetic. Check out the Josef's website for yourself before deciding whether it might be for you.

DESIGN
Contemporary

STATS
Rooms: 109 rooms
Rates: Start at €149 Low Season / €203 High Season including breakfast
Check-in: 14:00
Checkout: 12:00
Gym: Small; if a gym is important to you, I don't think you will be happy.
Internet: In-room high-speed internet (laptop required), Wi-Fi in lobby, and two computers in

business center. All services are free of charge.

Nightly turndown service
Bed and Linen Factor:
Lovely—almost as nice as my own bed
Bath Products: Aveda, including face wash! Bonus!
Daily Newspaper: Wide selection available in Breakfast Room
Pets: €24 per day
Parking: €18 per day

RECOMMENDATIONS & EXTRAS
Rooms with a view of the Prague Castle:
Rooms 704 & 801: Superior double room with glass bath and a terrace.
Room 803: Superior double room without glass bath; I'm confident that you will still be happy.
Room 802: Standard single room, which happens to have a great view at no extra charge.

NOTE: Superior Rooms have glass showers or baths; although some exceptions apply, this is what differentiates them from the standard rooms, not size.

EATING IN
Breakfast: 06:30–11:30
Buffet plus an extensive à la carte menu at no additional fee.
Request: A table next to the window overlooking the courtyard.
Room Service: 09:00–23:30

STAYING IN
Bar: 09:00–01:00
The bar at the Josef is hip and modern. Why not stay in for a cocktail or two?

ALSO WORTH NOTING
Josef's Choice, a booklet you'll find in your room that offers excellent suggestions for cafés, design shops, dining and enter-

tainment. It's updated on a regular basis.

Definitely watch the *Prague Welcome* video on your TV. It's very interesting and well edited; to my surprise, I really enjoyed it. When you get to Part II, on Konopiště Castle, skip it unless you want to watch a dog kill a rabbit, blood and all.

Books on Czech Design are offered for sale in the lobby at very reasonable prices.

■ ■ ■ ■ ■ ■ ■ ■ ■ ■ ■ ■ ■ ■
ICON hotel
V Jámě 6, Prague 1, Nové Město
www.iconhotel.eu
TEL 221 634 100
METRO Můstek ● ●
TRAM 3, 9, 14, 24 to Vodičkova

The ICON hotel opened in March 2007 and is definitely the most progressive hotel in town. I'd describe it as a boutique hotel for those in the under-45 set who are either extremely hip or simply love gadgets. The staff is very friendly and the protocol is informal, with reference to a first name basis (if you allow) and "uniforms" by Diesel. The beds won me over—I hardly moved from mine during my 18-hour stay, as it was simply too delicious to leave! They are by Hästens (a Swedish company rumored to have the best beds in the world) and have sheets far more deluxe than I'd expected. The hotel's close proximity to Old Town Square (as well as to numerous metros and trams) is also a definite plus. The daylong breakfast is another great bonus, as there's nothing I hate more then forcing myself out of bed just to avoid missing

breakfast! I have opened a corporate account here, as the location—while not exactly picturesque—is very convenient for hopping around downtown, and the rates are less expensive than any of the other hotels I've listed. However, this hotel is definitely *not* for everyone, as the informal protocol and trendy atmosphere simply will not agree with all tastes.

DESIGN
Contemporary with accents of Art Deco

STATS
Rooms: 31 rooms, including 2 suites
Rates: Start at €115 Low Season / €160 High Season including breakfast
Check-in: 15:00
Checkout: 12:00
Gym: No, but starting in August 2007 they will offer yoga and tai chi in the mornings. They also have a small wellness center (see below).
Internet: In-room high-speed internet (laptop required), Wi-Fi in lobby, and one computer at the bar. All services are free of charge.
Nightly turndown service
Bed and Linen Factor: So nice you want to steal the sheets.
Bath Products: Rituals
Daily Newspaper: Wide selection available in Breakfast Room
Pets: €18 per day
Parking: No

RECOMMENDATIONS & EXTRAS
Room 209: This suite actually feels more like a lovely little apartment than a hotel room. Of the two suites in the hotel, this one is my favorite, as it has more light.

stay in for cocktails and lounge on their purple leather bed-sized couches?

Zen Asian Wellness: 10:00–22:00

A peaceful massage studio offering everything from a 15-minute "Backscratch" (290 CZK) to a 90 minute Thai massage (1,290 CZK). I opted for the 60-minute (850 CZK) "Foot Joy" treatment that combines acupressure and reflexology—perfect after a long day of trekking around Prague!

ALSO WORTH NOTING

Urban Secrets is an excellent resource available on the hotel's website, offering suggestions for bars, cafés, clubs, shops, and dining. It's updated on a regular basis.

Gadget Factor: Standard in all rooms:
•Biometric safes
•iPod connection
•Skype connection
Optional (available for rent):
•GSP Travel Assistant
•Segway

PRAGUE CASTLE, C. 1934

Room 205: This deluxe room with super-high ceilings is very spacious and bright, and it has a surprisingly long and comfy bathtub. I'm confident that you will be as happy as I was staying here.

Room 404: This standard room features wood beams, as it happens to be on the top floor, making the space very cozy.

EATING IN

Breakfast: 06:30–24:00
Buffet plus an à la carte menu at no additional fee. Yes, the hours are correct (all-day breakfast), so there's no need to rush out of bed!

Dinner & Lunch: 12:00–24:00
Jet Set, the ICON hotel restaurant, offers a limited (but diverse) menu at very affordable prices.

Request: The communal table if you feel like being social. If not, sit in the back under the big skylight.

Room Service: 06:30–23:00

STAYING IN

Jet Set: 09:00–24:00
The bar at the ICON hotel is hip and chic. Why not

■ ■ ■ ■ ■ ■ ■ ■ ■ ■ ■ ■ ■

Mandarin Oriental, Prague

Nebovidská 1, Prague 1, Malá Strana
www.mandarinoriental.com/prague
TEL 233 088 888
METRO Malostranská ●
TRAM 12, 20, 22, 23 to Hellichova

The Mandarin Oriental just opened in September of 2006 and has unexpectedly become my home away from home and hotel of choice in Prague. No request is too big or too eccentric. I should know— I have stayed here more than a handful of times! The service is not just

31

impeccable but truly personable, making me feel very much at home (albeit a *much* nicer home than my own). The rooms in the historic parts of the building are my favorite because they all have parquet floors, which give me the feeling of spending the night in a *very* stylish home rather than a hotel. The bathrooms, with polished limestone, heated floors, and plasma screen TVs are large and the chicest in town. Their spa also happens to be the best in Prague, hands-down! Need I say more?

DESIGN
Contemporary Asian, housed in a beautiful monastery that dates back to the 14th century.

STATS
Rooms: 99 rooms, including 22 suites
Rates: Start at €269 Low Season / €359 High Season, including breakfast
Check-in: 14:00
Checkout: 12:00
Gym: Large and well equipped.
Internet: In-room high-speed internet (laptop required), Wi-Fi in lobby, and three computers in business center. Fees apply to all options.
Daily turndown service
Bed and Linen Factor: So nice you want to steal the sheets
Bath Products: Aromatherapy Associates
Daily Newspaper: *The International Herald Tribune* or *Wall Street Journal* (or whatever you wish) delivered to your room.
Pets: Not Allowed
Parking: 1000 CZK per day

RECOMMENDATIONS & EXTRAS
Presidential Suite: Imagine an intimate dinner party *al fresco* on your own private terrace overlooking the Prague Castle, Malá Strana, and Staré Město. This duplex suite provides one of the *all time* great views of Prague. Should you be a rock star, royalty, or just the girl next door with deeper pockets than mine, you'll certainly feel as special as ever in this fabulous temporary perch.
Lazar Suite: Located in the historic Baroque section of the building, this would be my own suite of choice, as I immediately felt at home in its very chic yet cozy setting. It would be ideal for a movie star staying for a month or two, as the 91 square meters gives you plenty of room to spread out and make yourself at home. Should you fear that you're missing out on the golden opportunity to dine *al fresco* on the private terrace listed above, this can be arranged if the Presidential Suite is not in use.
Room 509: This room is one of four on a private corridor, in the historic Baroque section of the building that served as cells for the monks; l love this corridor, as it features high vaulted ceilings, pigeonhole windows, and seating in the hall. This particular room is great to know about, as it's the "bargain" on this wing.

EATING IN
Breakfast: 06:30–10:30
Dinner & Lunch: 11:30–14:30 18:00–23:00
Essensia, the Mandarin Oriental Prague restaurant, is certain to hit the spot for virtually any palate, day or night, as it features both international and Asian offerings prepared to perfection (see p. 144).
Request: A table in the first room, where one waits to be seated. I find this to be the prettiest of the five rooms, and it always has wonderful floral arrangements.
Room Service: 24 hours

STAYING IN
Afternoon Tea: 14:00–17:00 Tea is served in the Monastery Lounge at the hotel. I won't ruin the surprise of what awaits, but I can assure you that the setting, tea and food will *not* disappoint.
Spa: 09:00–22:00 See p. 132 for a complete description.
Barego 09:00–02:00 Possibly the chicest bar in town; they make a fabulous martini, and you can actually hear the person next to you speak. No stay at the Mandarin would be complete without at least one visit here.

ALSO WORTH NOTING
If visiting the spa is on your agenda, book your treatments well in advance of your arrival, especially if you visit over a weekend, as it's often fully booked.

I always thought all hotel slippers were created equal, but I was wrong; the Mandarin's are better, plump and velvety.

■ ■ ■ ■ ■ ■ ■ ■ ■ ■ ■ ■ ■
Maximilian
Haštalská 14, Prague 1, Staré Město
www.maximilianhotel.com
TEL 225 303 111
TRAM 5, 8, 14 to Dlouhá třída

If Eileen Gray and Mies van der Rohe are what really speak to your heart, then the Maximilian, by the same owner as Hotel Josef, might be just right for you. It's located on a picturesque square a stone's throw from Old Town Square. The real selling point for me however, is the Zen Asian spa, as I love staying at hotels where you can get a great massage after a long day.

DESIGN
Art Deco glamour with Modernist sensibility

STATS
Rooms: 70 rooms, including 1 suite
Rates: Start at €149 Low Season / €203 High Season including breakfast
Check-in: 14:00
Checkout: 12:00
Gym: No, but they do have a very nice spa.
Internet: In-room high-speed internet (laptop required), Wi-Fi in lobby, and two computers in the lobby. All services are free of charge.
Bed and Linen Factor: Lovely—almost as nice as my own bed
Bath Products: The White Company
Daily Newspaper: Wide selection available in Breakfast Room
Pets: €24 per day
Parking: €18 per day

RECOMMENDATIONS & EXTRAS
Room 406: Suite with a very chic Philippe Starck bath tub.
Room 206: "Romantic room" superior double with balcony overlooking the square. The room is lovely and atypical of the other rooms in this hotel. The interior design, including the bathroom, is reminiscent of the Josef, but in a burgundy color scheme. This room was definitely my favorite, but it is on the small side.

Rooms 642 & 645: Superior single rooms with balcony overlooking a quaint and quiet square.

EATING IN
Breakfast: 06:30–11:30 Buffet plus a limited à la carte menu at no additional fee.
Request: Table next to the window overlooking the courtyard.
Room Service: 12:00–24:00
Honesty Bar: 12:00–24:00 Has the feeling of an airport business lounge rather than somewhere you want to hang out.

STAYING IN
Zen Asian Wellness: Massage studio (see p. 133).

ALSO WORTH NOTING
I have to be honest; if I had to choose between the Josef and Maximilian, the Josef would be my first choice. The Josef's service is more polished; they have a full time concierge on staff, a bar with a bartender, and absolutely better bathrooms and amenities—important factors to a girl like me.

The Maximilian's reception is magnificent, but other parts of the hotel's common areas seem somewhat cold and sterile. Single rooms are definitely tight; unless you really want a balcony, I'd recommend getting a double or better yet a superior double room, which are significantly more spacious and often include a sofa.

Maximilian's Choice, a booklet you'll find in your room, offers excellent suggestions for cafés, design shops, dining and entertainment, and is updated on a regular basis.

■ ■ ■ ■ ■ ■ ■ ■ ■ ■ ■ ■ ■ ■
Pachtuv Palace
Karolíny Světlé 34, Prague 1, Staré Město
www.pachtuvpalace.com
TEL 234 705 111
METRO Staroměstská ●
TRAM 3, 17, 18, 21 to Karlovy lázně

The Pachtuv Palace enjoys one of the most exceptional riverside locations in town, including a beautiful view of the Charles Bridge and the Prague Castle. It also happens to be a two-minute walk from the Charles Bridge and a five-minute walk from Old Town Square. The buildings that make up the hotel both have long histories. The Pachta family became the owners around 1700, and their houseguests included W.A. Mozart, who, as the story goes, composed six dances for Count Jan Pachta in his music salon before lunch one day, after which a ball was held at the house so that everyone was able to listen to the new pieces. The present hotel was created by combining two existing palaces into 60 unique apartments, each with a different layout and décor. The architectural features include antique wooden beams, frescos, vaulted ceilings, and fireplaces.

DESIGN
Baroque setting with old world interiors to match

STATS
Rooms: 60
Rates: Start at €245 Low Season / €295 High Season including breakfast
Check-in: 14:00
Checkout: 12:00
Gym: Small; if a gym is important to you, I don't think you will be happy.

Internet: In-room high-speed internet and Wi-Fi in lobby (laptop required). Both services free of charge.

Nightly turndown service

Bed and Linen Factor: Perfectly adequate

Bath Products: The White Company

Daily Newspaper: Wide selection available *for purchase* at reception, annoying!

Pets: Not Allowed

Parking: €20 per day

RECOMMENDATIONS & EXTRAS

Room 209: The Smetana suite—with its fresco ceiling, balcony, and windows overlooking the river, Charles Bridge and the Prague Castle—is a perfect option for first time visitors to Prague.

Rooms 305 & 405: One bedroom corner deluxe suite; excellent river view and very spacious.

Room 214: One-bedroom suite in the original Baroque palace, with windows giving onto the street. The room features fabulous original marble walls and a large dining table. If you like to dine in every now and then, even when traveling, or prefer room service for breakfast, this room is perfect. They are happy to arrange a catered dinner; just let them know in the morning. I'm thinking of throwing my Thanksgiving dinner here!

EATING IN

Breakfast: 07:00–11:30 Room service available at no additional charge.

Request: The terrace if the weather is good.

Tea: 15:00–17:00

Room Service: 12:00–15:00, 17:30–10:30 (menu is very limited)

STAYING IN

The courtyard is charming, a great little secret just two minutes away from the hordes of tourists that may be swarming the Charles Bridge. It's simply perfect for a late morning coffee or afternoon tea, before one heads out to hit more sights and shops. I love the fountain in the second courtyard; I'm dying to dip my feet in it!

ALSO WORTH NOTING

There are kitchenettes in all rooms, so if you like to eat in or have kids, this could be a very big help.

If room service is an essential element of your stay, however, I fear this hotel will disappoint you, as both the hours and menu are extremely limited.

Further Afield

▪ ▪ ▪ ▪ ▪ ▪ ▪ ▪ ▪ ▪ ▪ ▪ ▪

Le Palais

U Zvonařky 1, Prague 2, Vinohrady
www.palaishotel.cz
TEL 234 634 111
METRO Náměstí Míru ●
TRAM 6, 11 to Bruselská

PACHTUV PALACE COURTYARD (PHOTO COURTESY OF PACHTUV PALACE)

A member of the *Leading Small Hotels of the World*, Le Palais pays attention to small details like marble baths and heated floors. I've only received rave reviews from people who have stayed here. The hotel is located in the rather residential neighborhood of Vinohrady, where I happen to live, and, as it is several blocks from public transport, taxis or the hotel's car service will be an essential part of your stay. If your budget is sufficient, I'd *definitely* choose to stay in one of the Le Palais suites, as it is in these suites that the hotel's true colors *really* shine.

DESIGN
Belle Époque meets English country—seriously.

STATS
Rooms: 72, including 12 suites
Rates: Start at €295 Low Season / €335 High Season, including breakfast and VAT.
Check-in: 15:00
Checkout: 12:00
Gym: Impressive, shockingly large and well equipped for a hotel of this size, including a whirlpool for 12, sauna and steam baths, mood lighting, and the quirkiest thing yet—aromatic showers; I got to test eucalyptus and orange (eucalyptus was my preferred scent). Massages and facial treatments are also available.
Internet: In-room high-speed internet (laptop required), Wi-Fi in lobby and first floor, where several of the suites are located. One computer in the lobby. Fees apply to all options.

Nightly turndown service
Bed and Linen Factor: So nice you want to steal the sheets
Bath Products by: Escada in suites; Sutton & Foster in all other rooms
Daily Newspaper: Wide selection available at reception
Pets: €25 per day
Parking: €30 per day
Jogging map available

RECOMMENDATIONS & EXTRAS
Room 104: The Belle Époque Suite features an original ceiling fresco as well as a working fireplace in the very large living room.
Room 106: The Marold Suite boasts a molded wood ceiling and a working fireplace in the living room. Need I say more? I cannot think of a cozier place to spend a cold and snowy winter evening, enjoying a drink or two before turning in.
Room 216: The Balcony Suite is the only room with a balcony, and it has a panoramic view. My friends stayed here and thought they had found paradise.

EATING IN
Breakfast: 06:30–10:30 (until 12:00 on weekends)
Dinner & Lunch: 12:00–23:00 Le Papillon–Le Palais restaurant (see p. 150).
Request: A table on the terrace if it's warm enough; if not, choose one of the tables with wing chairs, which are a very comfy way to dine.
Room Service: 24 hours
Lobby Bar: 24 hours—now that's impressive! Offering cocktails, coffee, nibbles, dessert and cigars, of course.

STAYING IN
Summer Terrace: On a warm summer day have dinner or lunch on the terrace; it's charming and the food is superb.
Library: Cozy in that English country house way; a great place to meet for an aperitif or nightcap. It seems the hotel guests agree, as every time I've been there, more than a few tables are occupied.
Whirlpool: It's enormous! With lots and lots of mosaic tiles, it looks more than tempting.

ALSO WORTH NOTING
The mini bar is actually FREE! This is a first, and I hope my brother-in-law takes note, as he is a huge fan of the mini bar, regardless of price.

Bohemian Countryside Retreat Outside Of Prague— One-hour Drive
■ ■ ■ ■ ■ ■ ■ ■ ■ ■ ■ ■ ■ ■
Chateau Mcely
Mcely 61, Mcely
www.chateaumcely.com
TEL 325 600 000

You don't have to sacrifice deluxe accommodations during your dream trip to the Bohemian countryside; the Chateau Mcely, just one hour from Prague, is a member of the *Leading Small Hotels of the World*. The chateau, originally built in 1650, is an idyllic place to unwind. The interior, featuring grand public rooms on the ground floor, an attic library, and a roof top observatory complete with telescope, is elegant and comfortable. If your budget is sufficient I'd *definitely* choose to stay in one of the Chateau Mcely suites, as it is in these

CHATEAU MCELY
(PHOTO COURTESY OF CHATEAU MCELY)

suites that the hotel *really* shines. The interior designer, Oto Bláha, chose to use Czech talent and materials during the renovation; charmingly, 80% of what you find in the chateau is Czech-made.

DESIGN

Secluded chateau near the forest

STATS

Rooms: 24, including 8 Suites, 6 doubles and 10 singles (all with plasma TVs)

Rates: Start at €145 Low Season / €155 High Season including breakfast

Check-in: 14:00

Checkout: 12:00

Gym: None. But there's a sauna on the ground floor, with doors leading to an outdoor year-round Jacuzzi for 6—stargazing has never been so good! Massages are available upon request.

Internet: In-room high-speed internet (laptop required), Wi-Fi in lobby. One computer in the library. All services are free of charge.

Nightly turndown service

Bed and Linen Factor: Perfectly adequate

Bath Products by: Sutton & Foster

Daily Newspaper: Daily selection at reception

Pets: €10 per day (small); €25 per day (large)

RECOMMENDATIONS & EXTRAS

Room 120: Africa Suite Features two stuffed trophy heads and a massive desk overlooking the drive leading up to the chateau. Parquet floors, oriental area rugs, and accents of navy help to create the setting in this suite. Given that Bohemia is famous for hunting, this is a most appropriate setting for your stay.

Room 116: Mark Twain Named for the author who spent time at the chateau in 1899, this is one of the chateau's most popular rooms. With its handsome color scheme of chocolate brown and sage green, and a lovely *Ridinger* print over the desk, it's not hard to see why. There is no better room at the Chateau to view the blossoming of spring or the changing of the leaves in autumn, as it's located high up on the 3rd floor, providing an ideal view of the garden and valley beyond.

Room 118: America Another perennial favorite with guests, it also has a lovely view of both the valley and the drive. With subdued hues of red and cream and a wonderful display of antique china on the wall, it's certain to set an appropriate tone for your visit to the Bohemian countryside, regardless of its name.

EATING IN

Breakfast: 07:00–09:30 (but if you sleep past, as I did, breakfast will still be waiting for you). Room service available at no additional charge.

Lunch & Dinner: 12:00–24:00 The restaurant specializes in international cuisine, with a chef from France at the helm. However don't be shy if you want Czech specialties—it's clear they are here to please. The menu changes daily, and they are happy to meet all dietary requests.

Request: A table by the window.

Tea: 17:00

Room Service: 24 hours, menu is limited to sandwiches; however, ask and you shall receive all that your heart (and stomach) desires!

STAYING IN

Alchemist Bar: Located in the cellar, this boozy retreat offers "rejuvenating elixirs" created by the proprietor, as well as a fabulous Wurlitzer jukebox featuring the tunes of Aretha Franklin, Beach Boys, The Doors, etc. Time for a very fun evening!

The Theatre Hall: Located among the public rooms on the ground floor. If you wish to watch a movie (and the Plasma TV in your room just won't do) the staff will be happy to set it up for you.

ALSO WORTH NOTING

Wondering how to get to the chateau? No worries; for 3,000 CZK the chateau will send a car to Prague to pick you up.

The best bathrooms are in rooms 124 (Orient) and 125 (Legend); the latter includes a balcony overlooking the valley.

If you're on a budget and can only afford a single

MUSHROOM PICKING GUIDE BOOK, C. 1938

room that can easily sleep two, Room 103 (March) is my favorite, with its fresh, springlike colors. Room 105 (May) is also a nice choice, with warm lavender colors and slightly more space.

If you want to make a trip to the forest or stroll around the chateau's garden during wet weather, complimentary mackintoshes (raincoats) and Wellingtons are both available at reception.

ACTIVITIES

Pondering what one might do during the day? Here are a few suggestions:

Bikes: €5 for ½ day, €10 for full day

Golf: Benátky nad Jizerou (9 holes): 15 min away Poděbrady (18 holes): 25 min away

Horseback riding: 300 CZK per hour

Mushroom picking: This can be done in St. George Forest, including a guide and basket, and your forest finds can be cooked for dinner by the chef.

Pigeon shooting: 600 CZK per hour

STALKING DEER IN ST. GEORGE FOREST (PHOTO COURTESY OF CHATEAU MCELY)

Sights

I do not attempt to offer a comprehensive guide to all the sights in Prague here, operating on the assumption that you have already visited or will soon visit all the main attractions, such as Wenceslas Square, Old Town Square, Charles Bridge, Prague Castle and the Jewish Quarter—and perhaps even the little Prague Jesus for good measure. Rather than listing these standard (and, of course, essential!) destination points, I've simply opted to add a few of my own favorite sights, focusing in particular on those sights that I feel are usually overlooked.

Sights By Area

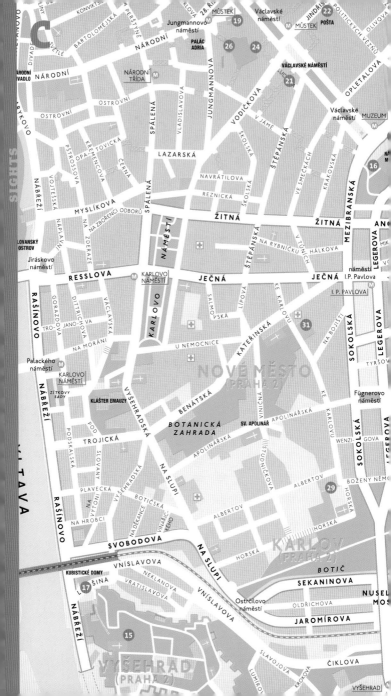

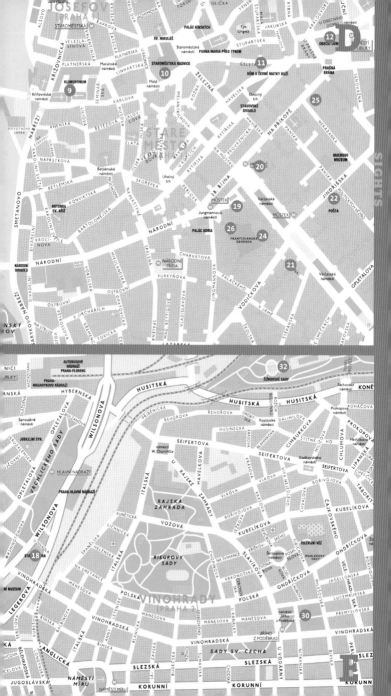

CASTLES & PALACES

Lobkowicz Palace

Jiřská 3, Prague 1, Hradčany
www.lobkowiczevents.cz
HOURS Daily: 10:30 – 18:00
ENTRANCE FEE 275 CZK
Adults; 175 CZK Children; 6
and under Free
METRO Malostranská ●
TRAM 22, 23 to Pražský hrad

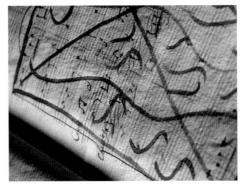

MANUSCRIPT OF HANDEL'S MESSIAH, WITH ANNOTATIONS
BY W. A. MOZART (detail); PHOTO BY EDWARD OWEN, COURTESY OF
THE LOBKOWICZ COLLECTION, LOBKOWICZ PALACE

Located within the Prague Castle complex, the Lobkowicz Palace houses a significant portion of what is one of the most important private collections in all of Central Europe. The paintings on view here rival those found in the world's top-tier museums, and include Pieter Brueghel the Elder's *Haymaking*, arguably the single most important painting in the Czech Republic. My favorite part of the exhibition, however, is the series of landscape paintings by Croll, which document, with Biedermeier clarity and informality, the Lobkowicz family's many estates and the stunning Bohemian countryside of the 1840s. The family's Music Archive is also quite impressive and features more than 4,000 scores, including original copies of Beethoven's 4th and 5th Symphonies (complete with his own corrections), and a manuscript of Handel's *Messiah* that was later revised and re-orchestrated by Mozart in a torrent of briskly inked annotations (the chutzpah!).

HAYMAKING (1565), BY PIETER BRUEGHEL THE ELDER, OIL ON WOOD
PANEL; PHOTO BY EDWARD OWEN, COURTESY OF THE LOBKOWICZ
COLLECTION, LOBKOWICZ PALACE

At least as impressive is the palace itself. Built in the mid-16th century and occupied by the family since that time, the palace was confiscated by the

ASSORTED HUNTING RIFLES FROM SILESIA AND BOHEMIA, 17–18TH
CENTURY (detail); PHOTO BY EDWARD OWEN, COURTESY OF THE
LOBKOWICZ COLLECTION, LOBKOWICZ PALACE

government in the 1940s, and the family relocated to Boston, Massachusetts. The fall of communism led to the passing of restitution laws in the early 1990s, which, in turn, led to the Lobkowicz family finally regaining ownership of many of their holdings throughout the Czech Republic, including the palace itself in 2002. The museum was opened to the public in April of 2007.

There is an excellent museum shop, as well as a restaurant that offers breathtaking views of the entire city. So ditch the hordes trampling the cobblestones of Prague castle, sneak beneath the archway of Jiřská 3, and spend some time absorbing Bohemian history in this unique setting. Don't miss it.

■ ■ ■ ■ ■ ■ ■ ■ ■ ■ ■ ■ ■ ■

Prague Castle
Hradčanské náměstí,
Prague 1, Hradčany
www.hrad.cz/en
TEL 224 373 368
HOURS May–Oct: 09:00–
17:00; Nov–Apr: 09:00–16:00
ENTRANCE FEE 140–350 CZK
Adults; 80–175 CZK Children
METRO Malostranská ●
TRAM 22, 23 to Pražský hrad

OK, to be honest (as noted) I had no intension of including an entry for the Prague Castle, as any other guide book worth its salt is going to have an extensive write-up on this all-important Prague sight. My editor, however, advised this would be self-sabotage. To avoid such a fate I reconsidered and have a following few suggestions for my readers. At the castle, as in so much of Prague, what I find most gratifying is to

ROOSTER ON ST. VITUS CATHEDRAL, C. 1940

CZECH CURRENCY FROM 1940
(DURING THE GERMAN OCCUPATION OF
BOHEMIA AND MORAVIA)

VYŠEHRAD, PRAGUE'S 'OTHER' CASTLE

walk through all the nooks and crannies to see the mesmerizing architecture. It's not about going inside to see every sight listed on your castle map. You don't need to pay to enter the Prague Castle, but you'll need tickets to see the main sights; St. Vitus Cathedral (completed on its 1,000th anniversary, in 1929) and the royal gardens being the two I'd encourage you to visit. I also recommend that before you visit the castle, you find out what art exhibitions might be going on at that time, as many of the venues on the castle grounds feature rotating exhibitions.

■ ■ ■ ■ ■ ■ ■ ■ ■ ■ ■ ■ ■ ■

Vyšehrad

V Pevnosti 5b, Prague 2, Vyšehrad
www.praha-vysehrad.cz
TEL 241 410 352
METRO Vyšehrad ● then a 10-minute walk; there will be signs to follow.
TRAM 3, 16, 17, 21 to Výtoň or 7, 18, 24 to Albertov, then 10 minute walk uphill (I recommend the metro option)

If you fancy a castle with more history than tourist crowds, Vyšehrad is just what you're looking for. Perched on a rocky hilltop above the Vltava River, Vyšehrad dates back to the 10th century and it was the longtime home of Prague's early Přemyslid princes. More ancient ruin than functioning castle, Vyšehrad is still very much worth your time, assuming the weather is nice. The winding paths and sweeping views attract many Czechs seeking picturesque strolls, though oddly, the sight is virtually ignored by tourists. While at Vyšehrad, take the time to walk through the leafy and serene National Cemetery, the final resting place of many famous Czechs, from the composers Dvořák and Smetana to the painter Mucha. Additionally, many of the sculpted memorials are simply fabulous. Dare I admit I have already chosen one mausoleum in particular as inspiration for a bathroom I plan to design in an apartment that I don't even own yet? There has been a church at this sight since the 14th century, though the present one, the Church of St. Peter and Paul, dates from the beginning of the 20th century and you'll immediately recognize the influence of Art Nouveau throughout the Neo-Gothic design of the church's interior.

Also, if you've fallen in love with Czech Cubist architecture, follow the steep path down to the river and stop at the following destinations to see several fabulous examples of this unique architectural style:
Neklanova 2 & 30: Two apartment blocks by Josef Chochol
Rašínovo nábřeží 6–10: Family houses by Josef Chochol
Libušina 3: Vila Kovařovic by Josef Chochol

Further Afield — Half Day Trip

■ ■ ■ ■ ■ ■ ■ ■ ■ ■ ■ ■ ■

Nelahozeves Castle

Nelahozeves
www.lobkowiczevents.cz
TEL 315 709 121
HOURS Tue–Sun: 09:00–17:00;
(Monday by appointment)
ENTRANCE FEE 330 CZK

Closed for re-installation; the Castle will re-open in the summer of 2007

Following the Velvet Revolution in 1989 and the passing of the restitution laws in the early 1990s, the Lobkowicz family received back from the state 13 castles and innumerable other properties, including vineyards and a brewery that's been in operation since 1466. Nelahozeves, a spectacular Renaissance palace perched above the Vltava River, is just one of these. It has been open to the public since 1997, and the family's impressive art collections are now divided between this location and the Lobkowicz Palace in the Prague Castle complex (see p. 46).

The castle's permanent art collection includes important works by Veronese and Rubens, and a new exhibition focuses on the more personal side of the family's life and history. Spanning 27 rooms, the exhibition features important furniture and major decorative arts from the Middle Ages through the 1930s, as well as thousands of objects used in daily life over the years. The family played an integral role in European politics, starting in the early 17th century as Chancellors of Bohemia under Emperor Rudolph II,

GAME BOARD (detail), FRUITWOOD, EGER, C. LATE 1600S
PHOTO BY EDWARD OWEN, COURTESY OF THE LOBKOWICZ
COLLECTION, LOBKOWICZ PALACE

and they continued to be involved up through the dark days of the German Occupation in the 1940s, when the last Duke served the Czechoslovak government-in-exile in England—and the new exhibition clearly reflects their intriguing history. Don't miss the giant lobster shell!

Like the Lobkowicz Palace in Prague, Nelahozeves has a terrific (and surprisingly chic) gift shop, as well as a great restaurant. Many Americans will recognize dishes from the beloved *Silver Palate* cookbook, which have been adapted by Alexandra Lobkowicz herself, and are a welcome change of pace from much of the

(pork-and-potato-based) food available in the Czech countryside!

TOURS

Every half hour daily during high season (May–Oct); Every hour, or by appointment, during low season (Nov–April)

DIRECTIONS

By Car: From Prague take D8 to Exit 18, drive south on the main road No.16. Turn left after 2 km in the direction of Veltrusy, then take a right after less than 1 km on to a road parallel with the river, this leads to the castle 4.5 km away. There should be signs clearly marking the way.
By Train: Although possible to reach Nelahozeves

Castle by train, it's far less flexible, given the infrequency of direct train departures. Trains depart from Prague's Masarykovo nádraží station, as well as Holešovice nádraží, approximately every 2 hours. Nelahozeves zastávka is where you get off, and the travel time is approximately 50 minutes. Ask your hotel concierge for assistance in making arrangements.

CUBIST FURNITURE DESIGNS, 1913
(SOURCE: NTM COLLECTION NO. 14)

MUSEUMS & MONUMENTS

. . . .

Museum of Czech Cubism at the House of the Black Madonna
Muzeum českého Kubismu Dům U Černé Matky Boží
Ovocný trh 19, Prague 1, Staré Město
www.ngprague.cz
TEL 224 211 746
HOURS Tue–Sun: 10:00–18:00
ENTRANCE FEE 100 CZK Adults; 50 CZK Children; 6 and under Free
METRO Náměstí Republiky
TRAM 5, 8, 14 to Náměstí Republiky

Now the Museum of Czech Cubism, The House of the Black Madonna was originally a department store with a famous coffee house, the Grand Café Orient (which has just been restored and re-opened), on the first floor (see p. 153). Itself a masterpiece of Czech Cubist architecture, the building was designed by the godfather of Czech Cubism, Josef Gočár and built in 1911. While artists such as Braque and Picasso applied Cubism to their paintings, only the Czechs explored

its possibilities in architecture and interior design. The use of this style, beginning in 1910, was extremely short-lived and came to a halt at the outset of WWI. Following the war, it briefly evolved into the so-called Rondo-Cubist style, which came to be called the 'Czech National Style,' but this later stage is less distinguishable from what is more generally known as Art Deco. So, a visit to this small museum focusing on the original phase of Czech Cubism in paintings, sculpture, furniture and ceramics is a *must*.

. . . .

Folk Art Museum
Historické muzeum
Kinský Summer Palace at Petřín Hill (Letohrádek Kinských)
Kinského zahrada 98, Prague 5, Smíchov
TEL 257 325 766
HOURS Tue–Sun: Oct–April: 09:00–17:00; May–Sept: 10:00–18:00
ENTRANCE FEE 80 CZK Adults; 40 CZK Children; 6 and under Free
TRAM 6, 9, 12, 20 to Švandovo divadlo

Beyond a few very general introductions, this museum is not exactly English-friendly; however, it's definitely high on my recommendation list. It reopened in 2005 after what was clearly a very loving restoration, and has been curated to perfection. The museum is filled with exquisite folk costumes, everyday wear and artifacts from the home and farm such as ceramics, farming tools and furniture. Anyone who is interested in textiles will have a special appreciation of the collection, as it shows off the intricate handiwork

BOHEMIAN FOLK COSTUME, c. 1941

50

of sewing, embroidery and weaving that only the deftest of hands could have executed; additionally, you'll see very interesting use of sequins and metallic threads. The exhibit with the baby clothing gets me every time, but I also love the dioramas that give you insight into how Czechs experienced everyday life.

Sadly, the gift shop has not embraced the glorious potential of modern consumerism, but there are a few items inspired by pieces in the museum collection that I feel are worth noting; the wooden toys; painted ceramic bowls; and traditional gingerbread in various forms (including Christmas ornaments), are especially nice; my personal favorites are wood pendant necklaces on leather twine, many of them hand-painted with religious icons. I bought a lamb I love for 150 CZK.

MORAVIAN MAIDENS PAINTING THE FACADE OF A HOUSE, C. 1941

Kampa Museum
Muzeum Kampa
U Sovových mlýnů 2,
Prague 1, Malá Strana
www.museumkampa.cz
TEL 257 286 141

HOURS Daily: 10:00–18:00
ENTRANCE FEE 120 CZK
Adults; 60 CZK children;
6 and under Free
METRO Malostranská ●
TRAM 12, 20, 22, 23 to
Hellichova

This museum houses the private collection of Jan and Meda Mládek, who, during their exile in the West, bought work by a wide range of Eastern European artists, some of whom were unrecognized at the time. The collection also includes works by such heavy-hitters as František Kupka, often thought of as the father of abstract painting; Otto Gutfreund, one of the outstanding 20th century Czech sculptures; and Jiří Kolář, a postwar surrealist known for his work in collage.

Before or after your viewing, be sure to stop for a coffee at the museum's café overlooking the river.

The National Museum
Národní muzeum
Václavské náměstí 68,
Prague 1, Nové Město
www.nm.cz
TEL 222 497 111
HOURS Daily: May–Sept:
10:00–18:00; Oct–Apr:
09:00–17:00
ENTRANCE FEE 110 CZK Adult,
50 CZK Children, 6 and under
Free
METRO Muzeum ● ●
TRAM 11 to Muzeum

VILLAGE PEOPLE, C. 1941

The 1891 Neo-Renaissance building housing the National Museum is more than striking enough to steal the show, but its Zoological collection runs a close second if you have a fetish for taxidermy. So, if Deyrolle happens to be your favorite shop in Paris, you might have just found heaven...minus the fact that you can't charge the polar bear to your AMEX and send it home. Highlights include an elephant head, an entire giraffe, as well as various bats, squirrels, and rats. And a very cute little baby penguin. It's interesting to note that the display vitrines are the original furnishings from 1891, giving the museum a wonderfully Victorian feel. The building also affords what must be about the best view of Václavské náměstí (Wenceslas Square) from the entry stairs.

NOTE: Closed the 1st Tuesday each month

TRANSPORT HALL, NATIONAL TECHNICAL MUSEUM
(PHOTO COURTESY OF NTM)

THE ST. WENCESLAS MONUMENT, COMPLETED IN 1912, WITH THE NATIONAL MUSEUM JUST BEYOND IT
(PHOTO C. 1920)

■ ■ ■ ■ ■ ■ ■ ■ ■ ■ ■ ■ ■ ■ ■
National Technical Museum
Národní technické muzeum
Kostelní 42, Prague 7, Holešovice
www.ntm.cz
TEL 220 399 111
HOURS Tue–Fri: 09:00–17:00; Sat & Sun: 10:00–18:00
ENTRANCE FEE 70 CZK Adult; 30 CZK Children; 6 and under Free
METRO Hradčanská ● or Vltavská ●
TRAM 8, 25, 26 to Letenské náměstí
Closed as of Sept. 12, 2006 due to reconstruction; re-opening planned for July 2008

This museum is just really, really fun. The transport hall, a great Functionalist space, is filled to the brim with Czech-made vehicles, including vintage steam engines, cars, trucks, motorcycles (many with the mud still on the tires), and bicycles, as well as airplanes suspended from the ceiling; this is my favorite room. I've also always loved the photography exhibit, which houses a very extensive collection of vintage cameras, including lots of Kodaks.

Further Afield But Not Too Far
■ ■ ■ ■ ■ ■ ■ ■ ■ ■ ■ ■ ■ ■ ■
National Gallery
Veletržní palác
COLLECTION 19TH, 20TH & 21ST CENTURY
Dukelských hrdinů 47, Prague 7, Holešovice

www.ngprague.cz
TEL 224 301 111
HOURS Tue–Sun: 10:00–18:00
ENTRANCE FEE 250 CZK
Adults; 120 CZK Children; 6
and under Free
TRAM 5, 12, 17 to Veletržní

Housed in a Functionalist masterpiece built in 1928, the interior space is in many ways just as worthy of a visit as the museum itself. The museum is bewilderingly large, so taking it all in is probably not realistic, and you should instead choose in advance what it is you want to focus on. Regardless of your plan, however, start up on the 4th floor, as this allows you to fully appreciate the building's structure. The collection is predominately painting and sculpture, but you'll also find some furniture, applied arts and even a few classic Czech motor cars, including the oh-so-chic 1960's Škoda convertible (see back cover). Although the gallery does have a nice representation of French masters, including Cezanne, Degas and Matisse, as well as other European masters, you'll probably find it more rewarding to focus on the sections focused specifically on Czech art, such as the 2nd floor's Socialist Realism section—a real favorite of mine. The bookstore is also worthy of a stop.

VÍTKOV MONUMENT, C. 1950
(SOURCE: ČTK / CZECH NEWS AGENCY)

Further Afield

■ ■ ■ ■ ■ ■ ■ ■ ■ ■ ■ ■ ■ ■
Police Museum
Muzeum policie ČR
Ke Karlovu 1, Prague 2,
Nové Město
www.mvcr.cz/policie/
muzeum.htm
TEL 224 923 619
HOURS Tue–Sun: 10:00–17:00
ENTRANCE FEE 30 CZK adults;
15 CZK Children; 6 and under
Free
METRO I. P. Pavlova ●
TRAM 6, 11 to Pod Karlovem

Housed in a former convent, the Police Museum has always been one of my favorite off-the-beaten-track and not-for-everyone museums. It's ghoulishly fun and surprisingly interesting, featuring wonderfully creepy scene-of-the-crime mock-ups, as well as photographs documenting crime scenes, including the capture of dissidents who did not succeed in their attempts to flee. All of which seems wonderfully inappropriate for a museum where school trips visit often, and, needless to say, the kids seem to love it. There's also a vast arsenal of weaponry. The text is in Czech, but with this much visual delight, it's hardly

necessary to know exactly what is going on. I'm confident you'll solve it all for yourself and that your conclusions will be dead on.

■ ■ ■ ■ ■ ■ ■ ■ ■ ■ ■ ■ ■ ■
Vítkov National Monument
U Památníku 1900,
Prague 3, Žižkov
www.pamatnik-vitkov.cz
TEL 222 781 676
HOURS Daily: 07:45–16:30
(by appointment only)
ENTRANCE FEE 30 CZK each +
150 CZK for guide; minimum
fee 450 CZK
TRAM 1, 5, 9, 26 to Ohrada

Take A Taxi! Advise the driver to go to Kověvova Street and then turn on Pražačka; this will take you right to the monument.

Capped with the world's largest equestrian statue, the Vítkov National Monument is already plenty noteworthy, but there's much more to it than that; far behind the massive

JOSEF STALIN, KLEMENT GOTTWALD AND FRIENDS, c. 1946

metal doors is a huge mausoleum that was built between the wars as a memorial to the Czechoslovak Legions who fought against the Austro-Hungarian forces in WWI. Don't worry—there are no longer dead bodies stored here, as these were removed in 1990, which—come to think of it—may be at least as creepy.... In any case, the interior space is of true architectural merit, incorporating 29 different marbles and granites, all from local quarries, as well as fabulous Art Deco furnishings in the Presidential suite. During WWII, the Germans used the monument for weapons storage; later, the Communists used it once again as a mausoleum, adding to the structure. The highlight during their occupation must have been the state viewing of Klement Gottwald's body, the first and most famous communist leader in Czechoslovakia. Not unlike Lenin in Russia, Gottwald was embalmed and laid out for

viewing. In 1989 after the fall of communism, the government sold the building for 1 CZK—yes, you read right, 1 CZK—to a clearly very well-connected former comrade. Thankfully, he went bankrupt, and the government was later able to reclaim the building.

Although difficult to see, this sight is definitely worth the effort. Alternatively, from time to time they do offer organ concerts and even raves, so you might have your concierge look into this. Sadly, there's virtually nothing to buy with which to commemorate your historic visit, but you certainly won't forget it.

NOTE: Open year round; however, there is no heating in winter.

CONTACT: Mrs. Purkrábková to make an appointment one week in advance, and request Dr. Junek for your tour guide if possible. Ask him to show you the underground technical spaces used for the embalming of Klement Gottwald, and for his corpse's upkeep.

ARCHITECTURE

Obecní dům
The Municipal House
náměstí Republiky 5, Prague 1, Staré Město
www.obecni-dum.cz
TEL 222 002 101
ENTRANCE FEE 150 CZK Adults; 100 CZK Children; 6 and under Free (Guided Tour)
METRO Náměstí Republiky
TRAM 5, 8, 14 to Náměstí Republiky

Obecní dům is the Art Nouveau architectural gem of the Czech Republic, and a visit to this exquisite building should be included on every person's visit to Prague.

The building officially opened in 1912, with interior decoration by the most prominent Czech artists of the day. Most of the building is open to the public, and you should definitely stick your nose into the café, the French restaurant, and the glass elevator on the ground floor, as well as the Pilsner pub and the American bar in the basement. It's also possible to take a tour of the upstairs

OBECNÍ DŮM (THE MUNICIPAL HOUSE), c. 1912

THE ČERNÍNSKÝ PALACE, SEAT OF THE MINISTRY OF FOREIGN AFFAIRS, C. 1940.

JAN MASARYK (MINISTER OF FOREIGN AFFAIRS FOLLOWING WWII) LIVED IN THIS BUILDING. IN 1948, HE WAS FOUND DEAD AFTER APPARENTLY FALLING FROM HIS BATHROOM WINDOW. IT REMAINS A MYSTERY, TO THIS DAY, WHETHER THIS WAS AN ASSASSINATION OR SUICIDE. THE BUILDING IS OPEN TO THE PUBLIC ONLY A FEW TIMES PER YEAR, BUT ON THESE OCCASIONS YOU CAN VISIT JAN MASARYK'S PRIVATE APARTMENT AND SEE THE NOW-FAMOUS BATHROOM. IT'S ALSO WORTH NOTING THAT IN 1991, THE WARSAW PACT WAS OFFICIALLY TERMINATED AT THIS BUILDING.

Müller Villa
ADOLF LOOS

Nad Hradním vodojemem 14, Prague 6, Střešovice
www.mullerovavila.cz
TEL 224 312 012
APR–OCT: Tue, Thurs, Sat & Sun: 09:00; 11:00; 13:00; 15:00; 17:00 (by appointment only)
NOV–MAR: Tue, Thu, Sat & Sun: 10:00; 12:00; 14:00; 16:00 (by appointment only)
ENTRANCE FEE 400 CZK Adults; 200 CZK Children
METRO Hradčanská ●
TRAM 1, 2,18 to Ořechovka walk up stairs to building

Along with Le Corbusier, Walter Gropius and Mies van der Rohe, Adolf Loos was one of the fathers of Classical Modern architecture (what we know in America as 'The International Style'). The Müller Villa, Loos's masterpiece, is perched in a hilly suburb high above Prague, and should not be missed, whether you're an architectural buff or simply interested in how the upper class lived in late 1920's Prague. The architect not only oversaw the design of the building, but also the entire interior, including furniture, lighting, wallpaper and even door handles. While the exterior certainly bears out his famous pronouncement, "Ornament is Crime," the interior is surprisingly rich and luxurious in its use of materials and furnishings, including extensive marble work and even the deployment of oriental rugs.

Each time I visit, I walk away having learned something new, noting a small detail I hadn't noticed

rooms, including Smetana hall, the concert hall where the Prague Symphony performs, and the Mayor's Hall, which features murals by Alphonse Mucha. The building was completely renovated from 1994–1997, drawing on the talents of the best craftsmen throughout the country to restore it back to its original glory. Mission most certainly accomplished.

NOTE: Definitely check out the gift shop located in the information center (see p. 110 for a complete description).

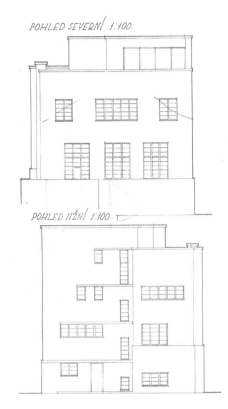

POHLED SEVERNÍ 1:100.

POHLED JIŽNÍ 1:100.

MÜLLER VILLA, PLAN OF NORTHEAST FACADE
AND SOUTHEAST FACADE (1928)
(SOURCE: UPM IN PRAGUE ARCHIVE, MM ESTATE
INV. NO. B1/167A, P. 3)

before, yet I'm always blown away by Loos's forward-thinking and re-sourceful use of materials, especially the wonderful veneers and marble. Indeed, it was my initial visit to this house that inspired the design of Artěl's private showroom in Vinohrady.

NOTE: I find it easier to take a taxi to the house and then public transport on the way back, as the tram stop is right below the house.

Church of the Most Sacred Heart of our Lord

Kostel Nejsvětějšího srdce Páně

náměstí Jiřího z Poděbrad, Prague 3, Vinohrady
TEL 222 727 713
HOURS Mon–Sat: 08:00 & 18:00; Sun: 07:00; 09:00; 11:00; 18:00
METRO Jiřího z Poděbrad ●
TRAM 11 to Jiřího z Poděbrad

Completed in 1932, this modernist church is

Modern Architecture In Prague

Modern architecture can be seen throughout Prague. I thought it would be great for Janek Jaros, the owner of Modernista (see p. 81), a shop that focuses primarily on household objects and furniture from this period, to give a brief overview on this period of architecture and to point out a few buildings he feels are particulary note-worthy.

Karen: Can you give me a quick overview of modern architecture in the Czech Republic?

Janek: The first seeds of Modern architecture in Bohemia were sown by Jan Kotěra and a handful of other young architects who studied in Vienna under the legendary professor Otto Wagner. While Kotěra mostly worked in the style of Wagner and contemporaries such as Josef Hoffmann, the slightly younger group of his assistants and pupils created the radical and internationally unique style of Czech Cubism. Nowhere else in the world was the Cubist style applied to such an extent. Indeed, for a time, the well-heeled of Prague could live in Cubist houses, furnished with Cubist furniture, drink coffee from Cubist cups and follow time on Cubist clocks. The movement was short-lived, though, and did not survive WWI. Towards the end of the 1920's, most progressive architects jumped on the Functionalist bandwagon, arriving via the Bauhaus. Some of the Modernist apartment blocks built in the 1930's still count among the best places to live in Prague. It's not too much of an exaggeration to say that Functionalism remained the dominant architectural style in the country until the Velvet Revolution—particularly in the area of public commissions. Its application in the 1960's and 1970's, however, was far removed from the original ideas proposed by its creators.

Karen: What are your favorite examples of the various modern styles of architecture in Prague?

Janek: For Cubist architecture, I'd say the Kovařovic house in Výtoň. And for Functionalist or Modernist architecture, the Müller Villa beats everything else, hands down. As far as I'm concerned, Stalinist architecture doesn't really deserve a mention. As far as the Communist architecture of the 1950's and 1960's goes, the National Assembly building near the museum, I would have to say, is notable for its utter monstrosity and sheer ignorance of its surroundings.

Karen: Thanks Janek. While I respect your answer for Stalinist architecture, I do think there's one building

NATIONAL ASSEMBLY BUILDING, 1973
(SOURCE: ČTK / CZECH NEWS AGENCY)

worth mentioning—the Crown Plaza Hotel (formerly The Hotel International) in Prague 6. I find it to be a striking example of Stalinist architecture. In fact, if I'm not mistaken, it's just been declared a national monument, no?

Janek: Well, now that we're stuck with it, it may as well be listed. Though I wonder what it symbolizes—either the Russians trying to impose something on us, or some zealous Czech trying to please the Russians out of their own initiative. Perhaps a combination of both. Certainly it is one of the most shocking examples of how brutal architecture can be when it ignores what surrounds it.

Addresses for buildings Janek has noted:

Kovařovic house in Výtoň
Libušina 3, Prague 2, Vyšehrad
METRO Vyšhrad ●
TRAM 3, 7, 16, 17, 21 to Výtoň

The Müller Villa
Listed on p. 55–56

Crown Plaza Hotel
(formerly The Hotel International)
Koulova 15, Prague 6, Dejvice
METRO Devická ● then
TRAM 8 to Podbaba

National Assembly Building
(currently RFE Radio Free Europe)
Legerova 75, Prague 1, Nové Město
METRO Muzeum ● ●
TRAM 11 to Muzeum
(You cannot miss it, it's the rectilinear building nestled between the National Museum and the State Opera House).

PLEČNIK'S MASTERPIECE, THE CHURCH OF THE MOST SACRED HEART

SUMMER VILLA BY DIENTZEN-HOFER, 1720 (NOW THE DVOŘÁK MUSEUM)

a masterpiece by the Slovenian architect Josip Plečnik, who also did extensive renovations at the Prague Castle. Sadly, most Czechs view it simply as an eyesore, when it is, in fact, one of the country's true architectural treasures. The interior is every bit as unique as the exterior, so try to time your visit so you can take in both. The building is open 30 minutes before morning services and one hour before other services, as well as one hour following all services.

■ ■ ■ ■ ■ ■ ■ ■ ■ ■ ■ ■ ■ ■
Dvořák Museum
Dvořák Muzeum –Villa Amerika
Ke Karlovu 20, Prague 2, Nové Město
www.nm.cz
TEL 224 918 013
HOURS Apr–Sept: Tue–Sun: 10:00–13:30; 14:00–17:30
Oct–Mar: Tue–Sun: 09:30–13:30; 14:00–17:00
ENTRANCE FEE: 40 CZK Adult; 20 CZK Children; 6 and under Free
METRO I. P. Pavlova ●
TRAM 4, 6, 11, 16, 22, 23, 34 to I. P. Pavlova

Truth be told, the building housing the museum

devoted to the great composer, a miniature Baroque summer palace built by Kilian Ignaz Dientzenhofer in 1720, is the true gem in the collection. Nestled behind wrought iron gates virtually in the center of Prague, it's a tidy architectural masterpiece. Were you curious to know what piece of real estate I dream of owning? Well, now you know, and if you visit, I expect you will start dreaming as well… Definitely worth a stop.

Sneak A Peek: A Few Arcades Or Buildings To Visit Before You Leave…

■ ■ ■ ■ ■ ■ ■ ■ ■ ■ ■ ■ ■ ■
Adamova lékárna
1920'S CABINETRY WITH WOOD INLAYS
Václavské náměstí 8, Prague 1, Nové Město
TEL 224 227 532
HOURS Mon–Fri: 08:00–18:00
METRO Můstek ● ●
TRAM 3, 9, 14, 24 to Václavské náměstí

Adamova lékárna has been in operation as a business since 1520 (a fact that this American, for one, found

most remarkable). Indeed, I called around to confirm it. It turns out that the current building housing this pharmacy went up only from 1911–1913, and the interior was installed in 1920. It's not an essential stop, but if you do happen to walk by, pop in to admire the wonderful original cabinetry with intricate wood inlay work…

■ ■ ■ ■ ■ ■ ■ ■ ■ ■ ■ ■ ■ ■
Bank of the Czechoslovak Legions (now ČSOB)
A SUPERB EXAMPLE OF RONDO-CUBIST ARCHITECTURE AND DECORATION
Na Poříčí 24, Prague 1, Nové Město
HOURS Mon–Fri: 09:00–17:00
METRO Náměstí Republiky ●
TRAMS 3, 24 to Masarykovo nádraží

This Rondo-Cubist masterpiece by Josef Gočár was built from 1923–1925. While the facade, featuring relief sculptures of Czech and Slovak legionnaires who fell during WWI, is certainly worth noting, the real treasures lie inside. First you will note the fabulous—indeed,

BANK OF THE CZECHOSLOVAK LEGIONS (MAIN HALL):
PERIOD PHOTOGRAPH

BANK OF THE CZECHOSLOVAK
LEGIONS (UPPER LEVEL HALL):
PRESENT CONDITION

fairytale-like—metalwork of the stairwell banister and elevator gate. Then, at the end of the passageway, you'll enter the main banking hall with its massive glass ceiling, undoubtedly the building's crowning jewel.

■ ■ ■ ■ ■ ■ ■ ■ ■ ■ ■ ■ ■

Koruna Palace

STAINED GLASS
DOME & SCULPTURAL
APPLICATION
Václavské náměstí 1,
Prague 1, Nové Město
METRO Můstek ●
TRAMS 3, 9, 14, 24 to
Václavské náměstí

Built on an angle at the intersection of Wenceslas Square and Na Příkopě from 1911–1914, by Antonín Pfeiffer, this Art Nouveau building, complete with arcade, is one of the oldest in Prague. In addition to the many impressive examples of heroic sculptural decoration, you'll want to take full appreciation of the building's magnificent clear and amber glass-bejeweled dome. Have a cup of coffee in the café right under the dome and be mesmerized by all the details. It's an experience not to be missed.

■ ■ ■ ■ ■ ■ ■ ■ ■ ■ ■ ■ ■

Lucerna Palace

STAINED GLASS DOME,
ORIGINAL METAL WORK, &
DAVID ČERNÝ'S HORSE
Vodičkova 36, Prague 1,
Nové Město
METRO Můstek ●
TRAMS 3, 9, 14, 24 to
Václavské náměstí

The Lucerna Palace is by far the most famous shopping arcade in Prague and was erected from 1907–1910 by Václav Havel, grandfather of the former Czech president. Here, too, the highlight is definitely the stained-glass dome. Take the grand marble staircase

KORUNA PALACE, UNDER CONSTRUCTION, 1913
(SOURCE: SVĚTOZOR MAGAZINE)

used to reach the cinema and bar on the second floor. Notice also the original metalwork and marble, much of which is original. The statue of St. Wenceslas on his upside-down horse is the work of David Černý, the artist behind the crawling babies on the TV tower and the Russian tank painted pink after the Velvet Revolution in 1989. (www.davidcerny.cz)

- - - - - - - - - - - - - - -

Main Post Office
Hlavní pošta
ATRIUM WITH WALL PAINTINGS
Jindřišská 14, Prague 1, Nové Město
TEL 221 131 111
HOURS Daily: 02:00–24:00
METRO Můstek ● ○
TRAM 3, 9, 14, 24 to Václavské náměstí

This Neo-Classical structure dating from 1871-1874 boasts a wonderful and extraordinarily large atrium in the main lobby that I encourage you to check out, regardless of your interest in sending a postcard or collecting stamps. Also of interest are the wall paintings, by Karel Vítězslav Mašek, which depict activities connected to the postal service and transport.

NOTE: If you're interested in stamp collecting and first-day covers, go to booth #29, which is where they offer all available stock.

- - - - - - - - - - - - - - -

The National Museum
Národní museum
THE LOBBY & GRAND STAIRCASE
Václavské náměstí 68, Prague 1, Nové Město
www.nm.cz

TEL 222 497 111
HOURS Daily: May–Sept: 10:00–18:00; Oct–April: 09:00–17:00; closed the 1st Tuesday each month.
ENTRANCE FEE: 110 CZK Adult; 50 CZK Children; 6 and under Free
METRO Muzeum ● ●
Tram 11 to Muzeum

The lobby and grand staircase of the 1891 Neo-Renaissance building housing the National Museum is absolutely worth a view, and you can explore both of these without paying admission. The building also affords what must be about the best view of Václavské náměstí (Wenceslas Square) from the entry stairs.

- - - - - - - - - - - - - - -

Světozor pasáž
STAINED GLASS WINDOW
Vodičkova 41, Prague 1, Nové Město
METRO Můstek ● ○
TRAM 3, 9, 14, 24 to Václavské náměstí

Built in the late 1940's, this Functionalist arcade culminates at the north end with a spectacular stained glass window made by the "Tesla" company. As a bonus, this window looks onto the Franciscan Gardens, one of the magic secret gardens mentioned in the next section.

- - - - - - - - - - - - - - -

Živnostenská banka
GLASS CEILING & ALLEGORICAL FIGURES
Na Příkopě 20, Prague, Nové Město
TEL 224 121 111
HOURS Mon–Fri: 08:30–17:00
METRO Můstek ● ○

Originally the Provincial Bank of the Bohemian Kingdom, this most

impressive building was erected in order to provide an environment appropriate for high-level finance. I do believe they succeeded! Walk up the main staircase with confidence and behold the main attraction on the second floor. Note the magnificent glass ceiling and the allegorical figures depicting various Bohemian regions looking down upon you. And then let the high finance begin… Just kidding.

SECRET GARDENS

Unless noted otherwise, all of these gardens are open from April to October.

- - - - - - - - - - - - - - -

Franciscan Garden
Františkánská zahrada
Jungmannovo náměstí, Prague 1, Nové Město
HOURS Daily: May–Sept: 07:00–22:00; Oct–Apr: 08:00–19:00
ENTRANCE FEE Free
METRO Můstek ● ○
TRAM 3, 9, 14, 24 to Václavské náměstí; if entering from Světozor pasáž, Vodičkova 41

The Franciscan Garden dates back to the beginning of the 17th century, but was closed to the public until 1950, when the communists decided it was worth sharing. Today the park is a secret retreat in the center of town, filled with fierce hedges and lots of benches (so bring a book or newspaper). If you enter from Vodičkova through the Světozor pasáž, first stop and get an ice cream at Hájek, the most famous ice cream shop in town under communism. Indeed, barring the recently opened Cremeria Milano on Pařížská, Hájek remains the favorite among locals, particularly for their cakes with fruit and gelatin.

■ ■ ■ ■ ■ ■ ■ ■ ■ ■ ■ ■ ■ ■
Vrtbovská Garden
Karmelitská 25, Prague 1, Malá Strana
www.vrtbovska.cz
TEL 257 531 480
HOURS Daily: 10:00–18:00
ENTRANCE FEE 40 CZK Adults;
25 CZK for Children; 6 and under Free
METRO Malostranská ●
TRAM 12, 20, 22, 23 to Malostranské náměstí

The Vrtbovská Garden is another gem that should not be missed if you enjoy formal Baroque gardens. Indeed, I'm embarrassed to admit that I only managed to get there in October 2005, years after they had re-opened. Of course, one could easily walk right by, as it is marked only by a rather modest doorway on Malá Strana's Karmelitská Street. Influenced by Italian terrace-style gardens, the Vrtbovská Garden was built at the Vrtbovský palace in the 1720's for the Count Jan Joseph Vrtba and represents the collective work of several prominent

Sneak A Peek Oddity: The Paternoster

A "paternoster" or "paternoster lift" is a dying breed of elevators which consists of a chain of open compartments that moves slowly up and down in a loop without stopping, so the passengers need simply hop on or off, as required. The name *Paternoster* ("Our Father," the first two words of the Lord's Prayer) was originally applied to the lift because it's in the form of a loop of rosary beads, which are used as an aid in reciting the paternoster. (Thank you, Wikipedia!)

These oddities, first built in 1884, were popular through the first half of the 20th century, for they could carry more passengers than an ordinary elevator, and the first one was installed in Prague in 1914. The construction of new paternosters, however, is no longer allowed, due to the high risk of accidents (mostly people tripping or falling while entering and exiting). And so, as the number of working paternosters continually decreases, they have achieved something of a cult status among especially nostalgic types (like me). Be sure to seek one out during your visit, as it's a sight to behold, and if you find yourself suitably brave and agile, take a leap of faith and enjoy the ride.

One Good Place Where You Can Brave A Working Paternoster:

■ ■
Palác YMCA
Na Poříčí 12, Prague 1, Nové Město
TEL 224 875 811
METRO Náměstí Republiky ●
TRAM 5, 26, 14 to Náměstí Republiky

The paternoster is on the left, directly beyond the reception desk.

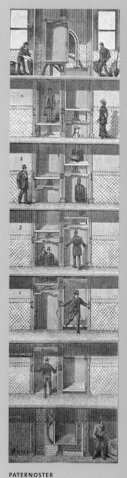

PATERNOSTER

artists. The garden itself was designed by Prague native František Maxmilián Kaňka, the sculptures were created by Matyáš Bernard Braun, and the painter Václav Vavřinec Reiner completed the frescoes. Walking all the way to the top, you'll be treated to an incredibly charming rooftop view of Malá Strana.

See p. 26 (Aria Hotel) to view a photograph of the Vrtbovská Garden.

NOTE: Should you stay at the Aria hotel, you may even get a room overlooking these gardens, in which case you're very lucky, and I'm most envious!

■ ■ ■ ■ ■ ■ ■ ■ ■ ■ ■ ■ ■

Wallenstein Garden
Valdštejnská zahrada
Valdštejnské náměstí 4, Prague 1, Malá Strana
TEL 257 071 111
HOURS Mon–Fri: 10:00–18:00; Sat & Sun: 10:00–17:00
ENTRANCE FEE 100 CZK Adults; 50 CZK for Children; 6 and under Free
METRO Malostranská ●
TRAM 12, 20, 22, 23 to Malostranské náměstí

This exquisite Baroque garden was designed by the Milanese architect Andrea Spezza between 1624–1630, at the same time as the adjacent palace, for General Wallenstein (of Thirty Years War fame), who razed some two dozen houses to make way for his own jaw-droppingly ostentatious vision. Fortunately he had the luck of finding and marrying not one but two rich widows who would foot the bill. The gardens are very geometric in design with several

WALLENSTEIN GARDEN
(SOURCE: ČTK / CZECH NEWS AGENCY)

Recommended Czech Architecture Books in English

Czech Cubism 1909–1925 Art / Architecture /Design
By Tomáš Vlček, Pavel Liška, and Jiří Švestka
– Modernista & i3 CZ 2006; 2,450 CZK

Famous Prague Villas
By Přemysl Veverka, Dita Dvořáková, Petr Koudelka, Petr Krajči, Zdeněk Lukeš – Foibos Art Agency, National Technical Museum in Prague 1999; 369 CZK

Prague 20th Century Architecture
By Stefan Templ – Springer Verlag Wien 1999; 480 CZK

peacocks in residence. Open to the public since 2002, they provide an excellent venue for outdoor summer concerts. The palace itself briefly housed the Czech Senate, and now serves as the base for the Ministry of Culture.

■ ■ ■ ■ ■ ■ ■ ■ ■ ■ ■ ■ ■ ■
Gardens Beneath the Prague Castle
Zahrady pod Pražským hradem
Valdštejnské náměstí 3, Prague 1, Malá Strana
www.palacovezahrady.cz
TEL 257 010 401
HOURS Daily: May & Sept: 09:00–19:00; June & July: 09:00–21:00; Aug: 09:00–20:00
ENTRANCE FEE 79 CZK Adult; 49 CZK Children; 6 and under Free
METRO Malostranská ●
TRAM 12, 20, 22, 23 to Malostranské náměstí

This magical group of terraced Baroque gardens practically spilling down from the castle grounds was originally laid out in the 16th century and then remodeled in the 18th. Exquisite stairways, statues, gazebos and other garden buildings punctuate the space. Again, although the Communists were kind enough to open these gardens to the public, preservation was never their first priority; after years of decay, they were finally closed for extensive restoration, which was completed only in the late 1990's. Thankfully, they have now been fully restored and re-opened once again for everyone to enjoy. Definitely not to be missed; these gardens are simply breathtaking!

VIEWS & PANORAMAS

■ ■ ■ ■ ■ ■ ■ ■ ■ ■ ■ ■ ■ ■
Astronomical Tower in the Klementinum
Mariánské náměstí 4, Prague 1, Staré Město
TEL 221 663 111
HOURS Daily: 11:00–20:00
ENTRANCE FEE 100 CZK Adult; 30 CZK children; 6 and under Free
METRO Staroměstská ●
TRAM 17, 18 to Karlovy lázně

Housed in the Czech Republic's massive national library, this is, hands-down, my favorite panoramic view in Prague, as it allows you to take in the whole city, including the Charles Bridge, and I'm confident that, upon leaving, you'll know why Prague is thought to be one of the most beautiful cities in the world. Sound too good to be true? OK, there is a catch: About 120 narrow spiral stairs, to be exact. But if you're up for the climb, the reward is well worth it. Until the 1920's the tower was used to calculate high noon,

VIEW INCLUDING CLOCK AT THE CHURCH OF ST. NICHOLAS: CIRCA 1940

STALIN STATUE IN LETNÁ PARK, C. 1950
(THE GIANT METRONOME NOW OCCUPIES THIS SPOT)

MY JSME CHLOUBA PRAHY ("WE ARE THE PRIDE OF PRAGUE"), 1910

with vaulted ceilings; the entire room is a wonderful turn-of-the-century mosaic celebrating Prague.

NOTE: To enter the clock tower, take the glass elevator to the 3rd floor.

Letná Park

METRO Hradčanská ●
TRAM 1, 8, 15, 15, 26 to Letenské náměstí

A vast and wonderful series of parks and gardens built high above the Vltava River, Letná Park allows for some striking city vistas. Under communism it was used for May Day parades, which do in fact still take place, though not with the same terrifying flair. It was also home to the largest statue of Stalin in the world, at 30 meters (100 ft.). Completed in 1955, even as his cult status was failing, the statue was sadly destroyed in 1962; in its place you now find the huge and very random red metronome.

Petřín Hill
Petřínské sady

Prague 1, Malá Strana
TRAM 12, 20, 22, 23 to Újezd, then take the funicular (lanovka) railway

Wonderfully free of tourists, Petřín Hill can be reached by taking a funicular up (using standard tram tickets), and the view is excellent. The park at Petřín is very peaceful in general, making it a wonderful place to spend a few hours or have a picnic.

See p. 181 for a complete description.

at which time a flag was raised for the castle to see, whereupon a cannon was fired to mark the hour. To get to the tower, you need to take the tour, which leaves hourly. On the way, you'll see the absolutely amazing library built by the Jesuits, decorated with fantastic frescoes depicting knowledge, learning and wisdom.

Clock Tower in Old Town Hall

Old Town Square (enter in rose-colored building marked *Turistické informace* to the left of the clock)
HOURS Tues–Sun: 09:00– 17:00; Mon: 11:00–17:30
ENTRANCE FEE 50 CZK Adult; 40 CZK Children; 6 and under Free
METRO Můstek ● ●
or Staroměstská ●

Rising above the very core of Prague, this clock tower affords an unbelievable view you won't find anywhere else in Prague. While many other observation points offer views overlooking the Old Town, this is the only one that is located in the Old Town itself. Take the stairs on the way down and be sure to note the fabulous wood-inlayed doors. At the bottom of the stairs, walk straight into the foyer

Shopping

Prague is a beautiful city steeped in history and teeming with culture, but it's not widely regarded as a shopper's heaven. As mentioned in my introduction, one of the lines I hear all too often is that "there's simply nothing to buy in Prague." Well, having lived here for over a decade, I can assure you, it's just not true. All the big brands are available in Prague and are clustered primarily on two streets: Pařížská, the "5th Avenue" of Prague, is where you'll find Christian Dior, Louis Vuitton, and Hermés; and Na Příkopě, Prague's "High Street," is where you'll find H&M, Zara, Mexx and Mango. But, as you can buy these brands in any major city, they will not be what I focus on. Instead I've featured stores that sell only, or at least primarily, Czech-made merchandise.

When shopping in Prague, you must keep in mind that the merchandising itself in many stores is disastrous, with customer service that leaves much to be desired—both holdovers from the Communist era. That leaves much of the work of finding what you're after up to *you*, so it will be good to think of each shopping attempt as a sports event, with a "win" being a bag in your hand upon exiting. So maintain a sharp eye and iron determination, and I guarantee you'll be rewarded with many fabulous finds that are *not* available everywhere else.

Visitors to Prague are always asking me for suggestions for gifts to take back home. Of course, there are hundreds of tourist shops selling extraordinarily tacky souvenirs, but should you be looking for something a little more authentic, I'd like to point you in another direction. I've even taken the liberty of including a number of gift suggestions at the beginning of the shopping section...

It's worth noting that while some things in Prague—beer, for instance—are inexpensive compared to America, many consumer goods with international brand recognition such as clothes, cosmetics, and electronics actually cost much *more* than if you were to buy them back home, so I definitely recommend you remove such brands as Levi's and Nike (as well as any electronics or iPods) from your Prague shopping agenda.

Unless noted otherwise, all the shops listed take credit cards. This can be a tricky business in Prague, however, as many stores that accept credit cards will claim they do not and try to persuade you to pay with cash; often by offering you a 10% discount. Many will claim this 10% is the processing fee charged by credit card companies; however, this is simply not true. So, if you only want to pay by credit card, you might want to mention this to the merchant at the outset. They may seem reluctant at first, but if you stick to your guns they should eventually relent. The maximum amount a credit card company will be charging them for their service, for the record, is 3.5%.

PRAGUE HARDWARE STORE, C. 1910

General Gift and Souvenir Ideas: Top 10 List

1. Local Liquor & Wine
Absinthe: Containing up to 70% alcohol, the famous "green fairy" has a real kick, and, needless to say, it is banned across much of Europe. The best brand on the market is Šebor, but honestly any brand will do, as the person consuming it won't remember anything the next day anyway.

Becherovka: A sweet herbal liqueur from Karlovy Vary with a secret recipe of 22 herbs that can be drunk straight, as the locals do, or with tonic, ice, and a slice of lemon (called a *Beton*, this is my personal favorite).

Fernet: A bitter local liqueur that is often compared to Jägermeister. It can be drunk straight or mixed with tonic (called a *bavorák*).

Slivovice: A plum brandy that is drunk as a shot by "old men in the worst pubs" according to my co-worker Kristýna. However, a homebrewed version, from garden plums, is viewed in a much more favorable light and one should feel honored if it is offered.

2. Glass and Crystal
(see p. 111–113)

3. Jewelry
Fine (Garnets or Moldalvite) or Costume (see p. 115–118)

4. Antiques (see p. 78–85)

5. Antiquarian Books, Prints or Stamps
(see p. 85–88)

6. Local Sports Paraphernalia
Slavia hockey or Sparta football (soccer) (see p. 123–124)

7. Music (see p. 121–122)
Classical Music: Dvořák, Smetana & Janáček

Country Music: "I See America" by Noví Zeleňáči (in English)

Country Music: "Nashledanou!" by Banjo Band Ivana Mládka (in Czech, but don't worry, it's really all about the music, which is terrific)

Swing: Originální pražský synkopický orchestr (any of their CDs are great)

Rock: Monkey Business (Funky in a George Clinton sort of way)

Rock: Tata Bojs (Rock with electronic effects, samples and loops)

Rock: J.A.R (Hugely influenced by Prince)

8. Czech Delicacies
Czech Wafer Cookies: My favorite brand is Kolonáda

CONTINUED >

Švestková povidla: A plum spread that is thicker than jam and simply delicious

9. Books
(see p. 90–92)

10. Ceramics with Traditional Folk Motifs
(see p. 94)

Top 10 List of Children's Gift Ideas

CZECH'S ANSWER TO PLAYMOBIL—IGRÁČEK TOYS: CEMENT WORKER AND BRICKLAYER, C. 1977 (SOURCE: WWW.IGRA.CZ)

1. Wooden Toys
(see p. 125, Hračky)

2. Marionette
(see p. 119–120)

WOODEN TOY DESIGN, C. 1957

3. Medieval Armor
(see p. 121)

4. Stuffed Animals or Other Accessories of Uniquely Czech Characters
(see p. 127, Sparky's)

5. Play Figures of Local Hockey Teams
(see p. 127, Sparkys)

6. Igráček
The Czech equivalent to Playmobil figures (see p. 82, Old Toys)

7. Books
(see p. 90–92)

8. Costume Jewelry
Either Wood Beads or Crystal (see p. 117–118 and p. 127, Sparkys)

9. Policeman, Postman and Trainman Uniforms and Play Sets
(see p. 127, Sparkys; if they don't have it, try one of the department stores in the Toys section, p. 101–102)

10. Road Signs
(see p. 127, Sparkys); if they don't have it, try one of the department stores in the Toys section, p. 101–102)

Shopping By Area

SHOPPING

SHOPPING

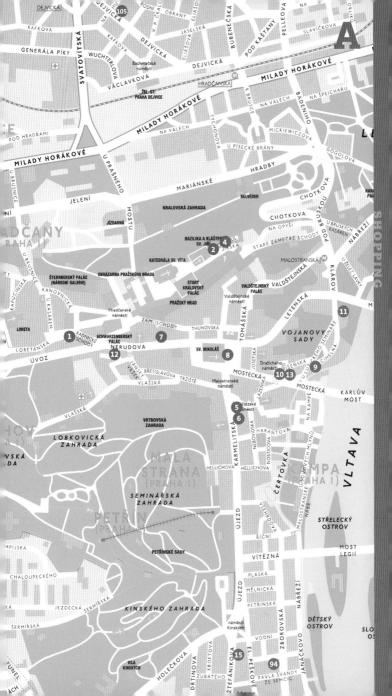

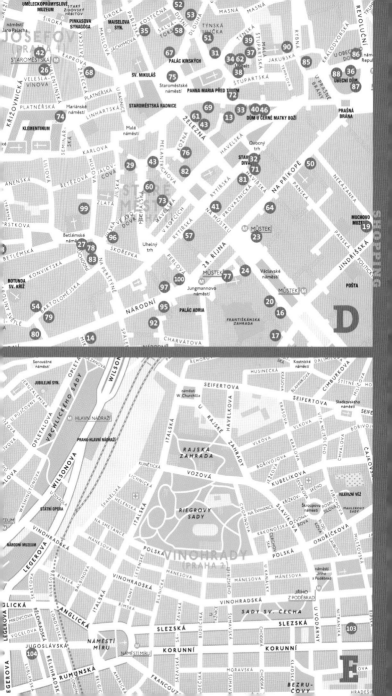

They sell very authentic-looking replicas of swords, battle-axes, daggers, knight's armor, bows and arrows and many similarly themed trinkets and souvenirs. Additionally, at the end of the exhibition hall there is a target range where, for 50 CZK, you can shoot 5 arrows from a medieval crossbow. I myself did not indulge on my most recent visit, but it sure looked like fun. This delightful exhibition/store is run by the owner of an establishment on the other side of the river, Gallery U Rytíře Kryštofa (see p. 121).

#12 — Manufaktura

A store selling Czech handicrafts, plenty of which are interesting. That said, Manufaktura has numerous stores throughout Prague, so if you like what you see, here, go to one of their other locations, where the selection will almost certainly be much larger. See p. 97 for a complete store description.

#19 — The Olga Havel Foundation

The late wife of the Czech Republic's first elected president, Václav Havel, Olga Havel was a noted philanthropist. The products in this shop are made by people with special needs and many of them are surprisingly fabulous. There are two things in particular that I love about this store; the first is that by buying something here, you're supporting a worthwhile charity; and the second is that most of the items for sale are totally unique and not to be found in any other stores.

THE GOLDEN LANE, HRADČANY, C. 1915

GOLDEN LANE AT THE PRAGUE CASTLE

A small 'lane' of shops within the Prague Castle walls, this just might be the very clearest example of a 'tourist trap' I can think of. Though, needless to say, I'm not a regular, I recently decided to pay it my first visit in twelve years, just to see what's going on there. After paying the 50 CZK entrance fee, I took a thorough look around every nook and cranny. The street itself is more charming than the shops, but there were a few surprises, and I've highlighted them below.

NOTE: The stores along the lane are numbered, and I've included their numbers below to make it easier for you to find them.

Perhaps the most welcoming surprise was the medieval armor and weapons exhibition upstairs, in the building on the left (oddly, it doesn't have a number). This place is great fun, and while you're up there you can peek out the windows for an exceptionally good view.

#20 — Antique Instruments

This shop sells just what its name suggests. I saw a wonderful accordion with pearl inlay for 12,000 CZK, as well as flutes, violins, harmonicas and recorders. In addition, they had antique sheet music and CDs.

#23 — Antikvariát

An interesting shop with very steep prices, Antikvariát carries antique paper-related items, such as sheet music, educational posters, etchings, stamps, and ex-libris decals, to name just a few.

#25 — Everything Mucha

This store purports to carry everything to do with the famous Czech artist, but frankly you're probably better off going to the Mucha Museum at the Kaunický palace on Panská 7 in Nové Město, as the museum really does have everything.

MARKETS

= = = = = = = = = = = = =

Havelská

METRO Můstek ●

An open-air market located on a street (Havelská) that bisects the heavily trod route between Wenceslas Square and Old Town Square. Once this was actually where people went to buy their fruits and vegetables, but today only a few such stalls remain. Sadly, most of the stalls are now run by merchants selling tourist wares, from wooden toys to sheepskins. Not too interesting (in my humble opinion), as the merchandise for sale is anything but unique and the prices are no better than what you'll find in other stores throughout Prague.

CASH ONLY

= = = = = = = = = = = = =

Old Town Square
Staroměstské náměstí
METRO Staroměstská ●

During the Christmas and Easter seasons, Old Town Square is transformed into a bustling holiday market, complete with vendors, seasonal music and entertainment. The vendors sell holiday-themed handicrafts and as well as lots of *grog* (hot rum and water) and *svařené víno* (hot red wine heated with cinnamon, sugar, dried oranges and other goodies).

CASH ONLY

FLEA MARKETS

= = = = = = = = = = = = =

Buštěhrad

Buštěhrad (near Kladno)
www.bustehradantik.cz
TEL 602 335 834
HOURS Fri: 08:00–14:00;
Sat: 08:00–12:00
ENTRANCE FEE 20 CZK
PARKING 30 CZK
DIRECTIONS Head to airport (letiště), follow signs to Kladno (route 7), exit at Kladno, take the first right, and you should see the flea market on your right.

A twenty-minute drive from the center of town, this is the granddaddy of flea markets in Prague. It's only open twice a month, so definitely check their website or have your concierge call. You'll find everything at this outdoor market, from knick-knacks to full bedroom suites. All prices are negotiable, so don't be shy about demanding a better one. The market is cash only, and as there is no bank machine close by, be sure to bring enough cash to do a little damage, because there's *always* something fun and worthy of buying. Try to bring smaller banknotes, too; if possible 100 CZK, 200 CZK, 500 CZK (it's difficult to negotiate when you only have 1,000 CZK or 2,000 CZK notes). If possible, try to go on Friday, as things are first-come, first-served; indeed, if you're a true die-hard, you'll want to get there at 7 am, while the vendors are still setting up, so you'll be assured of first dibs.

NOTE: The website has English, but it's hard to navigate. To move forward, simply click the link at the bottom that says "*Dále*," which means next.

CASH ONLY

= = = = = = = = = = = = =

Klementinum

Mariánské náměstí 5,
Prague 1, Staré Město
TEL 222 320 993
HOURS Sun: 09:00–15:00
ENTRANCE FEE 30 CZK
METRO Staroměstská ●
TRAM 17, 18 to Staroměstská or Karlovy lázně

Nestled in the outdoor courtyard of the Klementinum, in the heart of Old Town, this is a new flea market started in April 2006 by the owner of one of my favorite antique stores. Many local antique stores display just a few of their finds at this market. At my last visit I picked up a very unusual Bohemian turn-of-the-century

ceramic vase for 600 CZK and a fun little plate for 50 CZK. I was completely enamored with a huge late 1800's porcelain doll head, but at 30,000 CZK, the price was just too steep. Definitely worth a stop if you enjoy flea markets.
CASH ONLY

ANTIQUE STORES

If you love antiquing, Prague will be right up your alley. The city is filled with an endless number of antique stores and bazaars. Prices are *always* negotiable. Utilizing several of the resources below, I've managed to fully furnish my apartment, country house, and office, to say nothing of bestowing friends and family with any number of fabulous finds. Have fun, but be sure to leave a few items for me...

■■■■■■■■■■■■■■
Alma Mahler
ANTIQUE – LINENS & COSTUMES
Valentinská 7, Prague 1, Staré Město
www.almamahler.cz
TEL 222 325 865
HOURS Daily: 10:00–18:00
METRO Staroměstská ●
TRAM 17, 18 to Staroměstská

At this store you will find everything from china and crystal to toys and clothing. I stop in on a regular basis to look at their excellent collection of turn-of-century hand-embroidered clothing, bedding, tablecloths and nightgowns, all of which you'll find downstairs. They often have very interesting folk costumes at fair prices.

■■■■■■■■■■■■■■
Antikva Ing. Burger
CHANDELIERS
Betlémské náměstí 8, Prague 1, Staré Město (in courtyard)
TEL 222 221 595
HOURS Mon–Fri: 10:00–13:00 & 14:00–18:00; Sat: 10:00–16:00
METRO Můstek ● ● or Národní třída ●

If lighting fixtures such as chandeliers and lamps are on your shopping agenda, then definitely add this shop to your itinerary. I have not personally bought anything here, but I do enjoy stopping in, as they always have an interesting and varied collection.

■■■■■■■■■■■■■■
Antik v Dlouhé
TOYS, JEWELRY & MISCELLANEOUS
Dlouhá 37, Prague 1, Staré Město
TEL 224 826 347
HOURS Mon–Fri: 10:00–18:00; Sat–Sun: 12:00–17:00
METRO Náměstí Republiky ●
TRAM 5, 8, 14 to Dlouhá třída

While not my very favorite antique store on Dlouhá, this is certainly worth a stop. They have a good collection of antique toys and lots of other goodies such as jewelry, ceramics, paintings and often a fabulous chandelier or two. Prices are fair, if a bit higher than at most of my regular haunts, and they are usually negotiable.

■■■■■■■■■■■■■■
Antiques Ahasver
LINENS, FOLK COSTUMES & MISCELLANEOUS
Prokopská 3, Prague 1, Malá Strana
TEL 257 531 404
HOURS Tue–Sun: 11:00–18:00
METRO Malostranská ●
TRAM 12, 20, 22, 23 to Malostranské náměstí

Antique linens and clothing—including folk costumes from 1900–1938—is what this store really specializes in. But they also have jewelry, ceramics and other small items. This is one of my regular stops, as there's always something I want to go home with. The owner is delightful and speaks excellent English. Credit cards are accepted, but if you pay in cash, you should be able to negotiate 10% off the price.

■■■■■■■■■■■■■■
Art Deco Galerie
1920'S & 1930'S
Michalská 21, Prague 1, Staré Město
www.artdecogalerie-mili.info
TEL 224 223 076
HOURS Mon–Fri: 14:00–19:00
METRO Můstek ● ●

This shop seems to be closed more often than it's open, frankly, which is incredibly annoying. If you *do* catch them open, however, you'll enter the door of the best Art Deco and First Republic (1918–1938) antique store in Prague. It's a true anomaly among local stores in that it sticks to one period and does so with style and flair. They have an excellent collection of porcelain, ceramics, glass, clocks, lamps, clothing, and various other accessories, all from this period. The prices can be on the high side, but you can bargain with the owner. They accept credit cards, but cash is always better when negotiating.

MORAVIAN FOLK COSTUMES

Bazar Antik

CERAMICS, GLASSWARE & LINENS

Křemencova 4, Prague 2, Nové Město

HOURS Mon–Thu: 11:00–18:00; Fri 11:00–17:00

METRO Karlovo náměstí

TRAM 6, 9, 18, 21, 22, 23 to Karlovo náměstí

If you enjoy sifting through piles of junk in search of a fabulous find, this store is for you. You'll need more patience than money in your treasure hunt here, but the atmosphere is fun and the prices low. I've amassed a wonderful collection of hand-painted ceramic bowls from this store, making my morning cereal and afternoon soup consumption that much more fun. I've also had very good luck with hand-embroidered linens here.

CASH ONLY

Bazar Antique

GLASSWARE

Dlouhá 22, Prague 1, Staré Město

TEL 222 320 993

HOURS Mon–Fri: 11:00–18:00

METRO Náměstí Republiky

TRAM 5, 8, 14 to Dlouhá třída

This shop leans toward the higher end, and is my favorite for when I'm feeling slightly indulgent, which seems to be the case all too often. I've purchased interesting art, prints and glassware here, but no furniture. The owner is very sweet and definitely willing to negotiate. He also happens to be the organizer of the Flea Market at the *Klementinum* on Sundays (see p. 77).

Bric a Brac

OVERPRICED JUNK SHOP

Týnská 7, Prague 1, Staré Město

TEL 224 815 763

HOURS Daily: 11:00–19:00

METRO Můstek ●

or Náměstí Republiky ●

Here you will find two shops at the same address. The first, and smaller of the two, I find simply claustrophobic, so unless you really enjoy weeding through mounds of merchandise in the hope of a true find, I recommend you just skip it. The second shop, located in the courtyard, is much more genteel and fun to poke about in; they carry lots of historical items, most of which originate from 1900 and onward. Most of their items, however, are *ridiculously* overpriced. If you find something you absolutely must have, make the effort to negotiate hard, and you should be rewarded with a more reasonable price; if not, walk away in the knowledge that you haven't committed the sin of overspending.

REPRODUCTION OF CHAISE LONGUE IN MÜLLER VILLA (SEE P. 55),
AVAILABLE AT MODERNISTA (SEE P. 81)
(PHOTO BY DAVID A. LAND, 2006)

Dorotheum

ANTIQUE STORE &
AUCTION HOUSE
Ovocný trh 2, Prague 1,
Staré Město
www.dorotheum.cz
TEL 224 216 699
HOURS Mon–Fri: 10:00–
19:00; Sat: 10:00–17:00
METRO Můstek ●
TRAM 3, 9, 14, 24 to Václavské
náměstí

This is a frequent stop
for me. I simply love this
store, as the quality is
always great and the price
points are fair, considering
they have already done
the homework for you.
Prices start at 700 CZK
and they carry jewelry
(including an excellent
collection of garnets),
ceramics, porcelain, silver,
glass, paintings, and
furniture. Auctions are
held quarterly, but they do
also have a large section of
the store devoted to items
for immediate purchase.

Interier Servi

TOYS, GLASS,
COSTUME JEWELRY &
MISCELLANEOUS
Opatovická 7, Prague 1,
Nové Město
HOURS Mon–Fri: 10:00–18:00
METRO Národní třída ●
TRAM 6, 9, 18, 21, 22, 23 to
Národní třída

This shop carries a wide
assortment of items,
including clocks, glass-
ware, jewelry and linens—
all at reasonable prices.
Ask to see the back room,
where the owner keeps
some of the best merchan-
dise. I'm still not entirely
sure why all of this is
off-limits to the average
shopper, but owners have
their quirks. Typically,

VINTAGE CZECH TOYS
(PHOTO BY DAVID A. LAND, 2006)

you can negotiate 5–10% off
the price if you pay in cash.

Military Antiques

Charvátova 11, Prague 1,
Nové Město
TEL 296 240 088
HOURS Mon–Fri: 10:00–
18:00; Sat: 10:00–13:00
METRO Můstek ●
or Národní třída ●

The name says it all, so if
you're looking for vintage
helmets, weapons and
other equipment, be sure
to stop in.

CASH ONLY

Modernista

HOUSEHOLD OBJECTS &
FURNITURE
Celetná 12, Prague 1,
Staré Město
www.modernista.cz
TEL 224 241 300
HOURS Daily: 10:00–20:00
METRO Můstek ●

Located in the heart of
Prague's busiest street,
this excellent design and
furniture shop will be
hard to miss. Modernista
sells both originals and
reproductions of designs
by prominent Czech Cubist
designers like Pavel Janák,
Vlastislav Hofman and
Josef Gočár. Be certain to go
downstairs, as many of the
most interesting pieces of
furniture are housed down
there, including the 1930's
Halabal recliner, as well
as table lamps, floor lamps
and ceiling fixtures. In
addition to Cubist pieces,
the proprietor also offers
Art Deco and Bauhaus.
If you have a vision of
what you're looking for but
cannot find it, be sure to

PORCELAIN BUST OF T.G. MASARYK
(PHOTO BY STUART ISETT, 2006)

Pražské starožitnosti

CERAMICS, PORCELAIN & GLASS

Mikulandská 8, Prague 1, Nové Město

TEL 224 930 572

HOURS Mon–Thu: 10:00–12:00 & 14:00–18:00; Fri: 14:00–18:00

METRO Národní třída

TRAM 6, 9, 18, 21, 22, 23 to Národní divadlo

I've been going to this store since I first moved here in 1994. They carry a very wide range of antiques, including one of the best selections of blue and white porcelain and ceramics in Prague. They also have silver, jewelry, paintings and glass from Biedermeier through Deco. My most recent purchase was a porcelain bust of T. G. Masaryk, the first president of Czechoslovakia. This had been on my shopping agenda for two years, and I happily brought it to my country house for immediate installation.

CASH ONLY

Starožitné hodiny

CLOCKS & TIMEPIECES

Zborovská 31, Prague 5, Smíchov

TEL 257 329 767

HOURS Mon–Fri: 10:00–18:00

METRO Anděl

TRAM 12, 14, 20 to Švandovo divadlo

A great source for timepieces of any type, including pocket watches, wristwatches, as well as table clocks, mantle pieces, and grandfather clocks. They focus primarily on timepieces from the Empire period, but they stock other periods as well,

seek out the owner, Janek Jaros, as he has a large warehouse filled with inventory; alternatively, he can source the piece if it is not currently available.

Old Toys

Rybná 21, Prague 1, Staré Město

TEL 224 811 336

HOURS Mon–Fri: 10:00–18:00

METRO Náměstí Republiky

TRAM 5, 8, 14 to Dlouhá třída

This shop is certainly overpriced and frequently closed during their posted hours. That said, it's the only store in town that focuses on antique children's toys, so I always make an effort to pop in when I *do* find it open. I bought a fabulous Russian penguin here that walks, lights up, flaps its wings and opens its mouth—an obvious gem. If you're interested in old toys, ranging from dolls and wooden toys to metal trains, miniature furniture and appliances, it's definitely worth a stop.

NOTE: They also have the best selection of *Igráček*—the Czech equivalent of Playmobil figures—which feature some very atypical professions (for toys) such as coal miners and chimney sweeps.

all the way through Deco. Although clocks and watches are the primary reason I stop in this store, they also carry glass, silver and furniture ranging from Baroque to Biedermeier.

CASH ONLY

━━━━━━━━━━━━━
Starožitné hodiny Václav Matouš
CLOCKS & WATCHES
Mikulandská 10, Prague 1, Nové Město
TEL 224 930 172
HOURS Mon–Fri: 09:00–12:00 & 14:00–18:00
METRO Národní třída
TRAM 6, 9, 18, 21, 22, 23 to Národní divadlo

This little store focuses specifically on clocks, small and large, and wristwatches from the Czech Republic, Germany and Austria. Prices start at 500 CZK and go up from there. During my last visit, the oldest clock on site was a Biedermeier wall clock from 1820. They also perform repairs.

CASH ONLY

━━━━━━━━━━━━━
Starožitnosti Aja
FOLK COSTUMES
Radnické schody 9, Prague 1, Malá Strana
TEL 220 513 869
HOURS Tue–Sat: 10:00–16:00
METRO Malostranská ●
TRAM 22, 23 to Pražský hrad

This store focuses on Czech folk costumes and always has an excellent selection to offer. It's hardly cheap, with prices ranging from 5,000 CZK to 8,000 CZK; however, if you appreciate handiwork and embroidery, I encourage you to stop in, as you'll be amazed at the workmanship that goes

into each one of these costumes. The owner is very helpful.

━━━━━━━━━━━━━
Starožitnosti pod Kinskou
PAINTINGS, PRINTS, FURNITURE, & LIGHT FIXTURES
náměstí Kinských 7, Prague 5, Smíchov
www.antique-shop.cz
TEL 257 311 245
HOURS Mon–Fri: 10:00–18:00; Sat 10:00–17:00
METRO Anděl
TRAM 12, 14, 20 to Švandovo divadlo

An old favorite of mine, this shop has a very large and interesting collection of paintings and prints, and this is the primary reason I visit. My favorite purchase is a stately portrait of a cow, in oil, that now hangs above the mantle in my country house. They often also have very interesting pieces of furniture; a friend of mine found a wonderful turn-of-century set of hunting furniture with a hand-carved relief portrait of St. Hubertus (patron saint of the hunt) on the back of one of the chairs that reaches a breathtaking level of sculptural brilliance. Additionally, their lighting fixtures—table lamps in particular—are often very good.

1907 HUNTING CHAIR WITH HAND-CARVED RELIEF OF ST. HUBERTUS (PHOTO BY STUART ISETT, 2006)

Starožitnosti Ungelt

GLASS, CERAMICS, JEWELRY, & SILVER

Týn 1, Prague 1, Staré Město
TEL 224 895 454
HOURS Mon–Fri: 10:00–18:00; Sat & Sun: 10:00–17:00
METRO Staroměstská ● or Můstek ● ●
TRAM 17, 18 to Staroměstská

This shop is undeniably expensive, but they do carry very interesting collections of glass, jewelry (including garnets, diamonds, and enamel work), ceramics and furniture. If you're interested in good antiques, you should definitely stop in to see the store—even if it's beyond your budget—as there are always great pieces to see. On my most recent visit I saw a wonderful moldavite (see p. 116) bracelet from the 1850's that was particularly unusual, as the stone was not often used to make jewelry at that time.

Further Afield But Not Too Far — Two Tram Stops From Národní Třída)

Antic Aura

1920'S & 1930'S

Vyšehradská 27, Prague 2, Nové Město
www.antic-aura.cz
TEL 224 922 575
HOURS Mon–Fri: 11:00–18:00
METRO Karlovo náměstí ●
then TRAM 18, 24 to Botanická zahrada

If you fancy the Art Deco era but haven't been able to find something worth bringing home, add this shop to your itinerary and you surely won't be disappointed. The collection here is well edited and includes an excellent collection of handbags as well as jewelry, ceramics, glassware, linens, art and some furniture.

Starožitný nábytek Josef Liška

CHANDELIERS, LIGHTING, FURNITURE & MISCELLANEOUS

Vyšehradská 33, Prague 2, Nové Město
TEL 224 919 053
HOURS Mon–Fri: 09:00–18:00
METRO Karlovo náměstí ●
then TRAM 18, 24 to Botanická zahrada

Located in the very back of a rather crummy courtyard, the entrance to this shop is anything but inviting, but the items they carry make it well worth seeking out. They carry lots of interesting furniture and light fixtures, including an extensive collection of chandeliers, as well as miscellaneous small items. This shop is on my regular hit list, and happens to be where I bought my very first antique in Prague, a light fixture that hangs

Czech Vintage Furniture Available in New York City

It's unlikely that you'll want to purchase furniture in the Czech Republic and go through the hassle of shipping it home. However, if you have your heart set on incorporating some Czech pieces into your interior vision, I can recommend Prague Kolektiv in New York City, which was opened in 2005 by two former Prague expatriates.

Set in the heart of Dumbo, Prague Kolektiv sells exclusively Czech furniture and home accessories from the 1920's through the 1960's. The owners have an excellent eye and all of the pieces for sale have been restored to their former glory. While you certainly won't experience the delicious pleasure of underpaying here, you *will* find some fabulous things to buy. And at least you won't have the hassle of international shipping!

Prague Kolektiv

143-b Front Street, between Jay Street and Pearl Street, Brooklyn, New York
www.praguekolektiv.com
TEL 718 260 8013
HOURS Tue–Fri: 12:00–19:00; Sat & Sun: 11:00–19:00
SUBWAY Take F train to York Street

from the ceiling of my bedroom. Hand-painted with a Bohemian floral motif, this remains one of my all-time favorite finds. In addition, I've bought everything from coffee tables and ceramic canister sets for the kitchen to antlers for the country house at this fine establishment.

CASH ONLY

Further Afield — On the way to/from the Airport— an extra added bonus!

■ ■ ■ ■ ■ ■ ■ ■ ■ ■ ■ ■

Antikvita

Na Hutích 9, Prague 6, Dejvice
www.antikvita.cz
TEL 233 336 601
HOURS Mon–Fri: 10:00–17:00
METRO Dejvická ●
TRAM 1, 8, 15, 18, 20, 25, 26 to Dejvická

This is yet another of my favorite haunts, as it has been ever since I moved here in 1994. Whenever I make it here (usually on my way to the airport), I find a fabulous trinket or two that I simply can't leave behind. There's an excellent collection of jewelry, including an extensive selection of diamond rings, so if an antique engagement ring happens to be on your must-find list, definitely add this store to your agenda. Ceramics, porcelain, glass, and toys round out the list of items to be found at this store. Most items are small, although they also carry some furniture upstairs.

ANTIKVARIÁTS Rare Books & Prints

An *antikvariát* is a specific type of antique store that specializes in all things paper related. In and among the many *antikvariáts* in Prague, you will find books, prints, maps, postcards, banknotes, stamps, and the list goes on. One of my favorite aspects of these shops are pick-boxes of stamps, banknotes or old photos, a lovely tradition that has long since disappeared from similar shops abroad.

■ ■ ■ ■ ■ ■ ■ ■ ■ ■ ■ ■

Alfafila

STAMPS
Václavské náměstí 28, pasáž
U Stýblů (Alfa), Prague 1,
Nové Město
www.alfafila.cz
TEL 224 235 457
HOURS Mon–Fri: 11:00–18:00; Sat: 11:00–16:00
METRO Můstek ●
TRAM 3, 9, 14, 24 to Václavské náměstí

Stamps, postcards, banknotes, and coins are primarily what you'll find at this little hole-in-the-wall. If you don't mind weeding through extensive books and boxes organized by various themes, then you're bound to find a treasure or two. No English is spoken, but the owner usually manages to figure out what you're interested in and will point you in the right direction. This is one of my regular haunts, and I have yet to walk out of the

COMMEMORATIVE POSTCARD FOR PRAGUE JUBILEE 1908, FEATURING A PORTRAIT OF EMPEROR FRANZ JOSEF (ILLUSTRATION BY KOLOMAN MOSER)

door without buying something; with prices starting at 2 CZK, it's not hard to justify the expenditure.

NOTE: This store can also be entered from the Světozor pasáž off Vodičkova.

CASH ONLY

■ ■ ■ ■ ■ ■ ■ ■ ■ ■ ■ ■ ■ ■
Antikvariát Pařížská
MAPS & PRINTS
Pařížská 8, Prague 1,
Staré Město
TEL 222 321 442
Daily: 10:00–18:00
METRO Staroměstská ●
Tram 17, 18 to Staroměstská

Given its location on the most expensive street in Prague, this store is surprisingly affordable. I had actually avoided it for years, assuming it was simply out of my budget. When I did finally wander in, however, I was pleasantly surprised

by the number of gems to be found that were very much within my price range. I've bought several items here, ranging from old educational posters to first-day covers of Czechoslovakian stamps.

■ ■ ■ ■ ■ ■ ■ ■ ■ ■ ■ ■ ■ ■
Antikvariát Karel Křenek
MAPS, BOOKS & PRINTS
U Obecního domu 2,
Prague 1, Staré Město
www.karelkrenek.com
TEL 222 314 734
HOURS Mon–Fri: 10:00–18:00; Sat: 11:00–18:00
METRO Náměstí Republiky
TRAM 5, 8, 14 to Náměstí Republiky

There are no bargains to be found at this lovely little shop. They have books and maps dating back to the 1500's, and on my last visit, two items really

captured my interest. The first was a Russian book of folk tales from the turn-of-the-century illustrated by Ivan Bilibin (think Walter Crane with a Russian flair and sensibility). The second item was a collection of hand-painted prayer books from the 1700's that were as beautiful as they were unusual. If you're interested in folklore and folk art, this store is definitely up your alley.

■ ■ ■ ■ ■ ■ ■ ■ ■ ■ ■ ■ ■ ■
Antikvariát Galerie Můstek
MAPS, BOTANICAL PRINTS & BOOKS
Národní 40/34 (Palác Adria),
Prague 1, Nové Město
TEL 224 949 587
HOURS Mon–Fri: 10:00–19:00; Sat: 12:00–16:00;
Sun: 14:00–18:00
METRO Národní třída ○
or Můstek ●

This store features maps dating back to the 17th century, as well as an excellent selection of copperplate engravings and lithographs, including botanical and zoological books. If you do visit this store, be sure to take note of the fantastic Rondo-Cubist building (Adria Palace) it's housed in.

■ ■ ■ ■ ■ ■ ■ ■ ■ ■ ■ ■ ■ ■
Antikvariát U Pražského jezulátka
BOOKS, ADVERTISEMENTS & POSTCARDS
Karmelitská 16, Prague 1,
Malá Strana
TEL 257 532 441
HOURS Daily: 10:00–12:00 & 13:00–18:00
METRO Malostranská ●
TRAM 12, 20, 22, 23 to Hellichova

TWO FIRST-DAY COVER ENVELOPES, C. 1951 & 1957

Miscellaneous would be the best word to describe this *antikvariát*. My most memorable purchases from this store have both been interior design related—near-complete collections of the seminal turn-of-the-century design magazines, *The Studio* and *Die Kunst*, as well as an interior design book from this period. In addition, they tend to have an interesting collection of old product labels, photos and postcards.

CASH ONLY

. . . .

Antikvariát U Zlaté číše

BOOKS, ADVERTISEMENTS & RECORDS
Nerudova 16, Prague 1, Malá Strana
TEL 257 531 393
HOURS Daily: 10:00–18:00
METRO Malostranská ●
TRAM 12, 20, 22, 23 to Malostranské náměstí

This is a terrific store that I've only recently begun to patronize. The assortment of items for sale here is large and varied, so although you'll definitely need a bit of time to sort through it all, you might just happen upon a great find! I should also mention that the shop assistants here are most helpful, which, it must be said, is not the norm in most *antikvariáts*.

. . . .

Sběratel The Collector

POSTCARDS
Malá Štupartská 5, Prague 1, Staré Město
TEL 224 827 097
HOURS Mon–Fri: 10:00–12:00 & 13:00–18:00; Sat & Sun: 11:00–18:00
METRO Můstek ● ●
or Náměstí Republiky ●

ADRIA PALACE, C. 1940

There's an excellent selection of old postcards and photos at Sběratel, though you'll need to filter through several well-stocked boxes to find your gems. And do be careful, as you can quickly rack up a large sum if you get carried away. They also offer framed vintage postcards. Beyond this, there's a small offering of other antiques, including old paper money, coins, medals and a few other odd baubles.

FURTHER AFIELD

. . . .

Antikvariát

SHEET MUSIC
Vinohradská 66, Prague 2, Vinohrady
TEL 224 251 220
HOURS Mon–Fri: 10:00–19:00; Sat: 10:00–12:00; Summer: 10:00–18:00
METRO Jiřího z Poděbrad ●
TRAM 11 to Jiřího z Poděbrad

If you're looking for old sheet music, this is the best resource I've found in town. They also carry books and records, but

DANCERS (2006), BY DANIEL PITÍN (OIL ON CANVAS)
(COURTESY OF HUNT KASTNER GALLERY)

it's definitely the sheet music that I come here for—the graphics are often fabulous, and I've had several pieces framed and hung in my office. Prices begin at about 5 CZK.

ART GALLERIES

Galerie JBK
WORKS ON PAPER
Betlémské náměstí 8, Prague 1, Staré Město
TEL 222 220 689
HOURS Daily: 10:00–19:00
METRO Můstek ●
or Národní třída ○

This gallery focuses exclusively on works on paper, and the artists are primarily Czech, from the turn-of-the-century through the end of the First Republic. Recent shows have included work by Josef Lada, Vojtěch Preissig (a student of Mucha), as well as Mucha himself. The prices range from a few thousand crowns on up. They also have antiques in the basement, mostly furniture

and lamps from the 1920's and 1930's.

Hunt Kastner Artworks
PAINTINGS, PRINTS & PHOTOGRAPHY
Kamenická 22, Prague 7, Holešovice
www.huntkastner.com
TEL 233 376 259
HOURS Wed, Thu, Fri: 12:00–17:00; (or by appointment)
METRO Vltavská ●
TRAM 1, 8, 15, 20, 25, 26 to Kamenická

This is a new gallery, focusing exclusively on contemporary Czech art. They represent several highly regarded young artists, including Josef

Bolf, who is my own favorite Czech painter. Media include oil, acrylic, prints and photography. Works on paper range from 8,000 CZK to 40,000 CZK, while paintings range from 50,000 CZK to 150,000 CZK. Camille Hunt, one of the owners and founders of the gallery, is a native of Toronto and also a long-term expatriate like me. In order to put some of this new Czech work in perspective, I'd recommend visiting this gallery in combination with the *Veletržní palác*, the National Gallery's collection for 19th, 20th and 21st century art (see p. 52).

Jiří Švestka
PAINTINGS, PRINTS & SCULPTURE
Biskupský dvůr 6, Prague 1, Nové Město
www.jirisvestka.com
TEL 222 311 092
HOURS Tue–Fri: 12:00–18:00; Sat: 11:00–18:00
METRO Náměstí Republiky ●
TRAM 3, 8, 24, 26 to Bílá labuť

Having participated in such high profile international art fairs as Basel, Jiří Švestka is, unquestionably, the leading private art gallery in Prague. The gallery covers many different

Umělec Magazine, established in 1997, is the local equivalent of art magazines such as *Parkett* or *Frieze*. It can be found in galleries throughout Prague. Parts of it are in English.

Cover Price: 120 CZK

UMĚLEC MAGAZINE COVER
(COURTESY OF *UMĚLEC*)

periods, including Modern, Post-War, and Contemporary, as well as works in several different media. Most but not all of the artists represented are Czech. If you're curious to see the Czech Republic's answer to Larry Gagosian or Paula Cooper, this should be put on your must-see list. Prague isn't about to become a major contemporary art capital anytime soon; nonetheless this gallery is well worth a visit.

ART SUPPLIES

■ ■ ■ ■ ■ ■ ■ ■ ■ ■ ■

Altamira

Jilská 2, Prague 1, Staré Město
TEL 224 219 950
HOURS Mon–Fri: 9:00–19:00; Sat: 10:00–17:00
METRO Národní třída ●

This art supply store is just a block away from the one listed below. If you're mostly focused on crafts and hobbies, this is probably the better option to start at, as you'll find materials for candle-making, batik, ceramics, decoupage, glass painting, beading, and so on. They also have another store around the corner that is focused on professional art supplies such as paints, engraving materials, papers, canvases, easels, stretchers, brushes, portfolios and so on. The second store is located at Skořepka 1.

■ ■ ■ ■ ■ ■ ■ ■ ■ ■ ■

Zlatá loď

Národní 37, Prague 1, Staré Město (in the Passage Platýz)
www.zlatalod.cz
TEL 222 220 174

The České Budějovice-based *Koh-i-noor* company has been producing high quality art supplies since 1790, including water-soluble colored pencils, graphite pencils, chalks, and paints. In addition to their standard offerings, they also make beautifully packaged gift sets. You can find their products at the art supply stores listed, as well as *Hračky* (see p. 125). Some department stores also carry the line, usually in the paper section, but their offerings tend to be much more limited.

www.koh-i-noor.cz

HOURS Mon–Fri: 09:00–19:00; Sat: 10:00–17:00
METRO Národní třída ●

You never know when inspiration will strike, or when you'll need to keep the kids occupied with an art project. In either case, this store can supply you with materials for all your artistic needs. Located in the heart of downtown in the same passageway as Kava Kava Kava (a local coffee café that is certainly better marked than this store), Zlatá loď has an excellent selection of art supplies, and you should be able to find just about anything you need to realize your vision.

BEE KEEPING

■ ■ ■ ■ ■ ■ ■ ■ ■ ■ ■

Včelařské potřeby

Křemencova 8, Prague 1, Nové Město
TEL 224 934 344
HOURS Mon–Thu: 08:00–12:30 & 13:00–17:00; Fri: 08:30–12:00
TRAM 6, 9, 18, 21, 22, 23 to Karlovo náměstí or Národní třída

Have you always dreamed of becoming a beekeeper? If so, Včelařské potřeby provides you with the ideal opportunity to get your feet wet and stock up on all of the required accessories. Additionally, they carry a generous selection of gifts, including *medovina* (a local honey wine), beeswax candles, and a broad range of cosmetics.

CASH ONLY

BOOKS

Anagram Bookshop
ENGLISH LANGUAGE & CHILDREN'S BOOKS
Týn 4, Ungelt, Prague 1, Staré Město
www.anagram.cz
TEL 224 895 737
HOURS Mon–Sat: 10:00–20:00; Sun: 10:00–19:00
METRO Náměstí Republiky
TRAM 5, 8, 14 to Náměstí Republiky

This English language bookstore has an excellent collection of children's books, not to mention a very cozy reading corner. It also offers a good selection of classics and art books. Much less mainstream than Big Ben.

Ars Pragensis
CZECH HISTORY, ARCHITECTURE, BLACK & WHITE POSTCARDS, & FAIRY TALES
Malostranské náměstí. 27, Prague 1, Malá Strana
TEL 257 532 093
HOURS Mon–Fri: 10:30–18:00; Sat & Sun: 12:00–18:00
METRO Malostranská
TRAM 12, 20, 22, 23 to Malostranské náměstí

A great little bookstore in the heart of Malá Strana, Ars Pragensis focuses exclusively on books related to the Czech Republic, including history, architecture and even fairytales translated

SEMINÁŘSKÁ STREET, C. 1920

Twisted Spoon Press

Twisted Spoon is a Prague-based independent publisher founded in 1992. Focused on translating a variety of writing from Central & Eastern Europe, the press boasts an author list studded with internationally recognized names as well as up-and-coming authors. A few of their titles that are definitely worth seeking out while you're in Prague:

1. The Kafka series, including *Contemplation, A Country Doctor,* and A Hunger Artist

2. *Total Fears,* Bohumil Hrabal

3. *May,* Karel Hynek Mácha

4. *Severin's Journey into the Dark,* Paul Leppin

www.twistedspoon.com

into other languages. The store also offers a well-edited collection of black-and-white vintage postcard reproductions, most of them Prague-related, as well as a fun selection of writing tools from Koh-i-noor, making it the perfect stop before heading off to a local café for a postcard writing session.

▪ ▪ ▪ ▪ ▪ ▪ ▪ ▪ ▪ ▪ ▪ ▪ ▪ ▪

Big Ben Bookshop

ENGLISH LANGUAGE
GUIDE BOOKS, BEST
SELLERS, & SCIENCE
FICTION
Malá Štupartská 5, Prague 1,
Staré Město
www.bigbenbookshop.com
TEL 224 826 565
HOURS Mon–Fri: 09:00–
18:30; Sat: 10:00–17:00;
Sun: 12:00–17:00
METRO Náměstí Republiky
TRAM 5, 8, 14 to Náměstí
Republiky

This English language bookstore has the best selection of guidebooks in town. They also have a wide selection of current fiction and non-fiction best sellers.

▪ ▪ ▪ ▪ ▪ ▪ ▪ ▪ ▪ ▪ ▪ ▪ ▪ ▪

Fraktály

ART, ARCHITECTURE, &
DESIGN
Betlémské náměstí 5a,
Prague 1, Staré Město
TEL 222 222 186
HOURS Mon–Sat: 10:00–
20:00; Sun: 12:00–20:00
METRO Můstek
or Národní třída

Established in 2002, Fraktály is the first store in Prague to specialize in books on architecture, design, and contemporary art. If you're looking for books on Czech art, architecture or design, this

Czech Literature Translated Into English

Jaroslav Hašek
The Good Soldier Švejk, Penguin, 1923
By precisely following every order he is given without ever accomplishing anything, Švejk reveals the ludicrous (and hilarious) bureaucracy of war.

Bohumil Hrabal
Closely Watched Trains, Abacus, 1966
Set in Nazi-occupied Czechoslovakia during WWII, this coming-of-age story centers on Miloš Hrma, a young man apprenticing as a signalman at a railway station.

I Served the King of England
Vintage International, 1971
The life and ambitions of the story's protagonist, Ditie (waiter turned millionaire turned prisoner), provide clear insight into the tumultuous history of the Czech nation.

Total Fears, Twisted Spoon, 1995
Total Fears takes the form of a series of personal letters written to an American student before and during the Velvet Revolution of Czechoslovakia in 1989.

Milan Kundera
The Joke, Harper, 1967
Ludvík is a bright university student in early 1950's Czechoslovakia, popular with his peers, and an active supporter of the country's new Communist regime. Intending to be funny, he sends a postcard to his girlfriend criticizing the Communist regime and soon finds his world has turned on him.

The Unbearable Lightness of Being
Harper, 1984
The Unbearable Lightness of Being examines the lives of Czech artists and intellectuals following the Prague Spring in 1968.

Franz Kafka
The Trial, Schocken, 1925
A psychological examination of Josef K., an ordinary man who, for reasons that are never revealed, is arrested one morning and put through the rigors of the justice system for an unspecified crime he almost certainly did not commit.

Jan Neruda
Tales of the Little Quarter, Greenwood, 1877
Prague's answer to Charles Dickens; bittersweet stories of life in 19th century Malá Strana.

Children's Books

Lucie Seifertová, *Mysterious Prague*, Slovart, 2003
This is a wonderfully fun pop-up book that reveals the history of Prague.

Josef Lada, *Mike Cat* (1934–1936)
A fairy tale made up of four stories about a speaking cat, Mikeš, and his unbelievable adventures with his friends a pig (Pašík) and billy-goat (Bobeš).

Zdeněk Miler, *How Come Little Mole has Trousers*, 1956
The first book featuring Krtek, the Czech Republic's most famous and beloved animated character. See p. 125 for more information on Krtek's history.

Olga Strunová (Illustrations by Helena Zmatlíková), *Mother Mouse*, Albatros 1961
A picture book of nursery rhymes, from 1961, with wonderful Bohemian imagery.

Czech-Related Books Written by Foreigners

Bruce Chatwin, *Utz*, Penguin, 1988
The tale of a porcelain collector based in the Jewish quarter of Prague, *Utz* is not your conventional hero. In this slim volume, Chatwin draws a satirical portrait of life in a Socialist state and concludes by revealing that human nature is the same no matter what political winds may be blowing.

J.M. Ledgard, *Giraffe*, Penguin, 2006
Giraffe tells the true story of the extermination of the largest herd of giraffes ever held in captivity in a zoo in Czechoslovakia in 1975.

Michael Chabon, *The Amazing Adventures of Kavalier & Clay*, Picador, 2001
The beginning of this National Book Award-winning novel is set in the Jewish quarter in Prague, and it's clear from every bewitching detail that Mr. Chabon has spent time here.

NOTE: *Prague*, by Arthur Phillips (Random House, 2003), is *not* actually about Prague; rather, it is about Budapest. While there is certainly an artistic reason for this (Prague being the Budapest expatriate's notion of a better place in which to be young and lost), Phillips has undoubtedly sold many copies to unsuspecting buyers who thought they were purchasing something quite different.

is the best choice in town. They also have an excellent selection of art and coffee-table books in English from publishing houses such as Phaidon, Rizzoli, and Thames & Hudson.

■ ■ ■ ■ ■ ■ ■ ■ ■ ■ ■ ■ ■
Knihkupectví U černé Matky Boží
MISCELLANEOUS BOOKS ON PRAGUE
Celetná 34, Prague 1, Staré Město
TEL 224 211 275
HOURS Mon–Fri: 09:30–18:30; Sat & Sun: 10:00–18:00
METRO Náměstí Republiky
TRAM 5, 8, 14 to Náměstí Republiky

Maps and books on Prague are the order of the day here, including illustrated coffee table books and Czech children's books translated into English. They also carry lots of interesting postcards.

■ ■ ■ ■ ■ ■ ■ ■ ■ ■ ■ ■ ■
Shakespeare and Sons
NEW & USED ENGLISH LANGUAGE BOOKS
U Lužického semináře 10, Prague 1, Malá Strana
www.shakes.cz
TEL 257 531 894
HOURS Daily: 11:00–19:00
METRO Malostranská ●

If you're in Malá Strana and looking for the work of a local author translated into English, this is an excellent bet. Shakespeare and Sons carries both new and used titles, and the ambience of the place is wonderfully cozy.

PHOTOGRAPHER IN PRAGUE, C. 1930

CAMERAS

Foto Škoda

Vodičkova 37 Palác Langhans,
Prague 1, Nové Město
www.fotoskoda.cz
TEL 222 929 029
HOURS Mon–Fri: 8:30– 20:00;
Sat 9:00–18:00
METRO Můstek ● ●
TRAM 3, 9, 14, 24 to Václavské
náměstí

One-stop shopping for all
your photography needs:
cameras, film, lenses,
cases… You name it; they
carry it.

Jan Pazdera

FOTO KINO OPTIKA
VIDEO
Vodičkova 30, Prague 1,
Nové Město
TEL 224 235 404
HOURS Mon–Fri: 10:00–18:00
METRO Můstek ● ●
TRAM 3, 9, 14, 24 to Václavské
náměstí

If you fancy antique
cameras, look no further
than this store. They have
everything from 127 to
8x10. I usually focus
on medium-format 120
cameras and I particularly
like those that were
manufactured locally,
including Corina, Fex,
Folkafex, and Pionýr.
The sales staff does not
speak English, but with
a little patience and
perhaps your very best
mime performance *ever*,
you'll get to see what you
want.

CAMERAS MADE IN
CZECHOSLOVAKIA

LEFT: FLEXARET, C. 1940's

TOP: PIONÝR, C. 1948–1967

BOTTOM: CORINA
(THE CZECHOSLOVAKIAN
EQUIVALENT OF THE
FAMED RUSSIAN LOMO),
C. 1963–1980's

CERAMICIST PAINTING BOHEMIAN POTTERY, C. 1941

CERAMICS & PORCELAIN

In addition to glass, the Czech Republic is known for its high-quality ceramics and porcelain. Although the vast majority is designed on a white background, you may also come upon items with a black background, my personal favorite.

▪▪▪▪▪▪▪▪▪▪▪▪▪▪▪

Tupesy Lidová keramika
PAINTED CERAMICS
Havelská 1, Prague 1, Staré Město
TEL 224 214 176
HOURS Daily: 10:00–19:00
METRO Můstek ●

This store features hand-made ceramics from Southern Moravia. The style is reminiscent of the kind of Italian ceramics you often see today, but with a unique feeling of Czech folklore and a decorative aesthetic that traces back to the Swiss Protestants who relocated to this region in the first half of the 16th century. This store has been around for years and carries a wide selection of pieces, many of which make great gifts. Prices range from 60 CZK to 10,000 CZK.

Further Afield— But Not Too Far (One Metro Stop From Muzeum)
▪▪▪▪▪▪▪▪▪▪▪▪▪▪▪

Dům porcelánu
PORCELAIN
Jugoslávská 16, Prague 2, Vinohrady
www.cesky.porcelan.cz
TEL 221 505 320
HOURS Mon–Fri: 09:00–19:00; Sat: 9:00–17:00; Sun: 14:00–17:00
METRO Náměstí Míru ● or I. P. Pavlova ●
TRAM 4, 6, 10, 16, 22, 23, 11 to I. P. Pavlova

If you're interested in Czech porcelain, this is definitely the best place in town. The "blue onion" made by Český porcelán is the quintessential Czech porcelain motif, its design originating from the first half of the 17th century. It is now back in vogue, and the famed New York design store, Moss, no less, is selling a Meissen version at $491 per five-piece place setting, while local ultra-hip designer Maxim Velčovský has applied the motif to a fabulous bust of Lenin as well as the work boots (see Qubus, p. 104). As a result you might just want to consider getting your own five-piece place setting here for 1,465 CZK ($65), a mere fraction of what Moss is charging. Dům porcelánu also had a great little cow figurine with the "blue onion" motif for 500 CZK, which in the right setting could definitely be seen as very modern and hip. I was also taken by the work of Haas & Czjzek, another Czech porcelain manufacturer—specifically the decorative pieces with gold ornamental work that are reminiscent of KPM. They also carry porcelain by Thun and Royal Dux Bohemia. This store is not exactly in the center of town, but it's certainly easily accessible by both metro and tram. Alternatively, hop in a taxi; it will be a very short ride.

CHANDELIERS AND LIGHTING

▪▪▪▪▪▪▪▪▪▪▪▪▪▪▪

Arzenal
Valentinská 11, Prague 1, Staré Město
www.arzenal.cz
TEL 224 814 099
HOURS Daily: 10:00–24:00
METRO Staroměstská ●
TRAM 17, 18 to Staroměstská

If you're a fan of Bořek Šípek, currently one of the most famous contemporary Czech designers, then you won't want to miss stopping in at Arzenal, which carries a great many interesting contemporary chandeliers and lighting fixtures— colorful, whimsical, and unusual would be good adjectives to describe them. Prices range from 13,000 CZK (for a simple piece) to 240,000 CZK (for a very large and complex chandelier).

REPRODUCTION GOČÁR CHANDELIER (1913), AVAILABLE AT MODERNISTA (P. 96)

M. Material Glass
STORE & INTERIOR DESIGN
U Lužického semináře 7, Prague 1, Staré Město
www.i-material.com
TEL 257 530 046
HOURS Daily: 10:30–21:00
METRO Malostranská ●

This store carries a very good selection of contemporary chandeliers with clean designs that are anything but fussy. The display here is easily the most sophisticated in town, with the items carefully selected and curated so that each piece can be appreciated independently. Prices for chandeliers range from 17,000 CZK to 32,000 CZK.

Preciosa
Jindřišská 19, Prague 1, Nové Město
TEL 222 247 550
Mon–Fri: 10:00–19:00; Sat & Sun: 10:00–17:00
METRO Můstek ● ●
TRAM 3, 9, 14, 24 to Jindřišská

Preciosa is the dominant manufacturer for current Czech chandelier production. Prices range from 1,280 CZK for wall sconces to 186,430 CZK for a very large chandelier. Custom projects are also possible, and it's quite likely that you'll already have seen their work, since their chandeliers hang in hotels and cultural venues throughout the world, including the Prague Castle and Russia's Bolshoi Theatre.

The store also offers individual replacement pieces, starting at 6 CZK, as well as several metal fixture replacements.

If you're in the market for a new chandelier that is traditional in style, this is definitely an excellent starting point. The sales staff is neither especially friendly nor helpful, but if you seem to be a serious customer, I'm certain they can rise to the occasion.

ANTIQUE CHANDELIERS AND LIGHTING Including Reproductions

Antikva Ing. Burger
CHANDELIERS & LIGHTING
Betlémské náměstí 8, Prague 1, Staré Město (in courtyard)
TEL 222 221 595
HOURS Mon–Fri: 10:00–13:00 & 14:00–18:00; Sat: 10:00–16:00
METRO Můstek ● ●
or Národní třída ●

If lighting fixtures such as chandeliers and lamps are on your shopping agenda, then definitely add this shop to your itinerary. I have not personally bought anything here yet, but I do enjoy stopping in, as they always seem to have an interesting and varied collection.

Modernista

CHANDELIERS & LIGHTING
Celetná 12, Prague 1,
Staré Město
www.modernista.cz
TEL 224 241 300
HOURS Daily: 10:00–20:00
METRO Můstek ● ●

Located in the heart of Prague's busiest street, this excellent design shop is hard to miss. Modernista sells reproductions of the original designs by prominent Czech Cubist designers like Pavel Janák, Vlastislav Hofman and Josef Gočár. The collection includes a nice reproduction of a really fierce chandelier by Gočár (69,000 CZK), the same architect that designed the interior including the chandeliers of the Grand Café Orient at the Black Madonna Museum (see p. 50). The store also offers Cubist table lamps, as well Functionalist table and floor lamps.

Further Afield— But Not Too Far (Two Tram Stops From Národní Třída)

Starožitný nábytek Josef Liška

CHANDELIERS & LIGHTING
Vyšehradská 33, Prague 2,
Nové Město
TEL 224 919 053
HOURS Mon–Fri: 09:00–18:00
METRO Karlovo Náměstí ●
then Tram 18, 24 to Botanická zahrada

Located in the very back of a rather crummy courtyard, the entrance to this shop is anything but inviting, but the items they carry make it well worth seeking out. They carry lots of interesting 1930's–1960's furniture and light fixtures, including an extensive collection of chandeliers, as well as miscellaneous small items. This shop is on my regular hit list, and happens to be where I bought my very first antique in Prague, a light fixture that still hangs from the ceiling of my bedroom. Hand-painted with a Bohemian floral motif, this piece remains one of my all-time favorite finds. Money well spent!

CASH ONLY

CHOCOLATE

Czechs love chocolate. Just visit a grocery store and you will be shocked to see the disproportionately large amount of shelf space it gets. My own local favorite is Orion's *Studentská pečeť hořká*, a dark chocolate filled with peanuts, raisins and candied fruit. Orion is the most venerable local manufacturer, having been established in 1896 in Vinohrady (although they later moved to another quarter in Prague). That said, none of the local brands are the kind of real standout that I'd go out of my way to purchase and bring back home. Instead, I've listed a Belgian chocolate store that happens to make a delicious little truffle with dark chocolate filled with Becherovka, a local herbal liqueur, which *is* a standout and definitely worthy of air travel!

Gold Pralines

Rybná 2, Prague 1,
Nové Město
TEL 222 316 227
HOURS Daily: 09:00–20:00
METRO Náměstí Republiky ●
TRAM 5, 8, 14 to Náměstí Republiky

CHRISTMAS ORNAMENTS

Czechs have a long history of making Christmas ornaments. Sadly, today it seems that the bulk of this work is done for export, and it's difficult to find interesting new pieces for purchase here in Prague. However, I've listed two of the stores that I consistently have luck with. I also encourage you to look for ornaments in antique stores and bazaars, as this is where I often pick up some of my most cherished finds.

KOFILA CHOCOLATE BAR LABEL, 1962. THE WRAPPER WAS ORIGINALLY DESIGNED IN 1921 AND HAS SURVIVED ALMOST UNCHANGED TO THIS DAY... SO GO BUY A KOFILA!

GINGERBREAD PRODUCTION, C. 1990

downtown Prague. They offer a wide range of Czech traditional handicrafts, including old-fashioned Christmas ornaments made from either straw or varnished gingerbread, as well as hand-painted eggs which are used for ornamentation both at Christmas and Easter.

CZECH HANDICRAFTS

■ ■ ■ ■ ■ ■ ■ ■ ■ ■ ■ ■ ■
Dom Job Košára
Rybná 27, Prague 1,
Staré Město
TEL 221 700 111
HOURS Mon–Fri: 08:00–13:00
& 14:00–20:00;
(Closed Wednesday)
METRO Náměstí Republiky ●
TRAM 5, 8, 14 to Dlouhá třída

Part of a non-profit organization that helps get Prague youth off the streets, this store features charming hand-crafted baskets in all shapes, sizes and colors made by local teenagers right on-site. Not only are they conducting a productive social service, but the baskets are enchanting and the prices almost embarrassingly low.
CASH ONLY

■ ■ ■ ■ ■ ■ ■ ■ ■ ■ ■ ■ ■
Fabre Facta
Zlatá ulička u Daliborky
30/31, Prague 1, Hradčany
TEL 233 339 268
HOURS Daily: 09:00–17:00
METRO Malostranská ●
TRAM 22, 23 to Pražský hrad

Fabre Facta is located on the castle grounds; you'll see the shop on your left immediately *before* paying your entrance fee to Golden Lane. The store boasts an interesting collection of

■ ■ ■ ■ ■ ■ ■ ■ ■ ■ ■ ■ ■
Dana
Národní 43, Prague 1,
Staré Město (Perlova 10)
TEL 224 214 655
HOURS Mon–Sat: 09:00–
19:00; Sun: 10:00–18:00
METRO Můstek ● ●
or Národní třída ●

While this store also sells ceramics, porcelain and chandeliers, I tend to come here mainly for their Christmas ornaments, stopping in throughout the year to check out their

GINGERBREAD COOKIES
CHRISTMAS, 2006
(MADE BY KATEŘINA PAVLITOVÁ,
DIRECTOR OF PUBLIC RELATIONS
AT MANDARIN ORIENTAL PRAGUE,
AS A GIFT TO THE AUTHOR).

inventory, which is always clearly displayed at the counter. I should mention that if you're looking for natural handmade ornaments, this stop is *not* for you. What you will find here are wonderfully colorful and glittering ornaments in all shapes and sizes ranging from classic ball shapes to my personal favorite, the Christmas hedgehog! Prices start at 22 CZK per ornament.

NOTE: You will need to enter by walking through the passageway.

■ ■ ■ ■ ■ ■ ■ ■ ■ ■ ■ ■ ■
Manufaktura
Melantrichova 17 and
Železná 3a,
Prague 1, Staré Město
TEL 221 632 480
HOURS Daily: 10:00–19:00
METRO Můstek ● ●

You'll see this chain of stores throughout

TRADITIONAL HAND-PRINTED TEXTILE, 1939
(SOURCE: EVA MAGAZINE)

Two things in particular set Traditional apart from Manufaktura: First, its selection of vintage enamelware (including old street signs and house numbers, starting at 275 CZK); and second, the owner's unique collection of 19th through early 20th century woodblocks (originally used for printing textiles and wallpaper and now sold as decorative objects). The latter were acquired from a factory that dates back to the Austro-Hungarian Empire. Each block was hand-carved with various motifs from plum or pear wood (interestingly, the same material used in making molds for mouth-blown glass production). Prices range from 800 CZK to 4,000 CZK, with most hovering around 2,000 CZK. Discounts are given if you purchase more than one item, which is worth it in any case for aesthetic reasons alone (so much better to group!). The store also carries ceramics, blue-printed textiles, some very cute cornhusk dolls, and other curiosities that the owner has found in his travels throughout the Czech Republic.

historical reproductions and artifacts that I've *never* seen at any other store in Prague. All are handmade using traditional methods and materials. Among the offerings are linen shirts, leather goods, handmade paper, religious icons, forest glass, beeswax candles, and tin soldiers. A most pleasant surprise! They also have a second location at Nosticova ulice 8, Prague 1, Malá Strana, right off of Kampa Island (TEL 257 311 165).

■■■■■■■■■■■■■■
Manufaktura
Melantrichova 17 and Železná 3A, Prague 1, Staré Město
TEL 221 632 480
HOURS Daily: 10:00–19:00
METRO Můstek ● ●

You will see this chain of stores throughout downtown Prague. They offer a wide range of Czech traditional handicrafts including wooden toys with a natural finish, blue-printed textiles, embroidered table cloths, ceramics, kitchen utensils, bath products, wool sweaters and rugs, painted eggs, and old-fashioned Christmas ornaments made from either straw or varnished gingerbread. Melantrichova and Železná are my two favorite locations, but they have several other outlets, including one on Karlova 26, another on Golden Lane at the Prague Castle (see p. 76), and even a location at Terminal 1 in the airport. All of the stores will have a very similar range of merchandise and beautiful packaging, making them a terrific resource for gifts.

■■■■■■■■■■■■■■
Traditional
Haštalská 7, Prague 1, Staré Město
www.woodblocks.cz
TEL 222 316 661

PAINTING EASTER EGGS IN A BOHEMIAN VILLAGE, C. 1940

SHOPPING

WILL RUSSELL AND THE AUTHOR WITH OUR 1981 LADA, PURCHASED FOR $600 (1)

CZECH VEHICLES
Cars & Motorcycles

■ ■ ■ ■ ■ ■ ■ ■ ■ ■ ■ ■ ■ ■

Prague Classic Car Centre
Strakonická 1, Prague 5, Smíchov
www.old-timers.cz
TEL 257 213 904
HOURS Mon–Sat: 09:00–18:00
Take a Taxi

Have you been lusting for an antique Škoda, Tatra or Jawa to add to your car collection? Well, deliberate no longer! Simply stop in the Prague Classic Car Centre, where you can pick up a 1940 Škoda Popular for 199,000 CZK, or a 1960 Škoda Felicia convertible

Škoda, Tatra, and Jawa

The Czech motoring industry dates back to the end of the 19th century, and its most famous manufacturers are Škoda, Tatra, and Jawa.

Škoda, which ironically means "it's a pity" in Czech (though for some reason Czechs don't seem to find the humor in it), dates back to 1899, when the team of Laurin & Klement produced their first motorcycle. Its first car, the Voiturette, debuted in 1905, making it the first car manufacturer in the Austro-Hungarian Empire. In 1925, Laurin & Klement merged with a machinery company named Škoda in order to stay afloat during the severely weakened market after WWI. Later, under communism, Škoda's main competitors were Lada, produced in the Soviet Union, and Trabant from East Germany. In 1991, Volkswagen bought a 70% stake in the company, and it continues to enjoy a large piece of the Czech market, to say nothing of the 80% percent of their production that is exported to other countries throughout the world.

Still known primarily as the official producer of government cars for high-ranking communist officers, **Tatra**, also manufactured in the Czech Republic, focuses primarily on trucks these days. In its heyday, however, it produced one of the first aerodynamic cars. Kind of like Citroen's sexy older brother... Hot. *So* hot.

Jawa is the most famous Czech motorcycle manufacturer. It began in 1929, when the founder bought out the motorcycle manufacturer Wanderer, and then changed the name to the unforgettable one it still sports today.

MLADÝ TECHNIK MAGAZINE COVER, 1952

Museums Featuring Czech Cars

National Technical Museum

CARS, TRAINS & PLANES
CLOSED as of Sept. 12, 2006, due to reconstruction; Re-opening planned for July 2008
Kostelní 42, Prague 7, Holešovice; www.ntm.cz
TEL 220 399 111
HOURS Tue–Fri: 09:00–17:00; Sat & Sun: 10:00–18:00
ENTRANCE FEE 70 CZK Adult; 30 CZK Children; 6 and under Free
METRO Hradčanská ● or Vltavská ●
TRAM 8, 25, 26 to Letenské náměstí

This museum is *very* fun. My favorite room, an enormous Functionalist space called the transport hall, is filled to the brim with Czech-made vehicles, including vintage steam engines, cars, trucks, motorcycles, and bicycles, as well as airplanes suspended from the ceiling.

MR. HORÁK IN HIS VINTAGE TATRA, 1969

for 149,000 CZK (see back cover), as well as a 1932 Walter Junior convertible for 290,000 CZK—perfect for a Sunday drive and picnic in the countryside. There are also several Jawa motorcycles to choose from. And, should the vehicles themselves fall out of your price range, you can instead take home a 1:43 model of your favorite Škoda or Tatra. In addition, they sell old car parts, an excellent collection of books, leather driving gloves (made locally), and, of course, aviator goggles and caps that let you *really* nail that authentic look.

TRABANT ADVERTISEMENT, 1962
(SOURCE: WWW.TRABANT.CZ)

Trabants or "Trabis," as they are affectionately called, have, like the Beetle and the Mini, passed into motoring legend. What sets this East German car apart, though, is that they were made from Duraplast, a composite of Phenolic resin and cotton fibers (similar to formica, bakelite or fiberglass) developed at the end of WWII, when steel was in limited supply. The sedan and station wagon styles that you'll find in toy stores (miniatures of miniatures) were in production from 1964 through 1991, and retained the same basic shape throughout that entire period.

See p. 127 (Sparkys) if you're interested in acquiring the toy version.

Škoda Auto Museum in Mladá Boleslav

Třída Václava Klementa 294, Mladá Boleslav
www.skoda-auto.com/global/history/muzeum
TEL 326 831 134
HOURS Daily: 09:00–17:00
ENTRANCE FEE 50 CZK Adult; 25 CZK Children; 6 and under Free
30km northeast of Prague on the E65.

The exhibition incorporates over 25 old Škodas and Laurin & Klements, including a rather heroic fire engine from 1917. The bulk of the collection is from the 1920's and 1930's.

NOTE: You can take the train, which takes about 1 hour, but I highly recommend either driving or being driven.

Tatra Technical Museum in Kopřivnice

Záhumenní 369, Kopřivnice
(look for the red locomotive outside)
www.tatramuseum.cz
TEL 556 871 106
HOURS Tue–Sun: 09:00–17:00; (Winter till 16:00)
ENTRANCE FEE 75 CZK Adult; 45 CZK Children; 6 and under Free
The only way to get to this museum is by driving, and it's a long drive.

Old cars, trucks and trains are housed at this very off-the-beaten-track museum in Moravia. I brought my parents and we all loved it. Our only regret is that we did not actually purchase the Tatra 77 that was for sale at that time. Don't make our mistake!

KOTVA DEPARTMENT STORE, 1980 (PHOTO BY JAROSLAV VEBR)

DEPARTMENT STORES

Kotva

Náměstí Republiky 8, Prague 1, Staré Město
TEL 224 801 111
HOURS Mon–Fri: 09:00–20:00; Sat: 10:00–19:00; Sun: 10:00–18:00
METRO Náměstí Republiky
TRAM 5, 8, 14 to Náměstí Republiky

Built in 1975, Kotva was the chicest store in town under communism; sadly, this is no longer true. The store is now made of up various independently run kiosks offering everything from cosmetics, costume jewelry and clothing to sporting goods and major appliances. They even have a rather good sewing department.

I tend to pop in to check out the stationery section on the ground floor with office and school supplies. Europeans always have great plastic folders and binders, so if you are obsessively organized, you will love it. Kotva also has a kiosk offering the most comprehensive selection of Schleich plastic animals and figurines; these toys are surprisingly realistic and extremely well made. You'll find it on the ground floor, next to the stationery section. In the basement is an Albert supermarket.

Tesco

Národní 26, Prague 1, Nové Město
TEL 222 003 111
HOURS Mon–Fri: 08:00–21:00; Sat: 09:00–20:00; Sun: 10:00–20:00
METRO Národní třída
TRAM 6, 9, 18, 21, 22, 23 to Národní třída

KOTVA DEPARTMENT STORE GRAND OPENING, 1975
(SOURCE: ČTK / CZECH NEWS AGENCY)

Tesco is the largest department store in downtown Prague and my personal favorite, as its layout is more logical and better labeled than Kotva's. Here, too, you will find an excellent selection of office and school supplies, as well as cosmetics, clothing, shoes, sporting goods, household items and electronics. In the basement is a Tesco supermarket.

NOTE: In October 2006, the building in which Tesco is housed became a cultural monument, cited as an excellent example of 1970's Communist architecture. You might question my fact checking after seeing the building for yourself; however, I can assure you, it's true. The review committee must have focused on the escalators, which are indeed rather chic.

TESCO ESCALATORS, 1980
(PHOTO BY JAROSLAV VEBR)

DESIGN SHOPS

■ ■ ■ ■ ■ ■ ■ ■ ■ ■ ■ ■ ■

Beldafactory

JEWELRY & HOUSEHOLD
OBJECTS

Mikulandská 10, Prague 1,
Nové Město

www.belda.cz

TEL 224 933 052

HOURS Mon–Thu: 10:00–
18:00; Fri: 10:00–17:00

METRO Národní třída ○

TRAM 6, 9, 18, 21, 22, 23 to
Národní divadlo

While offering an
assortment of items, this
design shop specializes in
jewelry designed by the
owner, Jiří Belda, utilizing
various metals (including
silver, titanium, stainless
steel, platinum and white
and yellow gold) combined
with precious stones, as
well as onyx and turquoise
and even plastics such
as Perspex and Corian. The
store also features jewelry
and house wares by several
other Czech designers
including Bára Škorpilová,
a famous local architect,
and Olgoj Chorchoj, whose
work can be found at Moss
in New York City.

■ ■ ■ ■ ■ ■ ■ ■ ■ ■ ■ ■ ■

Kubista

HOUSEHOLD OBJECTS &
BOOKS

Ovocný trh 19, Prague 1,
Staré Město

www.kubista.cz

TEL 224 236 378

HOURS Tue–Sun: 10:00–
18:00; (Monday closed)

METRO Náměstí Republiky ○

TRAM 5, 8, 14 to Náměstí
Republiky

Located in the ground
floor of the Black Madonna
Museum, Kubista, like
Modernista, sells replicas
of the original designs by
prominent Czech Cubist

BOX WITH LID BY PAVEL
JANÁK, 1911
(COURTESY OF MODERNISTA)

designers like Pavel Janák,
Vlastislav Hofman and
Josef Gočár. The offerings
include ceramics,
furniture, metalwork, and
paper goods, including
some *very* cool Cubist
wrapping paper. The store
also offers an excellent
selection of literature
related to Czech Cubist
painting, architecture and
applied arts.

■ ■ ■ ■ ■ ■ ■ ■ ■ ■ ■ ■ ■

Modernista

HOUSEHOLD OBJECTS &
FURNITURE

Celetná 12, Prague 1,
Staré Město

www.modernista.cz

TEL 224 241 300

HOURS Daily: 10:00–20:00

METRO Můstek ● ○

Located in the heart of the
busiest street in Prague,
this excellent design shop
will be difficult to miss.
Modernista sells reproductions of the original de-
signs by prominent Czech
Cubist designers like Pavel
Janák, Vlastislav Hofman
and Josef Gočár. The ce-
ramic vases and coffee sets
are my personal favorites,
but the offerings also include furniture, metalwork
(including chandeliers),

and clocks, as well as
glass and toys by Ladislav
Sutnar. Be certain to go
downstairs, as many of the
most interesting pieces of
furniture are housed down
there, including the 1930's
Halabala recliner, as well
as table lamps, floor lamps
and ceiling fixtures. In
addition to these reproductions, the proprietor also
offers Art Deco, Bauhaus
and Czech Cubism. If
you have a vision of what
you're looking for and you
don't find it, be sure to
seek out the owner, Janek
Jaros, as he has a large
warehouse filled with in-
ventory, or alternatively he
can source the piece if it is
not currently available. The
store also carries glassware
by Artěl, as well as Olgoj
Chorchoj (also mentioned
above), a very prominent
Czech design group whose
work is carried at Moss in
New York City.

WALRUS TOY BY LADISLAV
SUTNAR, C. 1930
(COURTESY OF MODERNISTA)

PORCELAIN WELLIES WITH CZECH BLUE ONION MOTIF, FLANKED BY THE REAL THING
(PHOTO BY DAVID A. LAND, 2006)

■ ■ ■ ■ ■ ■ ■ ■ ■ ■ ■ ■ ■ ■

Qubus Design Studio

HOUSEHOLD OBJECTS
Rámová 3, Prague 1,
Staré Město
www.qubus.cz
TEL 222 313 151
HOURS Mon–Fri: 10:00–18:00
METRO Náměstí Republiky
TRAM 5, 8, 14 to Dlouhá třída

Prague's answer to the
aforementioned New York
design mecca, Moss, this
off-the-beaten-track shop
is well worth a visit. Qubus
features the work of the
Czech Republic's best up-
and-coming designers,
first and foremost, Maxim
Velčovský, who works
primarily in porcelain. My
friend recently bought a
porcelain head of Lenin
decorated with the famous
Czech blue onion motif,
while I have the Wellies.
The store also sells work in
other media including
glass, jewelry (by Belda),
and plastic.

Czech 100 Design Icons
by Tereza Bruthansová and Jan Králíček
(CzechMania, 2005)

This wonderful paperback book focuses exclusively
on 20th century design in the Czech Republic
and includes excellent images and captions
in English. This is a fabulous resource for anyone
interested in design.

Dolce Vita Magazine

Far and away the best local design magazine, *Dolce
Vita* is so hip it hurts. The closest comparison would

be *Wallpaper*. For
anyone interested
in design, fashion, or
interior design, this
publication will give
you great insight
to what is happening
in the Czech market.

DOLCE VITA
MAGAZINE COVER
(COURTESY
OF *DOLCE VITA*)

FASHION
Children's

Balet
Karolíny Světlé 22, Prague 1, Staré Město
TEL 222 221 063
HOURS Mon–Thu: 10:00–18:00; Fri: 10:00–17:00; July & August: 11:00–17:00
METRO Národní třída ●
TRAM 6, 9, 18, 21, 22, 23 to Národní třída

I've always dreamed of having a tutu, and I don't even dance. Should you, on the other hand, have a little twinkle toes who actually *is* a ballerina, you absolutely must stop into this little, less-than-glamorous shop featuring every manner of tutu, both with and without appliqués, as well matching bun covers, ballet slippers, leotards, leg warmers, and tights. The tutus are made on site and start at 550 CZK, with sizes small enough to fit a two year old (and how's *that* for healthy early encouragement?!). Should you prefer a color that is not available, custom work is available with a lead-time of one week. They also have supplies for rhythmic gymnastics.
CASH ONLY

Bim Bam Bum
Karolíny Světlé 19, Prague 1, Staré Město
TEL 222 519 559
HOURS Mon–Fri: 12:00–18:00; July & August: 14:00–17:00
METRO Národní třída ●
TRAM 6, 9, 18, 21, 22, 23 to Národní divadlo

Czech-made clothing for children up to age 12.

The look is classic, with many natural fabrics and neutral colors. The collection includes hand-knit sweaters, gloves and hats, as well as fun textured leggings, dresses and jackets. What caught *my* eye were the linen dresses beautifully screen-printed with charming images such as giraffes, elephants and various forms of sea life. These are done in very limited editions. In fact, the one I bought for 1,280 CZK was a one-off. If they don't have the size you want, it can be ordered with a lead-time of one week. Although they do

accept MC and Visa, it's clear they prefer CASH.

FASHION
Men's

Adam Steiner
Václavské náměstí 24, Prague 1, Nové Město
TEL 224 220 594
HOURS Mon–Fri: 09:00–19:00; Sat: 10:00–18:00
METRO Můstek ● ●
TRAM 3, 9, 14, 24 to Václavské náměstí

If you're curious about where Prague's power players go to have their suits made, now you know. Bespoke suits at Adam Steiner start at 21,400 CZK, not including material. You'll also find their line of ready-to-wear suits in the back of the store. Additionally, on the off chance that you've managed to plan a day of golf at Karlštejn (the Winged Foot of the Czech Republic), they can, of course, provide you with just the right outfit to tee-off in. Golf attire includes women's wear as well.

MEN'S FASHION SHOW, LUCERNA PALACE, 1948
(SOURCE: ČTK / CZECH NEWS AGENCY)

■ ■ ■ ■ ■ ■ ■ ■ ■ ■ ■ ■ ■
Hedva
Na Příkopě 16, Prague 1, Staré Město
TEL 224 212 566
HOURS Mon–Fri: 10:00–18:00
METRO Můstek ● ●
or Náměstí Republiky ●

This charming little tie shop is a holdover from the first republic, having originally opened in 1926. Note the beautiful wood cabinetry and the plasterwork on the right (above the heater), which is reminiscent of Dagobert Peche. All of the ties, scarves and accessories (including cufflinks) are Czech-made. Even if ties don't happen to be one of your Prague visions, you might want to reconsider, as many of the styles are, dare I say, chic! Who knew? And the prices make these ties the bargain of the century (the "expensive" ties are 350 CZK). Eat your heart out Paul Smith! I will, however, warn you that the merchandising is *terrible*, so you'll need to hunt through the display cases that are organized by color. The window display will prove very helpful for cross-referencing.

■ ■ ■ ■ ■ ■ ■ ■ ■ ■ ■ ■ ■
Jozef Sloboda
Týnská ulička 4, Prague 1, Staré Město
www.jozefsloboda.cz
TEL 221 014 408
HOURS Daily: 11:00–19:00
METRO Můstek ● ●

A real rarity in Prague, this young Czech designer's store caters exclusively to men. And if you would describe your fashion sensibility as metro-sexual, then you'll definitely want to stop in to check out his fun, unique, and actually quite affordable collection of casual wear, including t-shirts, jeans, dress shirts and jackets. All items are made in limited editions not exceeding 25 pieces and often limited to as few as 3. The designer also offers bespoke suits, with a lead-time of two to three weeks, starting at 15,000 CZK (price is dependent on material chosen). This store has the best customer service of any store I've

visited in Prague; I only wish his staff worked for *me*. Ask if Petr is working when you stop in, as he's my favorite, and his English is exceptional. They also have a second location at Na Příkopě 12 (Černá Růže Shopping Center, level 2), Prague 1, Staré Město.

FASHION
Women's

■ ■ ■ ■ ■ ■ ■ ■ ■ ■ ■ ■ ■
Boheme
Dušní 8, Prague 1, Staré Město
www.boheme.cz
TEL 224 813 840
HOURS Mon–Fri: 11:00–20:00; Sat: 11:00–17:00
METRO Staroměstská ●
TRAM 17, 18 to Staroměstská

The Boheme brand was started in Sweden, where Czech designer Hana Stocklassová studied for a year at the University of Design and Craft in Gothenburg. In 2002 she opened her first store in

Prague. The collection now includes knitwear, separates, leather and suede with designs that are classic and yet at the same time very fresh. Timeless, I suppose you'd say.

■ ■ ■ ■ ■ ■ ■ ■ ■ ■ ■ ■
Helena Fejková Design
FASHION GALLERY
Lucerna Palace
Štěpánská 61, Prague 1,
Nové Město
(Vodičkova entrance as well)
www.helenafejkova.cz
TEL 224 211 514
HOURS Mon–Fri: 10:00–19:00; Sat: 10:00–15:00
METRO Můstek ●
TRAM 3, 9, 14, 24 to Václavské náměstí

Located on the 2nd floor of the Lucerna Palace, up the staircase featuring Černý's St. Wenceslas mounted on an upside-down steed, Helena Fejková Design was established in 1989. Indeed, Fejková was one of the first Czechs to enter the fashion industry after the Velvet Revolution. She is known for her use of natural materials and her often *very* inventive designs. The collection includes both day and evening wear in a variety of fabrics. The gallery carries her clothing exclusively and the jewelry and accessories of several other Czech designers. Truth be told, it's the accessories that interest me most at this store.

■ ■ ■ ■ ■ ■ ■ ■ ■ ■ ■ ■
Ivana Follová Art & Fashion Gallery
Ungelt-Týn 1, Prague 1,
Staré Město
www.IvanaFollova.com
TEL 224 895 460
HOURS Daily: 10:30–19:00
METRO Náměstí Republiky or Můstek ●
Tram 5, 8, 14 to Náměstí Republiky

The Ivana Follová Gallery, located within the Týn courtyard, is a real hodge-podge of fashion, accessories, jewelry, ceramics, and glass made by local talent. I'll warn you in advance: some are clearly more talented than others, but with a sharp eye, you're sure to find a great little bauble or two to snap up. I like to come here to look for jewelry in particular. When shopping for clothing, I prefer her other store (Ivana Follová, Vodičkova 36, Prague 1, Nové Město Mon–Sat: 10:30–19:00), as it's smaller and better edited. If you do make it to the latter location, be sure to seek out clothes by Iva Šimandlová.

■ ■ ■ ■ ■ ■ ■ ■ ■ ■ ■ ■
Klara Nademlynska
Dlouhá 3, Prague 1,
Staré Město
www.klaranademlynska.cz
TEL 224 818 769
HOURS Mon–Fri: 10:00–19:00; Sat: 11:00–18:00
METRO Staroměstská ●
TRAM 17, 18 to Staroměstská

Super-chic high fashion designed by a local talent is what you'll find at Klara Nademlynska. One may not be surprised to learn that the proprietress of this very refined establishment worked in Paris before establishing her own

VI.SLET VŠESOKOLSKÝ V PRAZE.
28.29.30/VI. a 1./VII. 1912

F. Horník

brand in Prague. If you're any bigger than a size 8, however, you may be out of luck…

Móda Original
CLOTHING, ACCESSORIES, JEWELRY & CERAMICS
Jungmannova 13, Prague 1, Staré Město
TEL 296 245 033
HOURS Mon–Fri: 10:00–18:00
METRO Můstek ● ● or Národní třída ○
TRAM 3, 9, 14, 23, 24 to Lazarská

This store actually fits into many categories, as their range of merchandise includes dresses, blouses, skirts and pants—all made from natural fabrics, including linen, silk and wool—as well as tablecloths, jewelry, and ceramics made by local designers in the Czech Republic. Most of the items are sold exclusively in this store. They even had a modern version of a *zavinovačka*, a very traditional wrap for a baby, used when carrying the baby or placing it in a pram. It is perfect one-stop shopping for gifts.

Navarila
Elišky Krásnohorské 4/11, Prague 1, Staré Město
www.navarila.cz
TEL 271 742 091
HOURS Daily: 10:00–19:00
METRO Staroměstská ●
TRAM 17, 18 to Staroměstská

This shop focuses on everyday knitwear designed by Czech designer Martina Nevařilová, who designs two collections annually that are manufactured locally. The quality and workmanship is, it should be said, excellent. The

store also carries a linen collection by another local designer named Iva Šimandlová, as well as leather handbags and jewelry by various local designers. Clothing prices start at 1,200 CZK, and they accept most credit cards, though *not* AMEX.

Tara Jarmon
Rytířská 9, Prague 1, Staré Město
TEL 272 075 356
HOURS Mon–Fri: 10:00–19:00; Sat: 10:00–19:00; Sun: 12:00–18:00
METRO Můstek ● ●

OK, you got me! This is *not* Czech-made, however, as the French designer Tara Jarmon has very limited distribution in the U.S. and U.K., I figured it was worth squeezing her in, as her store just might have that lovely little something that your wardrobe absolutely *needs*. I love the fabrics she works with, especially for winter, as they're very richly textured and decorative. I must say, I've been tempted more than once to add something to my own wardrobe. The average price for skirts is 5,000 CZK, while dresses run about 10,000 CZK. She also carries accessories, including handbags, shoes and jewelry, few of which, however, are of her own design.

Tatiana Boutique
Dušní 1, Prague 1, Staré Město
www.tatiana.cz
TEL 224 813 723
HOURS Mon–Fri: 10:00–19:00; Sat: 11:00–16:00
METRO Staroměstská ●
TRAM 17, 18 to Staroměstská

Started in 1995 by two Czech designers, Tatiana's offers classic lines with a definite element of glam in more than a few pieces. For spring/summer 2006 the use of jersey and cotton was seen throughout the collection. A very cute jersey dress with obvious 1940's inspiration, for instance, was 6,900 CZK.

Timoure Et Group TEG
V Kolkovně 6, Prague 1, Staré Město
www.timoure.cz
TEL 222 327 358
HOURS Mon–Fri: 10:00–19:00; Sat: 11:00–17:00
METRO Staroměstská ●
TRAM 17, 18 to Staroměstská

Designers Alexandra Pavalová and Ivana Šafránková have been a designing team since 1992, and opened this store in 2001. Here you will find classic clothing with great lines that is perfect for everyday wear for even the chicest New Yorker. For spring and summer they utilize mostly linen and cotton, and in the winter wool is primary. Prices begin at 2,400 CZK for skirts and 2,500 CZK for trousers. TEG also has a second location at Martinská 4, Prague 1, Staré Město
TEL 224 240 737.

FUR
Kožešinky
RETRO FABULOUS
Na Poříčí 8, Prague 1, Nové Město
TEL 222 328 317
HOURS Mon–Thu: 10:00–18:00; Fri 09:00–17:00
METRO Náměstí Republiky ○

Prague Fashion

In a word, Věra Korandová is the most fashionable person I know in Prague. Having studied textile design in high school, she designed and sold clothing for several years, and currently works exclusively as an interior designer. Věra's interest in fashion started early; she began dyeing her shoes and applying buttons to them at 15. By 16 she started designing her own clothing, often working with wonderful old dresses her grandmother would find for her. "People under communism were very creative about what they wore; they had to be, since no fashion was available in stores," Věra points out. Under communism, Věra created 60% of her wardrobe, as it was the only way to be original. Věra feels that the necessity of having to make your own clothes under communism has proved beneficial to Czech fashion design, as it forced people to be very creative in finding a way to "make it work."

Karen: Who is currently your favorite Czech fashion designer?

Věra: Monika Drápalová. I was just introduced to her collection this year. What I like is that her pieces combine two very important elements: they are highly original, but also very wearable.

Karen: What are your favorite stores that focus on Czech fashion?

Věra: My favorite is Pour Pour, a store behind the National Theatre; this store sells clothes designed by students who are currently studying fashion design in Prague, so often they have very original pieces that are not too expensive. They also offer second-hand pieces.

My other favorite is Leeda, which focuses on young up-and-coming designers. They often have several very interesting pieces; I would describe the look as minimalist and severe, and it definitely will not be for everyone's taste.

Karen: Both of the stores you mentioned are definitely off-the-beaten track of the Prague Fashion Center on Dlouhá, Dušní, and V Kolkovně. Are you less interested in the Czech designers based there?

Věra: No, I'm definitely interested in those ones, too; in particular I like the work of Klára Nademlýnská and Timoure Et Group—TEG, but I often find their work too expensive for my own budget. From time to time I'll purchase pieces at these stores and combine them with pieces from other stores.

Karen: So if you were going to recommend *one* store to visit, what would it be?

Věra: I can't! I don't have a favorite, and I don't have a store that I can always depend on to find what I need; it's always about chance, so I recommend visiting a couple.

Stores Recommended by Věra:

Leeda
Bartolomějská 1, Prague 1, Staré Město
www.leeda.cz
TEL 224 234 056
HOURS Mon–Sat: 11:00–19:00
METRO Národní třída ●
TRAM 6, 9, 18, 21, 22, 23 to Národní divadlo

As Věra notes, the overall look is minimalist and severe, so it will definitely not be for everyone's taste. Prices start at 500 CZK, and go up to 7,500 CZK. The store offers clothing for men as well.

Pour Pour
Voršilská 6 (entrance on Ostrovni), Prague 1, Nové Město
www.pourpour.com
TEL 777 830 078
HOURS Mon–Fri: 11:00–19:00; Sat & Sun: 12:00–18:00
METRO Národní třída ●
TRAM 6, 9, 18, 21, 22, 23 to Národní divadlo

This is a great store to know about; thank goodness I decided to interview Vera for this book, as I never knew about it before. It's as close to shopping on Elizabeth Street in Nolita as you'll find in Prague, only here it's one-stop shopping! Prices start at 50 CZK, and go up to 3,000 CZK. Trust me, this store is filled with very fun and totally unique items.
CASH ONLY

The establishment of a fur shop at this location dates back to 1880, and the shop remained under one family until 1962, since which time it has belonged to the Czech fur collective. The last renovation was completed in 1980, so if you're curious to see what a downtown store looked like under communism, stop in to note the orange and brown linoleum flooring, as well as the chair at the center of the room that looks vintage 1960's, but is in fact from the 1980's. The merchandising, it must be said, is equally reflective of that former period.

CASH ONLY

■ ■ ■ ■ ■ ■ ■ ■ ■ ■ ■
Kreibich kožešiny & rukavice
Michalská 14, Prague 1, Staré Město
www.kreibich.cz
TEL 224 222 522
HOURS Mon–Fri: 10:00–18:00; Sat & Sun: 10:00–17:00
METRO Můstek ● ●

Looking for some fabulous fur? How about a sheepskin or a bunny dyed pink? Perhaps a fox throw in blue, or would a cowhide from South America be more to your taste? If so, this is your dream store. I recently had this store make two rabbit fur carpets for my country house in Southern Bohemia, as well as a sheepskin carpet. The owner is more than willing to accommodate special orders, but he also has lots of stock on smaller items. Baby slippers are 340 CZK, gloves start at 660 CZK, longhaired sheepskin pillows are 2,400 CZK, and an absolutely delicious chinchilla scarf is 24,000

CZK. Scarves, hats, and coats in various furs are all available for immediate purchase.

■ ■ ■ ■ ■ ■ ■ ■ ■ ■ ■
Liška
Železná 1, Prague 1, Staré Město
TEL 224 221 928
HOURS Mon–Fri: 10:00–19:00; Sat: 10:00–15:00
METRO Můstek ● ●

Mink, sable, chinchilla, and fox are among the furs you can find at this Austrian store right off Old Town Square. Prices begin at 28,000 CZK and run up to about 250,000 CZK, though there are some excellent sales during the summer season. Accessories are on the ground floor, while the coats are upstairs, along with the best selection of Wolford stockings in town, so don't be shy and be sure to head upstairs. Thankfully, they offer tax-free shopping, which could add up to a pretty penny if you're as big a fan of chinchilla as I am…

GIFTS
General

■ ■ ■ ■ ■ ■ ■ ■ ■ ■ ■
Botanicus
Ungelt – Týn 3, Prague 1, Staré Město
www.botanicus.cz
TEL 234 767 446
HOURS Daily: 10:00–18:30
METRO Náměstí Republiky or Můstek ● ●
TRAM 5, 8, 14 to Náměstí Republiky

Botanicus features organically cultivated, hand-made products with exceptional packaging, making it an ideal resource for gift buying. The range includes soaps, bath

oils, shampoos, hand-made paper, candles and condiments—all made in the Czech Republic.

■ ■ ■ ■ ■ ■ ■ ■ ■ ■ ■
Manufaktura
Melantrichova 17 and Železná 3A, Prague 1, Staré Město
TEL 221 632 480
HOURS Daily: 10:00–19:00
METRO Můstek ● ●

You will see this chain of stores throughout downtown Prague. They offer a wide range of Czech traditional handicrafts, including wooden toys with a natural finish, blue-printed textiles, embroidered table cloths, ceramics, kitchen utensils, bath products, wool sweaters and rugs, painted eggs, and old-fashioned Christmas ornaments made from either straw or varnished gingerbread. Melantrichova and Železná are my two favorite locations, but they have several other outlets, including one on Karlova 26, another on Golden Lane at the Prague Castle (see p. 76), and even a location at Terminal 1 in the airport. All of the stores will have a very similar range of merchandise and beautiful packaging, making them a terrific resource for gifts.

■ ■ ■ ■ ■ ■ ■ ■ ■ ■ ■
The Municipal House Culture and Information Center
Náměstí Republiky 5, Prague 1, Staré Město
www.obecni-dum.cz
TEL 222 002 101
HOURS Daily: 10:00–18:00
METRO Náměstí Republiky
TRAM 5, 8, 14 to Náměstí Republiky

Oddly enough, the information center at the Obecní dům (The Municipal House) happens to have a very nice gift store that features a limited selection of items from Modernista (see p. 103) and the Art Deco Galerie (see p. 78). Often they have a very interesting display of antique buttons for sale. They also carry reproductions of Art Nouveau tiles used in the Obecní dům building that would make a stylish hot plate, as well as silk scarves inspired by the design of the building. The sales staff is anything but helpful; nonetheless you're sure to find some unique items here.

GLASS
Crystal

▪ ▪ ▪ ▪ ▪ ▪ ▪ ▪ ▪ ▪ ▪ ▪ ▪ ▪

Artěl
FUNCTIONAL/DECORATIVE
www.artelglass.com
TEL 271 732 161

At the time of writing Artěl does not *yet* have a flagship store in Prague; however the two stores listed (see p. 112) each carry extensive selections of Artěl products.

Is it inappropriate to toot my own horn? Although I'm a humble person, I feel I would be doing my readers an injustice not to put in an entry for Artěl, as we absolutely fill a niche in the luxury crystal market, not only in Prague but throughout the world (our work is carried in stores ranging from Barneys Japan to Paul Smith in Los Angeles, London, New York, and Paris). Artěl focuses on mouth-blown

GLACIER DOUBLE OLD FASHION BY DAVID WISEMAN FOR ARTĚL

BAROKO STEMLESS COLLECTION BY ARTĚL

VERDURE LARGE BOWL IN BLACK BY ARTĚL

TRINKET BOWL BY ARTĚL
BACK ROW: ATLANTIS IN AQUA, BUBLINKA IN OLIVE, PARIZ IN BLUE
FRONT ROW: VERDURE IN PURPLE, FINCH IN AMBER, NARCISSUS IN ROSE

SHOPPING

hand-engraved crystal for the table and home, and while certainly decorative as well, all of our pieces are primarily functional. One of our claims to fame is that we make the drink sets for the Rolls-Royce Phantom, but we have also worked on a limited edition of tumblers for the minimalist artist Sol LeWitt, and, more recently, we have collaborated with product designer David Wiseman.

Where to Find Artěl:
Lobkowicz Palace
Jiřská 3, Prague 1, Hradčany, (see p. 46).

Modernista
Celetná 12, Prague 1, Staré Město (see p. 103).

Arzenal
FUNCTIONAL/DECORATIVE
Valentinská 11, Prague 1, Staré Město
www.arzenal.cz
TEL 224 814 099
HOURS Daily: 10:00–24:00
METRO Staroměstská ●
TRAM 17, 18 to Staroměstská

Arzenal is an odd place—half contemporary glass store and half Thai restaurant—but then, I guess it's never a good

idea to put all your eggs in one basket. If you're a fan of Bořek Šípek, this is a great place to stop, as it's his store and features his work. The store carries a lot of very interesting contemporary chandeliers and lighting fixtures. Additionally, it has various items for the home made from glass, porcelain and metal as well as a few pieces of jewelry. I've only been to the restaurant once, but I remember it being quite good.

Design Glass
FUNCTIONAL/DECORATIVE
U Lužického semináře 42, Prague 1, Malá Strana
TEL 257 531 232
HOURS Daily: 10:00–19:00
METRO Malostranská ●

A lovely new glass store opened by the glassworks factory Květná, Design Glass features several collections designed by noteworthy Czech designers, including Olgoj Chorchoj, Mimolimit and Rony Plesl. If glass is on your list and you like a clean, modern look, I'd definitely put this shop on your list. I especially

like the drinks set by Olgoj Chorchoj.

Galerie Meridian
ART GLASS
Široká 8, Prague 1, Staré Město
www.galeriemeridian.cz
TEL 224 819 154
HOURS Daily: 11:00–18:00
METRO Staroměstská ●
TRAM 17, 18 to Staroměstská

If form over function rings true to your heart, then stopping into this glass gallery is a must. Prices begin at 65,000 CZK, with some pieces even exceeding 2,000,000 CZK, so this is for serious collectors only. Tomáš Hlavička, Pavel Hlava and Stanislav Libenský are among the artists whose work is carried. Galerie Meridian also exhibits at SOFA.

NOTE: On a recent visit, the staff of the shop was neither helpful nor friendly, and the English of the saleslady helping me was, frankly, less than terrific. So, if you're serious about buying something, you might want to bring along a translator to assist.

■ ■ ■ ■ ■ ■ ■ ■ ■ ■ ■ ■
M. Material Glass Store & Interior Design

FUNCTIONAL/DECORATIVE

U Lužického semináře 7, Prague 1, Staré Město

www.i-material.com

TEL 257 530 046

HOURS Daily: 10:30–21:00

METRO Malostranská ●

The display here is easily the most sophisticated in town; the items are carefully selected and curated, so that each piece can be appreciated independently. The store features work by Ajeto, the firm owned by Bořek Šípek, Forest Glass (the type of glass Juliška makes—often green and either inspired by or copied from medieval drinkware from this region), and Peter Rath (of the Lobmeyer family). The items include glassware, vases, plates, bowls and a very good selection of contemporary chandeliers.

■ ■ ■ ■ ■ ■ ■ ■ ■ ■ ■ ■
Moser

FUNCTIONAL/DECORATIVE

Na Příkopě 12, Prague 1, Staré Město

www.moser-glass.com

TEL 224 211 293

HOURS Mon–Fri: 10:00–20:00; Sat & Sun: 10:00–19:00

METRO Můstek ● ○

A decade ago I requested an unpaid internship here, and although they failed to so much as reply to my job inquiry, I still feel they deserve a place in my book. Moser is, after all, the most renowned Czech crystal manufacturer, as it has been since their establishment in 1857.

The store on Na Příkopě, which opened its door in 1925, was Moser's first shop. The dark wood-paneled showroom, alluring with elaborate inlay work, is well worth a look, regardless of your interest in glass. And while Moser is certainly available throughout the world, it's only in this store that you'll be able to see the very widest selection of merchandise. My favorite set is called "Bar." Originally designed in 1934 by Rudolf Eschler, it is every bit as contemporary today as it was then, and comes in a variety of delicious colors.

Moser, who was Jewish, fled when the Nazis invaded and the Communists later seized the company. It is one of a handful of Czech companies that did not suffer a serious decline in either quality or reputation during this period.

■ ■ ■ ■ ■ ■ ■ ■ ■ ■ ■ ■
Umělecká huť sklenářská

STAINED GLASS

U Milosrdných 14, Prague 1, Staré Město

www.vitraz.com

TEL 737 666 851

HOURS Mon–Fri: 08:00–17:30

METRO Náměstí Republiky ○

TRAM 5, 8, 14 to Dlouhá třída

This stained-glass workshop was established in 1935, and the founder's claim to fame was executing the windows designed by Alphonse Mucha for the Prague Castle's St. Vitus Cathedral. The workshop currently offers significantly less monumental pieces for purchase, including both new works and antiques, with prices starting at around 900 CZK. I've found the staff extraordinarily helpful and extremely nice. This is a *real* off-the-beaten-track find, by the way; I've been living and shopping in Prague since 1994 and only just found this place earlier this year.

NOTE: Don't be intimidated by the less-than-inviting entryway; this is a workshop, not a store. Just give a knock on the door, and someone will come to open it.

CASH ONLY

HATS

Hat-making has been a tradition in the Czech lands since the 13th century, and TONAK, a firm dating back to the second half of the 19th century, is still producing its traditional felt hats today—as softly textured as velvet. They are one of only eight remaining felt-hat manufacturers in the world, as a matter of fact, and their customers are every bit as varied as the hats themselves, including the Czech Army, Hasidic Jews in Brooklyn, Muslims in Saudi Arabia... and me!

So if you're in the market for a fez, fedora, knit cap or, God bless you, a top hat, I can only encourage you to seek out one of the stores listed below.

■ ■ ■ ■ ■ ■ ■ ■ ■ ■ ■ ■
Družstvo Model Praha

Václavské náměstí 28, Prague 1, Nové Město

TEL 224 216 805

HOURS Mon–Fri: 09:00–19:00; Sat & Sun: 10:00–17:00; (closed on Sunday in summer)

METRO Můstek ● ◐
TRAM 3, 9, 14, 24 to Václavské náměstí

This hat shop, nestled in an arcade on the right, is where I head each autumn to choose a hat or two for the winter to come. It carries an excellent selection of TONAK for both men and women, and is, frankly, the best hat store in Prague that I'm aware of. The range on display includes top hats, hunting hats, fedoras and exquisite straw hats for summer (perhaps a day at the races?)… Prices start at 500 CZK.

■ ■ ■ ■ ■ ■ ■ ■ ■ ■ ■ ■ ■ ■

Myslivost
Jungmannova 25, Prague 1,
Nové Město
www.myslivost.cz
TEL 224 949 014
HOURS Mon–Fri: 09:00–
18:00; Sat 09:00–12:00
METRO Můstek ● ◐ or
Národní třída ◐

If you're specifically seeking a hunting hat, this store should be your starting point. See entry on this page for a complete store description.

■ ■ ■ ■ ■ ■ ■ ■ ■ ■ ■ ■ ■ ■

Personality
OD Kotva
náměstí Republiky 8,
Prague 1, Nové Město
TEL 224 215 468
HOURS Mon–Fri: 09:00–
20:00; Sat: 10:00–19:00;
Sun: 10:00–18:00
METRO Náměstí Republiky
TRAM 5, 8, 14 to Náměstí
Republiky

This store within a store is located in the ground floor of Kotva, Prague's old Communist-era workhorse of a department store. Personality carries one of the widest collections of TONAK in Prague, as well as hats by other manufacturers. Both men's and women's styles are carried. Also

for sale are scarves, umbrellas, handbags and handkerchiefs. They have a second location right down the street at Na Poříčí 21
TEL 222 326 494
HOURS Mon–Fri: 09:00–19:00 and Sat: 09:00–16:00. It's also worth noting that their second location actually has a broader collection of men's hats than the one at Kotva.

HUNTING SUPPLIES

■ ■ ■ ■ ■ ■ ■ ■ ■ ■ ■ ■ ■ ■

Myslivost
Jungmannova 25, Prague 1,
Nové Město
www.myslivost.cz
TEL 224 949 014
HOURS Mon–Fri: 09:00–
18:00; Sat: 09:00–12:00
METRO Můstek ● ◐ or
Národní třída ◐

This is one-stop shopping for all things hunting (minus the guns, which you can get at the store listed next). The lower floor here is devoted primarily to clothing, including formal hunting hats by TONAK, a famous Czech hat manufacturer, starting at 290 CZK, as well as pants, shirts, sweaters, socks, and even ties. Upstairs, you'll find glassware, porcelain, flatware and pewter, all decorated with hunting motifs. One liqueur set with decaled motifs, including a decanter and six glasses, definitely bordered on kitsch and sold for a mere 370 CZK. Other items that caught my fancy included a wood carving of St. Hubertus, the patron saint of hunting, at 3,870 CZK, and Saint Hubert's Liqueur, definitely *not*

FEZ HATS IN PRODUCTION, C. 1948

If You Love Taxidermy, Put This Castle on Your Must-Hit List:

Konopiště Castle

Benešov; www.zamek-konopiste.cz

TEL 317 724 271

HOURS Tue–Fri: 09:00–15:00; Sat & Sun: 09:00–16:00; (Monday closed); Open: April – November

Konopiště is a Renaissance-style castle (originally Gothic) that was erected at the end of the 13th century on 14,600 acres. In subsequent centuries, it went through several renovations, the most recent of these being ordered by Archduke Franz Ferdinand d'Este (the successor to the Austro-Hungarian Empire's last emperor, Franz Josef), who was famously assassinated during a state visit to Sarajevo in 1914, triggering WWI. Right up until the day he himself was shot, Franz Ferdinand had been *obsessed* with hunting, and his entire castle is at once gloriously and ghoulishly decorated with his trophies. He recorded some 300,000 animals shot, including fox, deer, wild boar, bear, and even tigers! The castle itself has 100,000 of his triumphs on display.

NOTE: Three tours are offered, with entrance fees ranging from 180 CZK to 300 CZK; in November tours are limited. Check their website for availability.

Directions by Car: 45km south of Prague. Take highway D1 and then the E55 south towards Brno take exit 21, direction České Budějovice and Benešov. Alternatively, you can take the train to Benešov, which takes about 1 hour (the castle is 2.5km from the station), though I highly recommend either driving or being driven.

---

available everywhere, at 390 CZK a bottle.

- - - - - - - - - - - - - -

Zbraně a střelivo Brymová

Staroměstské náměstí 8, Prague 1, Staré Město

TEL 222 310 773

HOURS Mon–Fri: 09:00–18:00; Sat: 09:00–13:00

METRO Můstek ● ●
or Staroměstská ●

While I myself don't hunt, I decided to sneak a peak at this sportsman's emporium and, to my surprise, found lots of goodies that piqued my interest in all things hunting. The store is focused on weaponry, including an extensive range of guns, knives (medieval as well as modern) and bullets. They also offer proper hunting attire, trophy mounts, as well as hunting-themed items like cufflinks, pins, pipes, and glassware. I fully enjoyed my visit to this store (even purchasing a pair of cufflinks with Irish Setters on them for a friend), and will definitely be back.

JEWELRY
Fine

Garnets are the official gem of the Czech Republic, and you'll find them just about everywhere in downtown Prague. They were first found in the Czech lands in the 11th century, and the first guild was established in 1715 in Turnov, which is still the center of garnet production today.

If you've already been window-shopping and have started to notice that *all* the new garnet items, regardless of the store, look exactly the same, I can assure you, you're not going crazy, and, in fact, have a wise eye. They all look the same because they *are* all—yes, all of them—made by Granát Turnov, a collective that was established in 1953. This collective is responsible for getting the products from the ground all the way to the display cases, including excavating, sorting, cleaning, cutting, and setting the stones in one of the 6500 designs that they currently offer. Minus the very infrequent exception, I find virtually all of the new products both boring and unoriginal, which is why I must encourage you to consider the idea of purchasing antique garnets; I'm confident you'll find something far worthier this way…

Moldavite is the other local gemstone that you might have read about or seen. Olive green in color, it is unique to the Czech Republic, having been formed by the impact of a meteorite in southern Bohemia millions of years ago. The stones are sometimes cut and polished as precious stones, and when finished this way, they often look similar to Russian green garnets; this is how I prefer them. More often they are left in their natural state, with the surface covered in the wrinkles characteristic of meteorites.

■ ■ ■ ■ ■ ■ ■ ■ ■ ■ ■ ■

Antique Vladimír Andrle
GARNETS
Kaprova 12, Prague 1, Staré Město
www.antiqueandrle.cz
TEL 222 329 003
HOURS Mon–Sat: 10:00–19:00; Sun: 10:00–18:00
METRO Staroměstská ●
TRAM 17, 18 to Staroměstská

If your taste in garnets is similar to mine, and you favor antique jewelry rather than new, this shop will be a good starting place. They have a wide selection of earrings, brooches, necklaces, bracelets and even some unusual (albeit expensive) hair ornaments.

The pieces are well edited, and while prices are on the high side, negotiation is definitely possible. As a matter of fact, they have emphasized their willingness to negotiate on each of my visits, so haggling 25% off the price here feels especially satisfying (most stores won't budge more than 10%).

■ ■ ■ ■ ■ ■ ■ ■ ■ ■ ■ ■

Beldafactory
CONTEMPORARY DESIGN
Mikulandská 10, Prague 1, Nové Město
www.belda.cz
TEL 224 933 052
HOURS Mon–Thu: 10:00–18:00; Fri: 10:00–17:00
METRO Národní třída ●
TRAM 6, 9, 18, 21, 22, 23 to Národní divadlo

While offering an assortment of items, this design shop specializes in jewelry designed by the owner, Jiří Belda, utilizing various metals (including silver, titanium, stainless steel, platinum and white and yellow gold) combined with precious stones, as well as onyx and turquoise and even plastics such as Perspex and Corian.

■ ■ ■ ■ ■ ■ ■ ■ ■ ■ ■ ■

Český granát
GARNETS
Celetná 4, Prague 1, Staré Město
TEL 224 228 281
HOURS Daily: 10:00–19:00
METRO Můstek ● ●

As noted, I'm not the biggest fan of new garnet jewelry, for the simple reason that I find both the settings and aged patina of older pieces far more interesting. That said, I'm not everyone; so if you want to purchase

some *new* garnet jewelry during your visit, let me suggest this store. They offer a very wide range of settings and metal options, so I'm certain you'll find something to your taste. Unfortunately, the merchandizing is poor, so you'll have to be patient and take the time to look through the many different options, but the sales assistants tend to be very helpful with this.

■ ■ ■ ■ ■ ■ ■ ■ ■ ■ ■ ■

Dorotheum
ANTIQUE STORE & AUCTION HOUSE
Ovocný trh 2, Prague 1, Staré Město
www.dorotheum.cz
TEL 224 216 699
HOURS Mon–Fri: 10:00–19:00; Sat: 10:00–17:00
METRO Můstek ● ●
TRAM 3, 9, 14, 24 to Václavské náměstí

This is a frequent stop for me. I love this store, as the quality is always great and the price points are fair, considering that they've already done the homework for you, in terms of *what* something is, *when* it was made, and by *whom*. Prices start at 700 CZK, and they have an extensive section devoted to jewelry, including an excellent collection of garnets.

See p. 81 for a complete store description.

■ ■ ■ ■ ■ ■ ■ ■ ■ ■ ■ ■

Minerály Praha
MOLDAVITE
Celetná 12 (Hrzánská pasáž), Prague 1, Staré Město
TEL 224 234 573
HOURS Daily: 10:00–22:00
METRO Můstek ● ●

A mineral store that carries

jewelry made of the earthy green stone unique to the Czech Republic. Minerály Praha has jewelry set in its natural state as well as cut. The store also carries a nice collection of beaded garnet necklaces, which can be fairly hard to find.

■ ■ ■ ■ ■ ■ ■ ■ ■ ■ ■ ■
The National Museum
Národní muzeum
MOLDAVITE
Václavské náměstí 68, Prague 1, Nové Město
www.nm.cz
TEL 222 497 111
HOURS Daily: May–Sept: 10:00–18:00; Oct–April: 09:00–17:00
ENTRANCE FEE: 110 CZK Adult; 50 CZK Children; 6 and under Free
METRO Muzeum ● ●
Tram 11 to Muzeum

The gift store on the second floor of the National Museum has what is, quite simply, the best collection of cut moldavite that I've seen anywhere in Prague.

See p. 51 for a complete museum description.

NOTE: Closed the 1st Tuesday of each month.

■ ■ ■ ■ ■ ■ ■ ■ ■ ■ ■ ■
Studio Šperk
Dlouhá 19, Prague 1, Staré Město
www.drahonovsky.cz
TEL 224 815 161
HOURS Mon–Fri: 10:00–19:00; Sat: 10:00–18:00
METRO Náměstí Republiky ○
TRAM 5, 8, 14 to Dlouhá třída

This small store is an anomaly among garnet shops, because many of the settings they offer are absolutely contemporary, with clean modern lines. What caught my eye one day, passing by,

was a necklace strung with Japanese pearls interchanged with hand-cut, hand-polished garnets, at 40,000 CZK. If this is too steep for your pockets, the store has other pearl and garnet pieces that begin at 4,000 CZK. Garnets set with diamonds are another unusual find here. The store is owned by the Drahňovský family, who have been involved in the garnet industry since the late 1800's, and the family designs and manufactures all of the pieces in the store, making this a very unique find.

JEWELRY
Costume

The Czech costume jewelry industry dates back some 300 years. Like the Austrian firm Swarovski, Czech factories also produce machine-cut faceted beads, and while it's truly impossible to see any difference, they sell for less than Swarovski. Sadly, none of the Czech producers ever developed the consumer brand recognition Swarovski has. Within the industry, however, "Czech beads" are synonymous with excellent quality and variety. Unfortunately, there are no stores in Prague that sell loose beads, but you'll find earrings, bracelets, brooches and necklaces that incorporate them throughout the city.

■ ■ ■ ■ ■ ■ ■ ■ ■ ■ ■ ■
Artěl
JEWELRY FROM BOHEMIAN CRYSTALS
www.artelglass.com
TEL 271 732 161

At the time of writing Artěl does not *yet* have a flagship store in Prague; however the two stores listed below each have extensive collections of Artěl.

In addition to our crystal collection (see p. 111), Artěl designs a line of costume jewelry (which, until 2007, has only been available in the U.S.). Due to the matte-finished stones utilized throughout the collection, the look is classic with a contemporary edge. The collection includes earrings (pierced and clipped), necklaces, rings, brooches, and hair accessories, all in a dazzlingly wide range of colors.

OVAL CLUSTER & STAR FLOWER RINGS BY ARTĚL

LEAF CHOKER WITH SMALL & LARGE FLOWER EARRINGS BY ARTĚL

Where to Find Artěl:

Lobkowicz Palace
Jiřská 3, Prague 1, Hradčany,
(see p. 46).

Modernista
Celetná 12, Prague 1,
Staré Město (see p. 103).

FOXTROT
JEWELRY FROM
BOHEMIAN CRYSTALS,
BEADS AND ENAMELWARE
Palác Koruna
Václavské náměstí 1,
Prague 1, Staré Město
TEL 224 473 069
HOURS Mon–Fri: 10:00–
20:00; Sat: 10:00–18:00; Sun:
12:00–18:00
METRO Můstek ● ●

Definitely worth a stop
if the look you're after
is "beyond glamorous."
They actually carry a
better beaded jewelry
collection then Jablonex
(see next column) and also
have a second outlet in
Kotva department store
at náměstí Republiky 8;
however, their offerings
at Palác Kornua include
additional items, such
as beaded handbags and
clutches.

118

Frey Wille
JEWELRY FROM
ENAMELWARE
Havířská 3, Prague 1,
Staré Město
www.frey-wille.com
TEL 272 142 228
HOURS Mon–Sat: 10:00–
19:00; Sun: 11:00–16:00
METRO Můstek ●

I'll tell you straight away
that this store is not Czech,
but rather Austrian. As the
Austro-Hungarian Empire
once encompassed the
Czech Republic, however, I
figure I can get away with
it… The jewelry here in-
cludes enameled bracelets,
earrings, necklaces rings
and cufflinks, set in gold
or silver or silver-plate.
Their newest collection
honors Alphonse Mucha
and Sarah Bernhardt; this
is, of course, very apro-
pos, as Prague is indeed
the land of Mucha. What
caught my eye here were
the wide rings, though
hardly cheap at 5,000 CZK,
and the bracelet cuffs, at
9,000 CZK.

Jablonex
JEWELRY FROM
BOHEMIAN CRYSTALS &
BEADS
Kotva Department Store
náměstí Republiky 8,
Prague 1, Nové Město
www.jablonex.cz
TEL 224 101 114
HOURS Mon–Fri: 09:00–
20:00; Sat & Sun: 10:00–
18:00
Metro Náměstí Republiky ●
TRAM 5, 8, 14 to Náměstí
Republiky

Costume jewelry produc-
tion in Czechoslovakia
peaked just before WWII,
when it was the center for
worldwide production

---

and, although it no longer
holds this position, production of costume jewelry
is still significant. Jablonex
was founded in 1952 and
remains the leading
exporter. Among its many
baubles are imitation pearls
and diamonds in positively
every size and color.

Swarovski
SWAROVSKI CRYSTAL
Celetná 7, Prague 1,
Staré Město
www.swarovski.com
TEL 222 315 585
HOURS Daily: 10:00–23:30
METRO Staroměstská ●
TRAM 17, 18 to Staroměstská

Now made in Austria,
Swarovski did *originate* in
the Czech Republic, so for
our purposes, it makes
the cut (no pun intended).
Due to the current strength
of the Czech crown against
the U.S. Dollar and the
value added tax, however,
the same items here are
actually more expensive
than if purchased in the
United States. So, unless
there's an item that you
haven't seen before, or
that you know is not
available in the States, I
must advise you to wait
until you get home to make
your purchase. Sorry to
disappoint. They also have
a second, smaller location,
at Pařížská 16, Prague 1,
Staré Město.

NERUDOVA STREET, C. 1920

MARIONETTES

Home of the International Puppetry Association (UNIMA), established in 1929, Prague is, of course, famous for its marionettes and puppets. And the history dates back even further. Foreign troops during the Thirty Years War (1618–1648) first introduced Bohemia to the magic of puppetry, and toward the end of the 18th century Czechs began to make their own puppets. By the turn of the 20th century, puppet theatre underwent a renaissance here, with famous artists and designers of the day supporting it as a valid form of art. Hundreds of theatres and even schools for puppetry formed during the golden age of the First Republic.

While there are puppets for all budgets for sale throughout Prague, what is really amazing to see are the pieces that could just as easily be classified as art, with no two exactly the same. So, even if you're not interested in purchasing any puppets, I encourage you to stop into a few stores to see the truly impressive levels of workmanship out there.

▪ ▪ ▪ ▪ ▪ ▪ ▪ ▪ ▪ ▪ ▪ ▪ ▪ ▪

Obchod s loutkami
Nerudova 47, Prague 1, Malá Strana
www.marionettes.cz
TEL 257 532 735
HOURS Daily: 10:00–19:00
METRO Malostranská ●
TRAM 12, 20, 22, 23 to Malostranské náměstí

The traditional marionettes carried at this store are not as well executed as

Spejbl & Hurvínek

A father and son marionette team who made their debut in the 1920's, this is the best-known puppet show in the Czech Republic. They even have their own theatre in Prague. Unfortunately, the performances of this very comic and dynamic duo are only in Czech. Rounding out the crew is Žeryk, their beloved dog; Mánička, Hurvínek's friend; and Mrs. Kateřina, his babička (grandmother). In addition to their stage shows, they appear regularly on TV and have become beloved characters of the Czech nation, similar to Mickey Mouse or Bugs Bunny in the U.S.

It's not hard to find good reproductions, and they would make great souvenirs for adults and kids alike. You'll also find stuffed animals, coloring books, and bedding featuring the famous duo.

SPEJBL & HURVÍNEK, 1938
(SOURCE: ČTK / CZECH NEWS AGENCY)

Puppet Museum
Muzeum marionet
Karlova 44, Prague 1, Staré Město
www.puppetart.com
TEL 222 220 913
HOURS Daily: 15:00–16:30
(for groups, possible to arrange a different time)
ENTRANCE FEE 100 CZK
METRO Staroměstská ●
TRAM 17, 18 to Staroměstská or Karlovy lázně

This museum is run by the International Puppetry Association (UNIMA), which, as noted above, has its headquarters in Prague. They have a wonderful collection of puppets—mostly from the 19th and early 20th centuries. Be sure to take in the wonderful miniature theatre while you're there!

those at the other store I've listed; however they do have an excellent selection of simple felt puppets starting at 290 CZK. They also have a Prague Castle Guard doll in a very charming box for 790 CZK, and this is an item I haven't seen in any other store.

■ ■ ■ ■ ■ ■ ■ ■ ■ ■ ■ ■ ■

Pod Lampou
Marionety
Marionety Truhlář

U Lužického semináře 5, Prague 1, Malá Strana
www.marionety.cz
TEL 606 924 392
HOURS Daily: 10:00–19:00
METRO Malostranská ●

Truth be known, marionettes are not my favorite thing, but this store won me over. They have a very broad range of puppets, from simple, generic 300 CZK puppets, to one-of-kind creations that cost 60,000 CZK. Needless to say, it was the one-of-a-kind selection that did it for me. Ask to see puppets by Antonín and Martin Müller, as these two brothers are my personal favorites. Jan Růžička is another renowned artisan to seek out. In total, this shop carries the work of over 60 Czech artisans.

The store has a very small workshop located right on the premises, so you can even *see* the puppets *being carved*. They have a second location near Old Town Square at Ungelt-Týn 1, but I prefer the store in Malá Strana.

Make Your Very Own Marionette in Just 3 Hours

Nosticova 5, Prague 1, Malá Strana;
www.marionety.cz
TEL 606 924 392
HOURS Daily: 10:00 – 17:00
METRO Malostranská ●
COST 1 person 3,000 CZK; 2 people 2,250 CZK per person; 3 people 2,000 CZK per person; 4 people 1,750 CZK per person; 5 or more 1,500 CZK per person
Reserve 24 hours in advance
Maximum 10 people
Course time 3 hours (Ages 6 and up)

Are you curious about how marionettes are made? Here's your chance not only to find out, but also to make one yourself. This ingenious activity was thought up by Pavel Truhlář, the owner of Pod Lampou, listed above. The workshop is nestled in the heart of Malá Strana, in a Baroque building I had always dreamed of entering. In addition to making your own marionette, you'll also have an opportunity to tour his professional workshop on the same premises, including the tailoring and head painting rooms. You'll have a chance to view his collection of vintage marionettes, some of which were used as prototypes for the initial collection that he sold on the Charles Bridge before opening his first store in 1993.

With 22 unique characters to choose from in creating your own marionette, you'll be set up at your own workstation, and either Pavel or his wife will help you complete all the necessary steps. Beverages and cookies will be served.

A Mini Me... Can I Have a Marionette Made that Looks Just Like Me?

Of course! Simply provide Pavel Truhlář, listed above, with the following photographs:
- Head Shot (a close-up taken head on)
- Profile Shot (a close-up)
- Full Body Shot

The marionette will be made of wood (the same material used in the workshop), and will stand 18 inches (45 cm) tall! The lead-time is one month, and they are, of course, happy to ship your finished marionette anywhere in the world. For more information, visit www.marionety.cz

COST 7,000–8,000 CZK

MEDIEVAL ARMOR

■ ■ ■ ■ ■ ■ ■ ■ ■ ■ ■ ■

Gallery U Rytíře Kryštofa
Kožná 8, Prague 1,
Staré Město
TEL 224 236 300
HOURS Daily: 10:00–19:00
METRO Můstek ●

Frodo and his fellow hobbits should have made a point of stopping in here to arm themselves before heading off to the land of Mordor, because they've got it *all* here! You can buy yourself a full set of armor starting from 65,000 CZK, but if you want to start more modestly, you can get a mighty fierce sword, mace, battle-axe, lance, chain mail and hatchet, starting at 2,500 CZK. I bought my nephew a wooden sword (140 CZK) and woven leather belt with holster (200 CZK), so he can fight off all the evil beings in his bedroom and backyard (his siblings' rooms being off-limits for now).

NOTE: This store is owned by the same folks who run the great medieval armor exhibition upstairs at the Golden Lane, just down the hill from the Prague Castle (see p. 76).
CASH ONLY, CREDIT CARDS FOR PURCHASES 3,000 CZK AND OVER.

MUSIC & MUSICAL INSTRUMENTS

■ ■ ■ ■ ■ ■ ■ ■ ■ ■ ■ ■

Amati-Denak
INSTRUMENTS
U Obecního domu,
Prague 1, Nové Město
TEL 222 002 346
HOURS Mon–Fri: 10:00–18:00; Sat: 10:00–13:00
METRO Náměstí Republiky ●
TRAM 5, 8, 14 to Náměstí Republiky

If you're the musical type, this store will toot your horn. Bugles, records, trumpets, harmonicas and all the rest; I love this store, and I can't even *play* any instruments! Many of the instruments sold here

are made by Czech firms, and several of the pieces on offer would be appropriate for children.

■ ■ ■ ■ ■ ■ ■ ■ ■ ■ ■ ■

Bontonland Megastore
MUSIC
Palác Koruna
Václavské náměstí 1,
Prague 1, Nové Město
TEL 224 473 080
HOURS Mon–Sat: 09:00–20:00; Sun: 11:00–19:00
METRO Můstek ●
TRAM 3, 9, 14, 24 to Václavské náměstí

Located in the basement of Prague's famed Palác Koruna building, Bonton is the largest music and video store in the Czech Republic. You'll find all music genres here and every sort of media, including DVDs and video games. They also have a mini Apple store, so if you need a new iPod, travel speakers or even a laptop, this is a great resource to know about. It's more central than the Apple store at the Anděl mall in

PETROF PIANOS HAVE BEEN MADE IN THE CZECH REPUBLIC SINCE 1864.

Prague 5, Smíchov, and the salesman who helped me here last time around was far more helpful, too, I might add.

See pp. 69, 175, 177–78 for a list of recommended Czech CDs and artists.

Petrof – Pianos

Jungmannovo náměstí 17, Prague 1, Staré Město, 3rd floor
www.petrof.com
TEL 224 222 501
HOURS Mon–Fri: 10:00–19:00; Sat: 10:00–15:00
METRO Můstek ● ○
or Národní třída ○

Petrof has been making pianos in the Czech Republic since 1864. If you can't afford a Steinway, but are in the market for a high performance piano, Petrof might be just the ticket. Uprights run from €2,600 to €7,555, while grands run €11,640 to €62,750. It's also worth noting that they have several dealers in the United States.

Talacko

SHEET MUSIC
Rybná 29, Prague 1, Staré Město
www.talacko.cz
TEL 224 813 039
HOURS Mon–Sat: 10:00–18:00
METRO Náměstí Republiky ○
TRAM 5, 8, 14 to Dlouhá třída

From Dvořák to Hayden to the Beatles and even Iggy Pop, this is one-stop shopping for all your sheet music needs. Rumor has it that such stores are now a scarcity in the United States, so if you're a student of Dr. Terwillikers (*5000 Fingers of Dr. T*), be certain to stock up for that 24/7 practice session.

WOODCUT FOR BOOK COVER, c. 1946

POSTERS

Agentura Pro Vás

HISTORICAL POSTERS 1880–1990
Rybná 21, Prague 1, Staré Město
www.AgenturaProVas.cz
TEL 224 819 359
HOURS Mon–Fri: 09:00–18:00
METRO Náměstí Republiky ○
TRAM 5, 8, 14 to Náměstí Republiky

Would your trip to Prague be complete without an image of Stalin, Pro Vás's best seller? Or perhaps one or two early advertisements from the Czech Republic? Surely not, so put this hidden gem on your must-hit list. Original posters start at 300 CZK and run up to 50,000 CZK. The store offers copies of original posters for either 80 CZK or 120 CZK, depending on sizes. The owner, Vojtěch Sedláček, is charming; his English is terrific; and, most importantly, he is a true capitalist, as he advised me "everything is for sale"... Now that is a *first* for me in the Czech Republic, so, needless to say, he charmed his way into my heart immediately. Oddly, the store shares its space with a children's store for clothing and toys, so don't be misled if the window happens to be featuring children's shoes rather than Stalin; you *are* indeed in the right place!

SHOES

▪ ▪ ▪ ▪ ▪ ▪ ▪ ▪ ▪ ▪ ▪ ▪ ▪

Baťa
Václavské náměstí 6,
Prague 1, Nové Město
TEL 224 218 133
HOURS Mon–Fri: 09:00–21:00; Sat: 09:00–20:00; Sun: 10:00–20:00
METRO Můstek ● ○
TRAM 3, 9, 14, 24 to Vodičkova

Founded by Tomáš Baťa in 1913 in the town of Zlín,

Baťa has long since become nothing less than a shoe empire, one of the first truly global companies. Their flagship store on Václavské náměstí, built in 1927, originally sold Baťa shoes exclusively. Today the store sells other brands as well, although Baťa certainly remains the primary brand carried. Baťa's shoe quality is not what it once was, so I'd only indulge if the pair of shoes you have your eye on are *really* cute and 1,500 CZK or less, so you won't need to worry if they only last one season.

The building, however, is Functionalist perfection, and should not be missed, especially at night when it's lit up all the way to its roof!

SPORTS PARAPHERNALIA

▪ ▪ ▪ ▪ ▪ ▪ ▪ ▪ ▪ ▪ ▪ ▪ ▪

FANzone.cz
HOCKEY
Myslbekova 128/1, Prague 6, Střešovice
TEL 603 888 205
HOURS Mon–Fri: 12:00–18:00
METRO Hradčanská ●
TRAM 15, 25 to Malovanka

BAŤA, WENCESLAS SQUARE, C. 1940

If you're after an *official* Czech hockey jersey from Slavia, one of the local favorites, as opposed to one of the knockoffs that can be found practically anywhere downtown, this is the place to go. You can get one on the spot for 1,200 CZK; and for an additional 100 CZK, you can put a name and number of your choosing on it, though this takes approximately one week (so you might want to ask your hotel to assist you with coordinating this in advance, and then simply pick it up while you're here). They are very cool, I have to say. I got one for a Canadian hockey fanatic with Czech heritage, who also happens to work for Artěl, and I just may have won him over for life. They also sell lots of other goodies, including official hockey pucks for 100 CZK; hockey sticks, including tiny ones for kids for 100 CZK; t-shirts; mugs; and scarves. The official jerseys are only available in adult sizes.

A CORNER IN OLD TOWN, C. 1918

■ ■ ■ ■ ■ ■ ■ ■ ■ ■ ■ ■
JB Sport
HOCKEY
Dlážděná 3, Prague 1,
Nové Město
TEL 224 210 921
HOURS Mon–Fri: 09:00–
18:00; Sat: 09:00–13:00
TRAM 3, 9, 14, 24 to
Jindřišská; 5, 9, 26 to
Masarykovo nádraží

JB is one-stop shopping for all of your hockey needs, including pads, skates and helmets, but what I think may really interest you is their jersey collection in the back of the store. You can get the official Czech or Slovak Olympic or World Cup jersey for 2,200 CZK, or alternatively, be a bit more creative and get one of the official shirts from the local favorites for 1,290 CZK, including Kladno, Jaromír Jágr's home town team; Pardubice, Dominik Hašek's home town; or the local favorite and current champs, Sparta. For an additional fee and a one-day lead-time, you can have your favorite number and name put on the jerseys, (45 CZK per number and 10 CZK per letter). XL is the only size available, I'm afraid. Obviously, they assume you're a player and intend to wear it while playing. Hah!

■ ■ ■ ■ ■ ■ ■ ■ ■ ■ ■ ■
Sparta Praha Association Club
SOCCER
Na Perštýně 17, Prague 1,
Staré Město
TEL 222 220 424
HOURS Daily: 10:00–17:00
METRO Můstek ● ●
or Národní třída

This place can pretty accurately be described as a 'hole-in-the-wall,' but if you're desperate for "official" team paraphernalia from AC Sparta and SK Slavia, then look no further. They have all the usual gear: jerseys, hats, scarves, banners, key chains, and so on. You name it; they have a sports logo on it!
CASH ONLY

We have Mickey Mouse, Bugs Bunny and Sesame Street, while the Czechs have got their own unique and beloved fictional characters. Here are a couple of my favorites:

Krtek Created in 1956

As the story goes, Zdeněk Miler was having trouble inventing a character that Disney wouldn't already have come up with. Then, one day, while pondering the idea, he tripped over a molehill and voilà—Krtek was born. This little mole does not talk and is constantly surprised by the outside world since he lives underground. All his friends are animals native to the Czech Republic. Krtek is now an international star, well known throughout Europe, as well as parts of Asia.

KRTEK
(CREATED BY ZDENĚK MILER)

Večerníček

Created in 1967

Večerníček is a nightly TV host who welcomes Czech children before their evening bedtime story begins and then says goodnight when it's over. Much beloved.

VEČERNÍČEK
(CREATED BY RADEK PILAŘ)

Spejbl & Hurvínek

Created in 1920 (Spejbl) and 1926 (Hurvínek)

Originally, Spejbl & Hurvínek were a father and son marionette team who made their debut in the 1920's, but the best-known incarnation of the act dates to 1964. Rounding out the crew is Žeryk, their beloved dog; Mánička, Hurvínek's friend; and Mrs. Kateřina, his babička (grandmother). See p. 119 for a more extensive history.

Each of the unique Czech characters listed above have begotten countless spin-off products, including stuffed animals, marionettes, coloring books, school supplies, clothing, and bedding, among other items, any of which would make a wonderful souvenir for a child.

TOYS & MODELS

■ ■ ■ ■ ■ ■ ■ ■ ■ ■ ■ ■ ■ ■

Classic Model

MODEL TRAINS

Bartolomějská 3, Prague 1, Staré Město

TEL 224 228 101

HOURS Mon–Fri: 10:00–18:00; Sat: 09:30–12:30

METRO Národní třída

TRAM 6, 9, 18, 21, 22, 23 to Národní divadlo

For all you electric train fanatics, this small, off-the-beaten-track shop is stocked to the brim with treasures from big firms, such as Roco and Wilesco & Faller, as well as smaller Czech brands like MB and SVD. The store also stocks a full range of accessories, including trees, houses and little-itty-bitty-teenie-weenie people to help create the perfect diorama for your train. I picked up a very cool plastic apartment building, gutters and all, for 120 CZK.

■ ■ ■ ■ ■ ■ ■ ■ ■ ■ ■ ■ ■ ■

Hračky

TOYS

Loretánské náměstí 13, Prague 1, Hradčany

TEL N/A

HOURS Daily: 09:30–18:30

TRAM 22, 23 to Pohořelec

Despite its prime location near the Prague Castle, this toy store charges extremely fair prices, and happens to have the best selection of Czech tin toys that I've seen in Prague, as well as an excellent collection of wooden toys (including a marvelous Noah's Ark with exquisitely carved animals, some of which verge on being Cubist in design). Also be sure to check out the magnetic marionette sets,

ABC TECHNICAL MAGAZINE COVER, C. 1981

Another excellent model shop, MPM is actually a bit larger than its competitors. Here you'll find miniature Škodas and Fiats, a Russian MiG-29MS, and an interesting collection of Czech-made wooden hobby kits from which to build miniature structures such as a fort, house, windmill or cottage.

Pecka Modelář

Karolíny Světlé 3, Prague 1, Staré Město
TEL 224 230 170
HOURS Mon–Fri: 09:30–18:00; Sat: 09:00–12:00
METRO Národní třída
TRAM 6, 9, 18, 21, 22, 23 to Národní divadlo

Oddly, Prague boasts more model stores per capita than any other city in the world. Perhaps this phenomenon can be explained by the fact that, under Communism, there was only one, yes *one*, magazine for boys—ABC, which was entirely devoted to engineering and modeling. So, if you happen to be a model enthusiast, you'll have ample opportunity to purchase models made by local manufacturers. Smer is my favorite, featuring all kinds of fighter jets, tanks, and cars. Additionally, Pecka carries some wonderfully creepy hand-painted styrofoam heads in varying sizes that are meant to be installed in the model jets

including dioramas—an excellent item for a 5 to 7 year old. Definitely worth a stop.

IVRE

Jakubská 3, Prague 1, Staré Město
TEL N/A
HOURS Daily: 10:30–17:30
METRO Náměstí Republiky
TRAM 5, 8, 14 to Náměstí Republiky

IVRE focuses exclusively on wonderfully colorful hand-sewn fabric toys and accessories ranging from animals and puppets to beanbags and rattles. They offer fabric wall hangings for children's rooms with nature and transport themes, among others.

All of the items in the store have a very appealing homemade feel to them.

MPM Plastikové modely

Myslíkova 19, Prague 1, Nové Město
TEL 224 930 257
HOURS Mon–Fri; 09:00–18:00; Sat: 09:00–13:00
METRO Národní třída
TRAM 6, 9, 18, 21, 22, 23 to Národní třída

TOY TRAM, CONSTRUCTED OF METAL

GRAPE HARVESTING, C. 1963
(SOURCE: ČTK / CZECH NEWS AGENCY)

as pilots—I bought a few of these for a little installation in my flat, as they were simply too strange to leave behind...

Sparkys

Havířská 2, Prague 1, Staré Město
TEL 224 239 309
HOURS Mon–Sat: 10:00–19:00; Sun: 10:00–18:00
METRO Můstek ● ○

The "Toys 'R' Us" of the Czech Republic, Sparkys carries a wide variety of good quality Czech-made toys. Items to look out for include toys and jewelry made of wood (ground floor); plastic hockey figurines featuring local teams (top floor), Trabants made of metal (top floor); and metal toys made by Kovap (ground floor). Not to mention a vast array of Krtek, Večerníček, and Spejbl & Hurvínek goodies!

WINE SHOPS

Cellarius Vinotéka Pasáž Lucerna

Palace Lucerna
Štěpánská 61, Prague 1, Nové Město (you can also enter from Vodičkova)
www.cellarius.cz
TEL 224 210 979
HOURS Mon–Sat: 09:30–21:00; Sun: 15:00–20:00
METRO Můstek ● ○
TRAM 3, 9, 14, 24 to Václavské náměstí

A serious yet unpretentious wine store located on the ground floor of the Lucerna Palace, Cellarius offers an extensive and diverse collection of Czech wines and spirits, as well as foreign choices. The store also offers a wide range of decorative wood boxes with which to create handsome presentation packaging for the wine. The sales staff is always extremely helpful.

▪▪▪▪▪▪▪▪▪▪▪▪▪▪▪

Dům vína U Závoje
Havelská 25, Prague 1, Staré Město
www.uzavoje.cz
TEL 226 006 120
HOURS Mon–Fri: 11:00–19:00
METRO Můstek ● ○

Dům vína U Závoje is a wine and accessories merchant that opened in 2004 as part of a food and beverage-oriented commercial passageway. It's obvious that the people working in this shop are serious wine lovers with a broad knowledge to draw upon. The shop, however, is surprisingly small, compared with the wine bar in the same passageway. Indeed, if the store does not have what you're looking for, you might try to purchase it directly from the wine bar, as the latter's selection is much more extensive.

WINE CELLAR, C. 1966
(SOURCE: ČTK / CZECH NEWS AGENCY)

Czech Wine

For years, simply out of ignorance, I've always advised visitors to avoid Czech wines, as I personally had none to recommend (I'm *not* a big drinker). But as this was hardly sufficient advice for my readers, I decided to interview Bohuslav Uher, the assistant restaurant manager of Essensia restaurant at the Mandarin Oriental, Prague, so that you can benefit from some insider's tips on what to order, buy, and, of course, AVOID!

Karen: What are your favorite red and white Czech wines from the Mandarin Oriental cellar and why?

Bohuslav: For red I would recommend Springer Cuvée Skale 2004, as it shows off the skills of Czech winemakers; it really demonstrates their ability to make a full and complex wine, despite the less-than-ideal weather conditions in the Czech Republic.
　For white I would recommend the Ryzlink rýnský (Rhine Riesling) 2002 from Vinselekt Michlovský. Its fruity bouquet, rich body and very fine acidity make it especially appropriate for the cuisine we offer at Essensia.

Karen: Beyond the Mandarin Oriental itself, where is your favorite place in Prague to enjoy a glass of wine?

Bohuslav: I always like "Dům vína U Závoje" in the Old Town. They offer a wide selection of wines by the glass, which is nice when you would like to try something new. At the same location, they have a wine shop where you can buy the bottle immediately, and the prices are reasonable. Several times a month they offer wine tasting; their food is excellent; and they have the best cheese shop in town.

Karen: What are your favorite wine stores in Prague?

Bohuslav: In addition to "Dům vína U Závoje," I've been buying wines for years at "Monarch wine cellar," also located in the Old Town.

Karen: Which Czech winemaker is your favorite?

Bohuslav: My favorite is Tanzberg; they produce only top quality wines, including sparkling, and their presentation—often a handicap of Czech wineries—is very smart. Another one I like is Sonberk; their straw and ice wines are really unique.

Karen: What are your two single favorite Czech wines?

SHOPPING

CELEBRATION, C. 1947
(SOURCE: ČTK / CZECH NEWS AGENCY)

Bohuslav: Red: Frankovka (Blaufrankisch) 2003 from Bíza company. It is simply the best Czech red wine I've ever tasted. Unfortunately it's already out of stock. White: Any simple Welsch Riesling from Tanzberg, Mikrosvin, or Reisten.

Karen: What should someone keep in mind when they visit a wine store and there's no one to assist them? What should they stay away from? What should they look for?

Bohuslav: Buying ordinary Czech table wines is a waste of money. If you don't know the Czech market, buy only wines with special attributes. For example: late harvest (pozdní sběr); selection of grapes (výběr z hroznů); selection of berries (výběr z bobuli); ice (ledové); and straw (slámové) wines. In terms of local grape varieties, among whites, Pálava (a cross between Gewurztraminer and Müller Thurgau) is very interesting, and I also recommend Welsch Riesling. Among reds, I would suggest trying the André variety (a cross between the St. Laurent and Blaufrankisch grapes).

Wine Shop Recommended by Bohuslav:

Monarch Wine Bar & Shop
Na Perštýně 15, Prague 1, Staré Město
TEL 224 239 602
HOURS Mon–Sat: 11:00–19:00
METRO Národní třida ●

Also, see Wine Bars (p. 157).

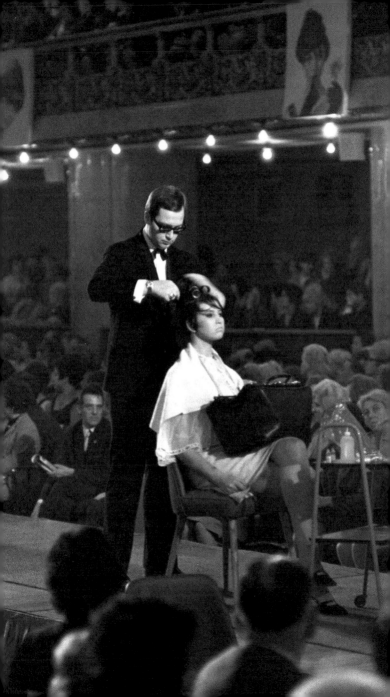

Services

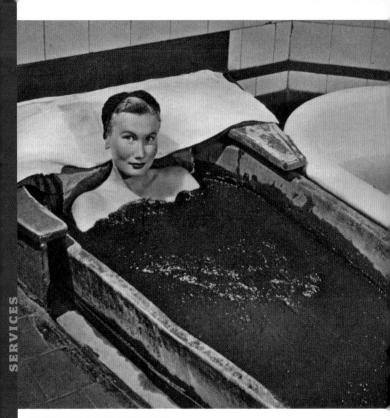

SPA TREATMENT IN KARLOVY VARY, C. 1940

MANICURES, PEDICURES, MASSAGES AND OTHER ESSENTIAL INDULGENCES

▪ ▪ ▪ ▪ ▪ ▪ ▪ ▪ ▪ ▪ ▪ ▪ ▪

Mandarin Oriental Prague Spa
Nebovidská 459/1, Prague 1, Malá Strana
www.mandarinoriental. com/prague
TEL 233 088 888
HOURS Daily: 09:00–22:00
METRO Malostranská ●
TRAM 12, 20, 22, 23 to Hellichova

The Mandarin Oriental Hotel opened in September 2006, and not only is their spa a fabulous addition to the local market; it has put all others to shame. The calm tranquil setting of the spa reception area, originally a Gothic church (remains of which can be seen through a glass floor), immediately sets the tone for your visit. The hotel is renowned for customer service and attention to detail, and my first visit only confirmed this. I opted for Oriental Harmony (1 hour 50 minutes for 5,100 CZK), which began with a soothing footbath, followed by a Linden Blossom Scrub (linden being the national tree of the Czech Republic), followed by a four-hand massage with two masseurs working in perfect unison. I followed the massage with a relaxing soak in the Vitality Pool located in my spa suite, Vltava. Heaven! Request this suite, if possible, as I found it to be the prettiest; they're all lovely, actually, but this is the only one with the Vitality Pool. Reservations are absolutely required, and I recommend you try to make them before you arrive in Prague, as this is currently the hot ticket in town, especially on weekends. For a full spa menu, visit the Mandarin Oriental website listed above, as they offer several different massages, facials and scrubs.

The Nail Shop / Darphin Salon

Slovanský dům, Na Příkopě 22, Prague 1, Nové Město
TEL 221 451 800
HOURS Daily: 10:00–20:00
METRO Můstek ● or Náměstí Republiky ○
TRAM 5, 8, 14 to Náměstí Republiky

The Czechs have yet to embrace the brilliance of the Korean walk-in nail salon, so making an appointment is absolutely necessary, though 24 hours notice will usually do. Located in the courtyard of the Slovanský dům, the Nail Shop opened in 2006, and I must admit, it's a new favorite of mine. If you're dying for a little TLC before hitting the town for the night, a stop here might be just what the doctor ordered. They also offer facials and waxing. Iva is my gal, and her English is exceptional (as she lived in the Wisconsin for two years, working in a salon there).

Manicures: 620 CZK including nail polish
Pedicures: 1,020 CZK including nail polish

Zen Asian Wellness

Maximilian
Haštalská 14, Prague 1, Staré Město
www.planetzen.cz
TEL 225 303 116
HOURS Daily: 10:00–22:00
METRO Náměstí Republiky ○
TRAM 5, 8, 14 to Dlouhá třída

Sabai is Thai for 'relax,' and that is precisely what you'll begin to do when you enter this serene Thai environment with accents of Art Deco deep in the Maximilian Hotel. They offer 10 different massages, ranging from the Silky Hand, a 30 minute massage that focuses solely on hands, for 450 CZK, to the Ritual, a 90 minute hot herbal massage utilizing tangerine and peppermint oils, for 1,650 CZK. During my most recent visit, I went for the Back Special, which left me very satisfied.

Topping off your massage with a visit to one of their two 'floating rooms'—basically enormous 7 meter baths —is certain to melt the stress away. The water is enriched with natural salt and mineral crystals for what they call 'The Dead Sea Effect,' by which you float virtually on the water, experiencing a unique feeling of weightlessness, absolute silence, deep relaxation and peace. Perfect after a long flight or an endless day of sight seeing. Floating 50 min will run you 890 CZK, but if you combine it with a massage, it's discounted approximately 30%.

Thai Foot Massage

Rytířská 19, Prague 1, Staré Město
TEL 224 226 105
HOURS Daily: 12:00–22:00
METRO Můstek ● ○

If you don't mind being in a very informal and communal room while being worked on, then this is a great stop to know about, as walk-ins are more than welcome. You'll have a choice of two options:

Foot Massage: 400 CZK
Full Body Massage: 600 CZK

Go for the full body; I assure you your money will be well spent! First, they will hand you a pair of shorts to change into, then you settle in your own comfy reclining chair and let them go to work. I have to say, I was pleasantly surprised by the quality of the massage. Ladda was my girl, and I measure her talents by the fact that I was not in the least bit distracted by all the relentless Thai chattering in the background. To take full advantage of the full body massages, be sure to take a T-shirt or camisole to change into, as it will allow them to work more comprehensively on your upper body.

CASH ONLY

PEDICURE, 1939
(SOURCE: EVA MAGAZINE)

Dining

A few words before we begin: the good news is that dining out in Prague has become a tastier and more pleasant prospect in the last few years. Indeed, I can assure you that you'll be pleasantly surprised by the quality, diversity, and sophistication you'll find.

The bad news: It may surprise you a bit that dining in Prague is *definitely* no longer a bargain. Indeed, I find some of the fancier places to be shockingly expensive. There are two factors I know of that help account for your expensive bills: 1. The U.S. dollar is at an all-time low against the Czech crown. 2. There is a 19% VAT tax on meals (included in the price on the menu), which hurts.

That said, I must be honest that I find myself, well, stunned to find that it costs me more to go out for a nice dinner in Prague than in New York. Something just doesn't add up... There's nothing you can do about it, though, so simply enjoy the meal, sign your receipt, and try to forget about it.

A Few Pieces of Basic Advice

CHECK THE BILL

It's always wise to check the bill before paying, as mistakes do happen. I myself have actually had very *few* problems with overcharging; however I've heard plenty of reports from other expats and visitors, so take a minute to double check.

TIPPING

Tips are rarely included in the bill so the assumption is that you'll add one yourself.

10% is more than acceptable from foreigners; Czechs themselves tend to leave about half that. It's up to you whether you want to tip based on the price of the meal only or on the full cost, including the 19% tax. I tend to tip on the meal only, unless the service has been really exceptional.

A new habit at the most expensive restaurants in town is to try and make you pay your tip in cash. Sometimes it will be done subtly, with a message at the end of your receipt, as in, "Tips in Cash Appreciated."

Other times they're a bit less subtle. For instance, the time I was handed back my charge slip with a big zero with a line through it on the tip line, not allowing me the option of choosing how I'd like to pay the tip. Sadly, that time around the waiter lost at his game, as I had no cash on me, so he ended up with nothing!

When I returned to the same restaurant two weeks later and handed my credit card to the waiter, I asked him to add a 350 CZK tip when he ran it through so that we wouldn't have the same problem. He then advised me, "We don't get the money if you leave us a tip on a credit card."

This was his unlucky day, however, as I had already discussed the incident with the General Manager, who had assured me that they do indeed get the money, but with taxes taken out of it. When I mentioned this to the waiter, he was a bit shocked.

He then revised his story, "Well yes, we do get the money, but most of it will be taken out for taxes, and do you really want to spend your money that way?"

Unfortunately for him, the answer was "*yes.*"

The fact of the matter is that the salaries waiters earn in Prague are good, not *low*, as in the United States, making tips far less of a desperately big issue for them. I also find this behavior annoying for the way in which it plays on the tourists' ignorance of what is customary, and the fact that it only happens at the most expensive restaurants in town. Do *not* let yourself be pushed around.

DRESS CODE

Dress code at most Prague restaurants is generally informal. Even the chicest places will be happy to seat you without a jacket, and ties are simply never required.

TABLE SHARING

At more informal restaurants, it's absolutely acceptable to share a table, should there be no other free ones available.

RESERVATIONS

Strongly recommended!

CREDIT CARDS

All the restaurants listed in this book accept them (unless otherwise specified).

Foods You Really Should Try While You're In Prague

Czech Main Courses

Svíčková: Roast beef slices served in a cream sauce, garnished with cranberries and lemon and served with bread dumplings.

Guláš: Pieces of beef or pork cooked in a hearty sauce and served with bread dumplings.

Vepřo, knedlo, zelo: Pork with cabbage and bread dumplings.

Kachna s bramborovými knedlíky a zelím: Roast duck with cabbage and potato dumplings.

Side Dishes

Krokety: Baked mashed potato balls.

Street Food

Sold at street stalls primarily located on Wenceslas Square and at Národní třída

Bramborák: Potato pancake.

Klobásy: Traditional sausages served with mustard and a slice of rye bread.

Párek v rohlíku: A hot dog slid into a hollowed-out roll with the condiment of your choosing; mustard or ketchup.

Smažený sýr: Fried cheese, a true Czech specialty, served either alone or in a roll with tatar sauce. The perfect way to end a heavy night of drinking, with a grease level that can only be called impressive.

Sweets

Sold at Cukrárnas, or Sweet Shops

Koláč: The closest thing to a cheese danish from a Jewish bakery that you're going to find here. Other fillings include apricot, poppy-seed and plum.

Bábovka: Pound cake.

Kokoska: Macaroon with chocolate base and a filling that includes either jam and/or chocolate.

Medovník: Layered honey cake.

Koblihy: Jelly doughnut.

Beer

Pilsner: The "Crème de la crème" of Czech beer, according to my co-worker Kristýna. The color is light but, at 12 degrees, it's heavier than some other beers on the market. Made in Western Bohemia, it is widely available in the United States.

Gambrinus: As Czech beers go, this is the lightest, at 10 degrees, but it also has the richest flavor. It's very popular among the locals both for taste and value, as it's about 25% less expensive than Pilsner. Since your average Czech can down quite a few beers in the course of an evening, this adds up. Gambrinus is owned by Pilsner and also brewed in West Bohemia.

Staropromen: Locals would say that this beer, brewed right in Prague, has a very specific scent and taste to it, due to the water used in the manufacturing process. The brewery is just a few minutes from downtown Prague, by the way, and you can easily arrange for a tour.

Budvar: Made in Southern Bohemia, Budvar is a very good beer with its own unique flavor. Not necessarily the obvious choice, Budvar nonetheless has its own die-hard fans, so it simply comes down to personal preference.

Kozel: This beer has a very specific, almost perfume-like taste that you will definitely notice. They, too, are owned by Pilsner, though their factory is located in Central Bohemia.

Each brewer has their own unique "top secret" recipe that they utilize, and I encourage you to try several, as each one will be slightly, or even not-so-slightly, different.

NOTE: always order draft or tap beer, never bottled. The tap beer tastes better, costs less, and happens to be the traditional method of consumption. If you've previously drunk Pilsner from a bottle, you'll notice a significant difference in taste from the draft Pilsner served here.

Soda

TopTopic: Kinda like Sprite.

Kofola: Kinda like Coke.

Restaurants by Area

MALÁ STRANA
HRADČANY – CASTLE
Lobkowicz Palace Café 1 B
Café, p. 154

U Černého vola 2 B
Pub, p. 156

MALOSTRANSKÉ NÁMĚSTÍ
CukrKávaLimonáda 3 B
Café, p. 152

U Zeleného čaje 4 B
Café / Tea House, p. 156

The Blue Duck 5 B
Czech, p. 142

Coda 6 B
International, p. 143

Hergetova cihelna 7 B
International, p. 145

Kampa Park 8 B
International / Mediterranean, p. 145

Square 9 B
International / Spanish, p. 148

U Zlaté studně 10 B
International, p. 149

Essensia 11 B
Thai / Indian / International, p. 144

SOUTH MALÁ STRANA & ÚJEZD
T.Z. Cukrárna 12 B
Cake Shop, p. 155

Café Savoy 13 B
International / Czech, p. 143

C'est La Vie 14 B
International / Asian Fusion, p. 143

STARÉ MĚSTO
OLD TOWN SQUARE & JEWISH QUARTER
NOSTRESS Café 15 A
Asian Fusion / French, p. 147

Au Gourmand 16 A
Café and Cake Shop, p. 151

Bakeshop Praha 17 A
Café and Cake Shop, p. 151

Coffee Heaven 18 A+C
Café, p. 152

Cremeria Milano 19 A
Café and Ice Cream, p. 152

Ebel Coffee House 20 A+C
Café, p. 153

Paneria 21 A
Café and Cake Shop, p. 155

Kolkovna 22 A
Czech, p. 146

Barock 23 A
International / Sushi, p. 142

Le Café Colonial 24 A
International, p. 142

Pravda 25 A
International, p. 148

Allegro 26 A+C
Italian / Mediterranean, p. 141

Amici Miei 27 A
Italian, p. 141

L'Angolo 28 A
Italian, p. 146

Pastacaffé 29 A
Italian, p. 147

Rugantino 30 A
Italian, p. 148

Country Life 31 C
Vegetarian, p. 152

Dům vína U Závoje 32 C
Wine Bar, p. 157

OBECNÍ DŮM
Grand Café Orient 33 C
Café, p. 153

Kavárna Obecní dům 34 C
Café, p. 154

Divinis Wine Bar 35 A+C
Italian, p. 144

Kogo 36 C+D
Italian, p. 146

U Rozvařilů 37 A
Czech Cafeteria, p. 155

NÁRODNÍ TŘÍDA
Culinaria 38 C
Café and Cake Shop, p. 153

Kavárna Slavia 39 C
Café, p. 154

U Medvídků 40 C
Pub, p. 159

NOVÉ MĚSTO
Hotel Evropa 41 C
Café, p. 154

Mánes *
Czech, p. 147

Lahůdky Zemark 42 C
Delicatessen, p. 155

Garden at the Opera 43 D
International, p. 144

Bredovský dvůr *
Pub, p. 158

Pivovarský dům *
Pub, p. 158

Bokovka *
Wine Bar, p. 157

FURTHER AFIELD
DEJVICKÁ
Perpetuum *
Czech, p. 150

KARLÍN
Pivovarský klub *
Pub, p. 159

LIBEŇ
Richter Brewery – Pivovar U Bulovky *
Pub, p. 159

VINOHRADY
Le Papillion *
International, p. 150

Aromi 44 D
Italian, p. 149

Radost FX Café 45 D
Vegetarian, p. 150

ŽIŽKOV
Štrúdl z taženého těsta *
Strudel, p. 156

*location not visible on featured maps

DINING

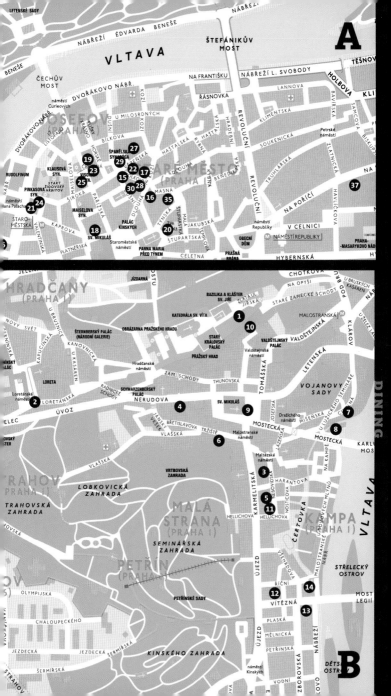

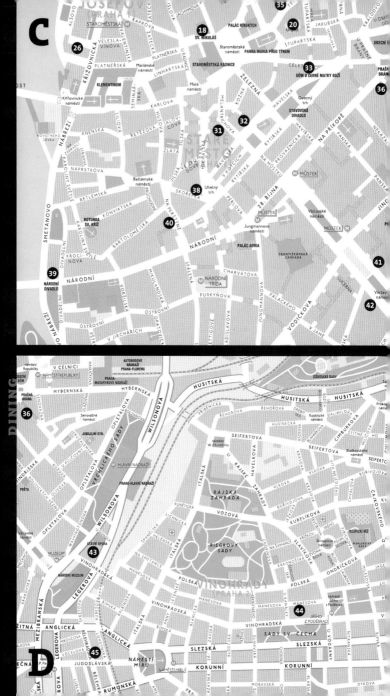

OLD TOWN SQUARE, C. 1930

if you want to splurge, this is well worth it (and hopefully your pockets are deeper than mine).

Starters: 520–740 CZK
Pasta: 520–570 CZK
Main courses: 640–1,700 CZK
Dessert: 295–495 CZK
Wine: 950–29,500 CZK
Pilsner beer: 155 CZK

■ ■ ■ ■ ■ ■ ■ ■ ■ ■ ■ ■ ■ ■

Amici Miei
ITALIAN
Vězeňská 5, Prague 1,
Staré Město
www.amicimiei.cz
TEL 224 816 688
HOURS Daily: 11:30–23:00
Average cost of a three-course meal, not including drinks: 1,020 CZK
METRO Staroměstská ●
TRAM 17, 18 to Staroměstská

Request: A table outside on the sidewalk, if the weather is nice.

If you want authentic Italian in Prague, Amici Miei is an excellent choice. The menu includes pastas, meat and fish; and their *scaloppini al limone* is the best I've had in Prague. The wine list is exclusively Italian. The restaurant also happens to make one of the best lattes in town, and their freshly baked bread, served with olive oil, is delicious. I particularly like the very private sidewalk dining area, which makes clever use of a hedge to create an intimate outdoor space. When the weather cooperates, this is always where I prefer to sit. The interior décor is Italian modern, with rather colorful chandeliers punctuating the otherwise neutral space (still not sure what I think of those, actually…).

RESTAURANTS

■ ■ ■ ■ ■ ■ ■ ■ ■ ■ ■ ■ ■ ■

Allegro Restaurant at the Four Seasons Hotel
ITALIAN /
MEDITERRANEAN
Veleslavínova 2a, Prague 1,
Staré Město
www.fourseasons.com/
prague/dining
TEL 221 426 880
HOURS Daily: 11:30–23:30
Average cost of a three-course meal, not including drinks: 1,845 CZK
METRO Staroměstská ●
TRAM 17, 18 to Staroměstská

Request: A table next to the window overlooking the river.

Year in and year out, Allegro is voted the best restaurant in Prague. I've eaten here several times and must admit it lives up to the hype. Once you're seated, you forget you're even at a hotel; indeed, over 50% of the people dining there on any given night are not hotel guests. The food is sublime, and the riverside location overlooking the Charles Bridge and the Castle is nothing short of dreamy. Three of the best meals I've ever had in Prague were eaten here. The prices are unquestionably high, especially for water, but

DINING

Starters: 260–620 CZK
Pasta: 250–650 CZK
Main courses: 390–720 CZK
Dessert: 130–190 CZK
Wine: 430–18,500 CZK
Pilsner beer: 60 CZK

■ ■ ■ ■ ■ ■ ■ ■ ■ ■ ■ ■ ■ ■

Barock
INTERNATIONAL / SUSHI
Pařížská 24, Prague 1,
Staré Město
www.barockrestaurant.cz
TEL 222 329 221
HOURS Daily: 10:00–23:30
Average cost of a three-
course meal, not including
drinks: 1,060 CZK
METRO Staroměstská ●
TRAM 17, 18 to Staroměstská

Request: The first banquette
table in the window,
overlooking the Old New
Synagogue and Pravda,
right across the street.

If you're bored with your
hotel's breakfast offerings
or it's not included in
your room rate, Barock

is an *excellent* morning
destination right in the
heart of Old Town. They
offer several different
breakfast options, but my
own favorite is the Yogurt
with Müsli and Fruit. On
my last visit this included
raspberries, blackberries,
blueberries, strawberries
and pineapple—a real
bargain at 105 CZK. Egg
dishes run 185 CZK, and
fresh-squeezed orange juice
rings in at 95 CZK.

The restaurant is also
open for dinner, but at
night I prefer Pravda,
which is across the street
and happens to be owned
by the same proprietor.

Starters: 335–445 CZK
Main courses: 395–595 CZK
Dessert: 130 CZK
Wine: 795–5,900 CZK
Pilsner beer: 85 CZK

Breakfast: Mon–Friday:
10:00–1:30; Sat & Sun:
10:00–16:00

KLEMENTIUM AND THE ROOFS OF OLD TOWN

■ ■ ■ ■ ■ ■ ■ ■ ■ ■ ■ ■ ■ ■

The Blue Duck
U Modré kachničky
CZECH
Nebovidská 6, Prague 1,
Malá Strana
www.umodrekachnicky.cz
TEL 257 320 308
HOURS Daily: 12:00–16:00 &
18:30–24:00
Average cost of a three-
course meal, not including
drinks: 940 CZK
METRO Malostranská ●
then tram 12, 20, 22, 23 to
Hellichova
TRAM 12, 20, 22, 23 to
Hellichova

Request: A table upstairs.

If you're after authentic
Czech cuisine, this is
a charming and pleasant
place to get it. The décor
upstairs is especially
quaint, and is warmed
up with antique fur-
nishings. The duck,
perhaps not surprisingly,
is as traditional as you
can get, and when you
pair it with lots of potato
and bread dumplings and
cabbage, you'll be dining
just as the Czechs once did.
There are two locations
for this restaurant, including another in the Old
Town, but I prefer the one
listed above.

Starters: 155–440 CZK
Main courses: 285–690 CZK
Dessert: 125–210 CZK
Wine: 560–12,820 CZK
Pilsner beer: 55 CZK

■ ■ ■ ■ ■ ■ ■ ■ ■ ■ ■ ■ ■ ■

Le Café Colonial
INTERNATIONAL
Široká 6, Prague 1,
Staré Město
www.lecafecolonial.cz
TEL 224 818 322
HOURS Daily: 10:00–24:00
Average cost of a three-
course meal, not including
drinks: 820 CZK

METRO Staroměstská ●
TRAM 17, 18 to Staroměstská

Request: A table in the bar area with low upholstered seating; this is far comfier, making for a more relaxed, leisurely meal.

This restaurant is a great place to stop for lunch or dinner while visiting the Jewish Quarter, as it is literally across the street from the Jewish cemetery and ticket office. An old standby of mine, it hasn't let me down yet. I especially like the salads, which are so big they constitute a meal in themselves.

Starters: 185–330 CZK
Main courses: 205–475 CZK
Dessert: 95–195 CZK
Wine: 325–1,750 CZK
Pilsner beer: 55 CZK

Breakfast: 10:00–12:00; average price of 350 CZK

- - - - - - - - - - - - - -
Café Savoy
CZECH / INTERNATIONAL
Vítězná 5, Prague 5, Malá Strana
www.ambi.cz
TEL 257 311 562
HOURS Mon–Fri: 8:00–22:30; Sat & Sun: 9:00–22:30
Average cost of a three-course meal, not including drinks: 735 CZK
TRAM 6, 9, 12, 20, 22, 23 to Újezd

For Dinner, Request: A table in the back room, ideally the center banquette table facing the archway.

For Breakfast or Lunch, Request: A banquette table in front room, facing the street (so you can watch the trams go by).

Housed in a handsome Neoclassical space, this café is a real find, as it serves breakfast, lunch and dinner, not to mention the best cake in town. Many people, including myself, have wondered why Czech café culture generally falls so far short of the Viennese model; but thankfully, with Café Savoy, I'm able to get around that problem without a six-hour drive to Demels. The food here is terrific, especially the soups, and priced very fairly. They also have a very good wine list. I would recommend this restaurant for breakfast, lunch, *or* dinner, as it's one of the very few places in Prague that is actually good with all three.

If you do go for breakfast, make sure to try a few of the classic Czech pastry offerings, as you won't see them at many other places. These include: *bábovka* (pound cake); *koláč* (similar to a Danish, with fillings that include *tvaroh* [cheese] and *mák* [poppyseed]); apple strudel; and *rebarborový koláč* (rhubarb pastry so rich and complex, it verges on the savory).

Starters: 185–290 CZK
Main courses: 139–325 CZK
Dessert: 180–195 CZK
Wine: 304–4,195 CZK
Staropramen beer: 49 CZK.

Breakfast: 08:00–11:00; average price 277 CZK

- - - - - - - - - - - - - -
C'est La Vie
ASIAN FUSION / INTERNATIONAL
Říční 1, Prague 1, Malá Strana
www.cestlavie.cz
TEL 721 158 403
HOURS Daily: 11:30–01:00
Average cost of a three-course meal, not including drinks: 1,600 CZK
TRAM 6, 9, 12, 20, 22, 23 to Újezd

Request: The riverside terrace

Located on the southern end of Kampa Park, away from the hustle and bustle of Malá Strana, this restaurant lets you eat right on the riverbank with a charming view of the river and the Charles Bridge. I've been here several times, and each time walked away extremely impressed with the food, which, I should mention, definitely emphasizes fish. It's less expensive than Kampa Park, though that's not saying much; this is still an expensive night out. The dining room is pretty, but I think this restaurant is best appreciated during the warmer months, when sitting by the riverbank is an option.

Starters: 295–895 CZK
Main courses: 695–895 CZK
Dessert: 295–395 CZK
Wine: 495–27,500 CZK
Staropramen beer: 55 CZK

NOTE: Several friends have mentioned that they have been overcharged at this restaurant, so be sure to double-check your bill before paying.

- - - - - - - - - - - - - -
Coda
INTERNATIONAL
Tržiště 9, Prague 1, Malá Strana
www.codarestaurant.cz
TEL 225 334 761
HOURS Daily: 11:30–01:00
Average cost of a three-course meal, not including drinks: 1,170 CZK
METRO Malostranská ●
TRAM 12, 20, 22, 23 to Malostranské náměstí

Request: A table on the terrace with seats facing Prague Castle and St. Nicholas Church.

DINING

Located on the roof terrace of the Aria hotel, Coda has become my place of choice for terrace dining, as it's nestled among the rooftops of Malá Strana—about as charming as it gets in Prague. The menu is mainly international, with a few Czech classics thrown in, and the food is consistently right on the mark. If you choose to dine inside, you should ask to be seated in the back dining room, preferably the table with the sofa for two.

Starters: 300–420 CZK
Main courses: 350–595 CZK
Dessert: 325–455 CZK
Wine: 695 –60,000 CZK
Pilsner beer: 120 CZK

■ ■ ■ ■ ■ ■ ■ ■ ■ ■ ■ ■ ■ ■
Divinis Wine Bar
ITALIAN
Týnská 19, Prague 1,
Staré Město
www.divinis.cz
TEL 224 808 318
HOURS Daily: 16:00–02:00
Average cost of a three-course meal, not including drinks: 990 CZK
METRO Staroměstská ●
TRAM 17, 18 to Staroměstská

Request: A table upstairs, preferably the round table for 4 or 5 set back in the alcove (a private little dining room, really).

A cozy and intimate wine bar with simple yet delicious Italian meals. There are just five or six choices on the menu to compliment your choice of wine, and both the owner and sommelier are on-hand to make recommendations. All my friends who drink wine have become quick fans. If you're not into wine, however, this probably won't be up your alley, as this, really, is their raison d'être.

Starters: 240–390 CZK
Main courses: 520–590 CZK
Pasta 290–380 CZK
Dessert: 110–160 CZK
Wine: 420–6,600 CZK
Pilsner beer: 60 CZK

■ ■ ■ ■ ■ ■ ■ ■ ■ ■ ■ ■ ■ ■
Essensia at the Mandarin Oriental Hotel
THAI / INDIAN / INTERNATIONAL
Nebovidská 1, Prague 1,
Malá Strana
www.mandarinoriental.com
TEL 233 088 888
HOURS Daily: 12:00–23:00
Average cost of a three-course meal, not including drinks: 1,175 CZK
METRO Malostranská ●
TRAM 12, 20, 22, 23 to Hellichova

Request: A table in the first room, as this room has a handsome centerpiece used for serving that is always outfitted with sublime flower arrangements.

You'll find the best Thai and Indian food in town at Essensia, and the service is simply impeccable. Should you be hankering for something other than Asian, they offer a more traditional menu as well. The Thai green chicken curry, in a soup base, melts in your mouth, and the papadam with Indian curry is to die for. In short, Essensia is a great addition to the Prague restaurant scene. And afterwards, why not cap off your meal with a nightcap at the hotel's ultra chic Barego bar? I particularly like the latter's lighting and strikingly modern architecture—a real departure from the rest of the hotel.

Starters: 250–495 CZK

Main courses: 450–745 CZK
Dessert: 200– 00 CZK
Wine: 700–20,000 CZK
Pilsner beer: 90 CZK

Afternoon Tea: 14:00–17:00; in the Monastery Lounge (520 CZK).

■ ■ ■ ■ ■ ■ ■ ■ ■ ■ ■ ■ ■ ■
Garden at the Opera
Zahrada v opeře
INTERNATIONAL
Legerova 75, Prague 1,
Nové Město
www.zahradavopere.cz
TEL 224 239 685
HOURS Mon–Sat: 11:30–01:00
Average cost of a three-course meal, not including drinks: 540 CZK
METRO Muzeum ● ●
TRAM 11 to Muzeum

Request: A table next to the window.

Garden at the Opera is a great option if you're planning to see a show at the State Opera. Located just next door to the famous music venue, this restaurant keeps serving until midnight to satisfy post-opera hunger pangs. The food is excellent and the prices are very reasonable. I should also mention the salad bar —a rare and welcome find in Prague. The rather funky modern décor was designed by the Czech architect Bára Škorpilová, who currently seems to be the "it" girl for restaurant design in Prague. If you're not going to the State Opera, however, it might not be worth the hassle of having to make it past the tight security around Radio Free Europe, the building in which it's located.

Starters: 125–250 CZK
Main courses: 165–530 CZK

KAMPA ISLAND, C. 1948

Dessert: 80–170 CZK
Wine: 245–2,990 CZK
Pilsner beer: 40 CZK

■ ■ ■ ■ ■ ■ ■ ■ ■ ■ ■ ■

Hergetova cihelna
INTERNATIONAL
Cihelná 2b, Prague 1,
Malá Strana
www.cihelna.com
TEL 296 826 103
HOURS Daily: 11:30–01:00
Average cost of a three-
course meal, not including
drinks: 1,180 CZK
METRO Malostranská ●
TRAM 12, 18, 20, 22, 23 to
Malostranské náměstí

Request: A table on the
terrace next to the wall.

This restaurant boasts
a fabulously expansive
terrace right next to the
river and a prime view of
the Charles Bridge. Less
expensive than Kampa
Park (next entry) but
with an equally inspiring
riverside view, it's certainly
a great option, though
hardly on par with the
former in terms of either
culinary sophistication or
total execution. The food is
international, with a little
bit of everything, and the
wine list is fairly expensive
relative to the rest of
the menu, with bottles
starting around 500 CZK.

Starters: 265–465 CZK
Main courses: 235–695 CZK
Dessert: 245–395 CZK
Wine: 500–23,900 CZK
Pilsner beer: 65 CZK

■ ■ ■ ■ ■ ■ ■ ■ ■ ■ ■ ■

Kampa Park
INTERNATIONAL /
MEDITERRANEAN
Na Kampě 8b, Prague 1,
Malá Strana
www.kampagroup.com/en/
TEL 296 826 102
HOURS Daily: 11:30–01:00
Average cost of a three-
course meal, not including
drinks: 1,700 CZK
METRO Malostranská ●
TRAM 12,18, 20, 22, 23 to
Malostranské náměstí

145

Request: A table on the downstairs terrace riverside, open year round.

Everything here is outstanding: food, service, and location. They really don't miss a trick, which is why this has been one of my favorite places in town for years. It's equally popular among locals, tourists and even A-list celebs. The best things about this restaurant is its location, which is literally *on* the river, beneath the strikingly lit arches of the Charles Bridge, making it very possibly the most romantic spot in town for dinner. Even if you're not able to get a table on the terrace, it's still *highly* recommended, as the food itself here is simply outstanding—utterly scrumptious.

Starters: 395–795 CZK
Main courses: 435–895 CZK
Dessert: 295–495 CZK
Wine: 425 –46,500 CZK
Pilsner beer: 55 CZK

■ ■ ■ ■ ■ ■ ■ ■ ■ ■ ■ ■ ■
Kogo Ristorante
ITALIAN
Slovanský dům, Na Příkopě 10 (in the courtyard), Prague 1, Staré Město
TEL 221 451 259
HOURS Daily: 11:00–23:00
Average cost of a three-course meal, not including drinks: 776 CZK
METRO Můstek ● ● or Náměstí Republiky ●
TRAM 5, 8, 14 to Náměstí Republiky

Request: A table under the covered terrace or in the winter garden.

If you're curious as to where the locals lunch, well, now you know. It also happens to be one of my own personal favorites, so I'm a regular. The food is always great and the service outstanding. An added bonus is the location in a very large, quiet courtyard right in the middle of downtown Prague, which gives you the pleasure of eating outside without the hassle of being bombarded by tourist traffic. The menu includes pastas, pizzas, and salads, as well as an excellent selection of fresh fish.

Starters: 180–1,660 CZK
Main courses: 350–950 CZK
Pasta 190–430 CZK
Dessert: 80–128 CZK
Wine: 520–9,900 CZK
Pilsner beer: 55 CZK

■ ■ ■ ■ ■ ■ ■ ■ ■ ■ ■ ■ ■
Kolkovna
CZECH
V Kolkovně 8, Prague 1, Staré Město
www.kolkovna.cz
TEL 224 819 701
HOURS Daily: 11:00–24:00
Average cost of a three-course meal, not including drinks: 539 CZK
METRO Staroměstská ●
TRAM 17, 18 to Staroměstská

Request: A table upstairs, away from front door.

Pilsner Urquell, the most famous Czech brewery, has brought the local tradition of pubs up-to-date at this hot spot right in the heart of downtown Prague, frequented by tourists and locals alike. They offer a wide selection of traditional Czech fare, all of it above average, as well as lots and lots of beer, including nonalcoholic brews. In winter I enjoy the intimate cellar downstairs, but at other times of year I prefer to eat upstairs, where the air circulation is a bit better. If you want a safe introduction to typical Czech food, this is a great spot to add to your must-hit list.

Starters: 119–255 CZK
Main courses: 125–419 CZK
Dessert: 105–129 CZ
Wine: 315–1,150 CZK
Pilsner beer: 37 CZK

■ ■ ■ ■ ■ ■ ■ ■ ■ ■ ■ ■ ■
L'Angolo
ITALIAN
Dlouhá 7, Prague 1, Staré Město
TEL 224 829 355
HOURS Daily: 08:00–23:00
Average cost of a three-course meal, not including drinks: 740 CZK
METRO Staroměstská ●
TRAM 17, 18 to Staroměstská

Request: The banquette table in the corner, which is totally private, while allowing you to take in the scene both at the restaurant and on the street.

A new restaurant from the owners of Kogo (see entry on this page), L'Angolo opened in the late spring of 2006 with a fabulous location and a chic interior to match. It's a perfect choice for breakfast, lunch or dinner, and there are lots of daily salads on offer, including several with exotic seafood, such as octopus. The staff isn't nearly as polished as at Kogo itself, but I'm confident that, given a little time, they will work out all the rough edges.

Starters: 195–380 CZK
Main courses: 350–670 CZK
Pasta: 195–280 CZK
Dessert: 90–155 CZK
Wine: 520–9,990 CZK
Pilsner beer: 55 CZK

Mánes
CZECH

Masarykovo nábřeží 250,
Prague 1, Nové Město
www.restaurace-manes.cz
TEL 224 931 112
HOURS Daily: 11:00–23:00
Average cost of a three course
meal, not including drinks:
350 CZK
TRAM 17, 21 to Jiráskovo
nábřeží

Request: If the weather is
warm, a table on the upper
terrace overlooking either
the National Theatre or
Gehry's Dancing Building.
If the weather is cold,
request a table near the
window, overlooking the
National Theatre.

If this is not yet a hot spot
in town, it's clearly an over-
sight on everyone's part, as
the location is fabulous. The
1930's Functionalist building is a historic landmark,
although I'll admit that the
space has seen better times
and is in great need of
renovation. In addition to
the restaurant, Manes also
has a large exhibition space
with changing exhibitions.
All the Czech classics are on
the menu, and the prices
are ridiculously low—120
CZK for pork with cabbage

and dumplings, for in-
stance (at other spots downtown it would be double or
triple that). It also happens
to have a remarkably great
view of Gehry's famous
dancing building, which I
prefer to see at night, when
it's all lit up.

Starters: 47–172 CZK
Main courses: 120–335 CZK
Dessert: 65–130 CZK
Wine: 220–395 CZK
Krušovice beer: 33 CZK

NOSTRESS Café
ASIAN FUSION / FRENCH
Dušní 10, Prague 1,
Staré Město
www.nostress.cz
TEL 222 317 007
HOURS Daily: 10:00–24:00
Average cost of a three-
course meal, not including
drinks: 780 CZK
METRO Staroměstská ●
TRAM 17, 18 to Staroměstská

Request: The table with the
four leather club chairs
in the back room on the
ground floor.

While this definitely wins
the prize for the Worst
Restaurant Name in
Prague, the cafe itself is ac-
tually lovely. Located in the
Old Town, close to the Old

Jewish Quarter (Josefov),
it's especially good for
lunch, and both the chick-
en salad and fried shrimp
with coconut sauce are
yummy. The atmosphere
here is great—it feels like
they're going for a 'Buddha
Bar in Paris' vibe—and I
can definitely recommend
it for a before-dinner drink
or a nightcap. I would eat
dinner elsewhere, however.

Starters: 205–480 CZK
Main courses: 220–580 CZK
Dessert: 90–180 CZK
Wine: 420–2,585 CZK
Pilsner beer: 60 CZK

Breakfast: 10:00–12:00;
average price 250 CZK

Pastacaffé
ITALIAN
Vězeňská 1, Prague 1,
Staré Město
www.ambi.cz
TEL 224 813 257
HOURS Mon–Sat: 08:00–
22:00; Sun: 10:00–22:00
Average cost of a three-
course meal, not including
drinks: 378 CZK
METRO Staroměstská ●
TRAM 17, 18 to Staroměstská

Request: A table on the
banquette along the wall.

At once sleekly Italian and
offbeat, this retro 1950's
restaurant is perfect for
breakfast, lunch or an
informal dinner. It's also
great for a quick espresso
or cappuccino—certain to
be one of the best cups of
coffee you'll find in town.
The menu is limited to
salads, paninis and pasta.
Frequented by locals and
tourists alike, Pastacaffé
also happens to be child-
friendly, with a large buck-
et of toys for kids to play
with, as well as a changing
table in the bathroom.

OLD-NEW SYNAGOGUE ON PAŘÍŽSKÁ STREET, C. 1900

MALOSTRANSKÉ SQUARE AND CHURCH OF ST. NICHOLAS, 1934

DINING

Starters: 118–178 CZK
Main courses: 118–189 CZK
Dessert: 87–129 CZK
Wine: 284–1,840 CZK
Stella beer: 55 CZK

Breakfast: 08:00–11:00; average price 236 CZK

- - - - - - - - - - - - - -
Pravda
INTERNATIONAL
Pařížská 17, Prague 1,
Staré Město
www.pravdarestaurant.cz/en
TEL 222 326 203
HOURS Daily: 12:00–24:00
Average cost of a three-course meal, not including drinks: 1,285 CZK
METRO Staroměstská ●
TRAM 17, 18 to Staroměstská

Request: A table along the banquette on the second level, facing Pařížská Street, with the large mirror just behind you.

This is international cuisine served in a very chic setting ideal for people-watching. Literally next door to the Old-New Synagogue, Pravda is a very convenient choice if you attend Friday evening services. The food may not be *as* exceptional as at Kampa Park, but I'm confident you will not be disap-

pointed; I myself eat here all the time. Although dessert here will inevitably be delicious, I recommend you skip it and go across the street to Cremeria Milano, Pařížská 20, which has absolutely the best ice cream in Prague. Crème Caramel is my personal favorite!

Starters: 365–425 CZK
Main courses: 325–625 CZK
Dessert: 295 CZK
Wine: 725–5,790 CZK
Krušovice beer: 85 CZK

- - - - - - - - - - - - - -
Rugantino
ITALIAN
Dušní 4, Prague 1,
Staré Město
TEL 222 318 172
HOURS Mon–Sat: 11:00–23:30; Sun: 12:00–23:30
Average cost of a three-course meal, not including drinks: 435 CZK
METRO Staroměstská ●
TRAM 17, 18 to Staroměstská

Request: A table in the non-smoking front section, where the room is much brighter.

Rugantino is an affordable, delicious, and informal stop for a sit-down lunch. They serve excellent pizzas,

including a wide selection of vegetarian options as well as pasta and salads. The restaurant is child-friendly, with a changing table in the bathroom.

Starters: 145–200 CZK
Main courses: 100–225 CZK
Dessert: 95–195 CZK
Wine: 285–980 CZK
Bernard beer: 45 CZK

- - - - - - - - - - - - - -
Square
INTERNATIONAL/SPANISH
Malostranské náměstí. 5/28,
Prague 1, Malá Strana
TEL 296 826 104
HOURS Mon–Fri: 08:00–01:00; Sat & Sun: 09:00–01:00
Average cost of a three-course meal, not including drinks: 825 CZK
METRO Malostranská ●
TRAM 12, 18, 20, 22, 23 to Malostranské náměstí

Request: A table on the terrace, if the weather is warm, and specify a table next to the hedge along the parking lot (trust me!). If you're eating inside, request a table by the window on the same side of the restaurant.

I don't think there could be a more convenient place to eat in Malá Strana, and, as the saying goes: location, location, location… It also happens to have a wonderful view of the fabulous buildings lining Malostranské náměstí. Although they're apparently famous for their tapas, I recommend you skip them, as I myself was not impressed. You'll do better, I think, simply to start with a hot or cold appetizer. The main courses are excellent; my salmon was cooked to perfection, the asparagus was done just right (a true achievement, given how much more reasonably priced it is than most of the upscale restaurants in Prague), and the service is absolutely on par with the food.

Starters: 155–275 CZK
Main courses: 175–545 CZK
Pasta: 175–295 CZK
Dessert: 145–345 CZK
Wine: 475–15,500 CZK
Pilsner beer: 55 CZK

Breakfast: 09:00–16:00; average price of 350 CZK
Lunch, prix-fixe: 295 CZK; includes a starter, main course, water and coffee/tea

■■■■■■■■■■■■■
U Zlaté studně
INTERNATIONAL
U Zlaté studně 4, Prague 1, Malá Strana
www.terasauzlatestudne.cz
TEL 257 533 322
HOURS Daily: 07:00–23:00
Average cost of a three-course meal, not including drinks: 1,370 CZK
METRO Malostranská ●
TRAM 12, 18, 20, 22, 23 to Malostranské náměstí

Request: A table on the terrace next to the railing; if eating inside, request a table next to the window.

The first thing I should say about U Zlaté studně is that, unless your legs are in spectacular shape, you'll want to take a taxi there, as it is nestled in a little nook high up Malá Strana's steeply sloped neighborhood, within the U Zlaté studně Hotel. They won't win any prizes for best signage or warmest welcome either, so just trust your instincts, keep heading up, and eventually you'll find the roof-top terrace, at which point you'll be rewarded with one of the most outstanding views of Prague—basically an all-encompassing panorama of the city; which is good, because, while the food is certainly fine, it's the view you're really paying for.

Starters: 235–750 CZK
Main courses: 420–950 CZK
Dessert: 295–350 CZK
Wine: 550–24,000 CZK
Pilsner beer: 70 CZK

Breakfast: 10:00–12:00; 290 CZK. On a beautiful day when you have a little time to spare, this could be a great option.

Further Afield
■■■■■■■■■■■■■
Aromi
ITALIAN
Mánesova 78, Prague 2, Vinohrady
www.aromi.cz
TEL 222 713 222
HOURS Mon–Sat: 12:00–23:00; Sun: 12:00–22:00
Average cost of a three-course meal, not including drinks: 775 CZK
METRO Jiřího z Poděbrad ●
TRAM 11 to Jiřího z Poděbrad

Request: In the summer, a table on the terrace; or, inside, a table next to the window, preferably in the back corner, next to the bookcase.

U ZLATÉ STUDNĚ (THE GOLDEN WELL), C. 1930

Aromi is located on a charming, tree-lined street in the residential district of Vinohrady, and they offer excellent authentic Italian food in a warm, cozy setting. You won't find any pizza on this menu, but what you *will* find is wonderful antipasti, pasta, meat and fish. Fish is their specialty, and the last time I was there, I had the grilled octopus, which was not only grilled to perfection but served in its gloriously monstrous entirety—something you don't see every day. Both helpful and quick, the staff doesn't miss a beat. I'm confident you will enjoy a meal here. Should you be staying across the river or in the city center, Aromi is very easy to reach by public transport, but you may simply want to have your hotel arrange for a taxi.

Starters: 145–295 CZK
Main courses: 245–425 CZK
Pasta: 165–225 CZK
Dessert: 95–165 CZK
Wine: 420–8,695 CZK
Stella beer: 55 CZK

■ ■ ■ ■ ■ ■ ■ ■ ■ ■ ■ ■ ■
Le Papillon at the Le Palais Hotel
INTERNATIONAL
U Zvonařky 1, Prague 2, Vinohrady
www.palaishotel.cz
TEL 234 634 111
HOURS Mon–Fri: 12:00–23:00; Sat & Sun: 13:00–23:00
Average cost of a three-course meal, not including drinks: 1,210 CZK
METRO Náměstí Míru ●
TRAM 6, 11 to Bruselská

Request: A table on the terrace if the weather is warm. Alternatively, inside, request a table with wing chairs next to the window.

Located in Le Palais Hotel in Prague's Vinohrady district, Le Papillon is ideal for summer dining, as they have a large garden terrace that affords a unique cityscape panorama unlike any other in Prague. Far from the river, the Charles Bridge and the Prague Castle, it looks out instead over the rooftops of Nusle, another Prague district. The food is as refreshingly well turned out as the view is unique. I had the pork tenderloin with a honey glaze, served with polenta and spring spinach; hands down, it was the best piece of pork I've ever had, *anywhere*. After dinner you can retire to the elegant library or the lobby bar (open 24 hours) for dessert, a nightcap, or even a cigar.

Starters: 350–550 CZK
Main courses: 620–660 CZK
Dessert: 180 CZK
Wine: 750–4,400 CZK
Pilsner beer: 100 CZK

■ ■ ■ ■ ■ ■ ■ ■ ■ ■ ■ ■ ■
Perpetuum
CZECH
Na hutích 9, Prague 6, Dejvická
www.cervenatabulka.cz
TEL 233 323 429, 602 666 550
HOURS Mon–Sat: 11:30–23:00
Average cost of a three-course meal, not including drinks: 470 CZK
METRO Dejvická ●

Request: A table in the first room, which I find more chic and appealing than the rest of the restaurant.

Duck is what it's all about at this off-the-beaten-track restaurant in Prague 6. During my most recent visit, it was free of tourists and filled with locals—always a good sign. This is the only restaurant I know of that specializes in duck and offers both classic Bohemian recipes more contemporary creations. I went for the classic, roasted duck served with bread and potato dumplings and red and white cabbage (190 CZK for a quarter; 290 CZK for a half). It was delicious. My friend had the sliced duck with honey, accompanied by a bacon soufflé—and based on the bite I snagged off her plate, this will definitely be my order next time! For dessert, absolutely try the homemade *buchty* (kinda like yeasty hot cross buns with sweet filling), which are definitely the best thing on the dessert menu and an item you won't find at any other restaurant, as it is typically eaten only at home.

Starters: 65–290 CZK
Main courses: 180–310 CZK
Dessert: 90 CZK
Wine: 200–7,150 CZK
Budvar beer: 30 CZK

■ ■ ■ ■ ■ ■ ■ ■ ■ ■ ■ ■ ■
Radost FX Café
INTERNATIONAL / VEGETARIAN
Bělehradská 120, Prague 2, Vinohrady
www.radostfx.cz
TEL 603 193 711
HOURS Daily: 11:00–05:00
Average cost of a three-course meal, not including drinks: 375 CZK
METRO Náměstí Míru ● or I. P. Pavlova ●
TRAM 4, 6, 11, 16, 22, 23 to I. P. Pavlova

Request: A table in the backroom, where the seating is more comfy and the lounge atmosphere more fun.

Lets Go On A Picnic!

Imagine a charming wicker picnic basket, all tucked in with a blanket, delivered right to your door. It can be arranged, and should you have time to spare, I can think of no better way to spend a warm sunny afternoon in Prague. Petřín Hill in Malá Strana or Riegerovy sady in Vinohrady are two of my favorite picnicking spots, both offering unique vistas of the city.

The following two baskets are available from Pachtuv Palace:

Royal Basket €50

4 Sandwiches (Cheese; Roast Beef; Grilled Vegetables; and Salmon)
Caviar and Toast
Eggs, Tomatoes, Fresh Fruit, Strawberries
Sweet Muffins & Cookies
Belgian Pralines
2 bottles of Champagne
2 bottles of Evian

Luxury Basket €30

4 Sandwiches (Cheese; Roast Beef; Grilled Vegetables; and Salmon)
Eggs, Tomatoes, Fresh Fruit, Strawberries
Sweet Muffins & Cookies
2 bottles of Bohemian Sekt (Champagne)
2 bottles of Evian

■ ■ ■ ■ ■ ■ ■ ■ ■ ■ ■ ■ ■ ■ ■ ■

Pachtuv Palace
Karoliny Světlé 34, Prague 1, Staré Město
www.pachtuvpalace.com
EMAIL fbm@pachtuvpalace.com
TEL 234 705 111, 608 053 481

Call food and beverage manager, Josef Kokos, 1 day in advance to reserve.

The best vegetarian restaurant in town, Radost also happens to be the hippest. The décor is at once charming and funky, and the food is simply terrific. It's perfect for a light supper—or even a not-so-light one, should you order the huge spinach burger—and it will let you see where all the painfully young and hip converge. They also serve an excellent brunch on the weekend, including their own highly unique interpretation of a bagel. Should you be traveling with your teenagers or 20-something children, they will definitely thank you for choosing this spot (especially if you give them their own café table away from any parental style-cramping). CASH ONLY; a 10% tip is added into the bill

Starters: 50–180 CZK
Main courses: 140–285 CZK
Dessert: 50–85 CZK
Wine: 155–895 CZK
Pilsner or Staropramen beer: 35 CZK

Breakfast: 11:00–15:00; average price of 220 CZK

CAFÉS
Quick Bites

I have not included average pricing for any of the listings in this section, as they are *all* inexpensive. At virtually any of these listings you can assume the total will be 200 CZK or less; the only exceptions, perhaps, being CukrKávaLimonáda and Lobkowicz Palace Café at the Prague Castle, at either of which your total might reach 300 CZK, depending on what you order.

■ ■ ■ ■ ■ ■ ■ ■ ■ ■ ■ ■ ■ ■

Au Gourmand
Dlouhá 10, Prague 1, Staré Město
TEL 222 329 060
HOURS Mon–Fri: 08:00–19:00; Sat & Sun: 09:00–18:00
METRO Staroměstská ●
TRAM 17, 18 to Staroměstská

This is a great stop for coffee, cake or a light lunch near the Old Town Square. Formerly a turn-of-the-century butcher shop, it still boasts the original floor mosaic and wall tiles illustrated with animals both before and after their trip to the slaughterhouse (fun!). Apart from anything else, they have the best mille-feuille in town. Au Gourmand also has a second location, across the river in Malá Strana at U Lužického semináře 23, but I like the one in Old Town better.
CASH ONLY

■ ■ ■ ■ ■ ■ ■ ■ ■ ■ ■ ■ ■ ■

Bakeshop Praha
Kozí 1, Prague 1, Staré Město
www.bakeshop.cz
TEL 222 316 823
HOURS Daily: 07:00–21:00
METRO Staroměstská ●
TRAM 17, 18 to Staroměstská

If you're strolling near Old Town Square and just want a quick bite or a good cup of coffee to go, this is your place. They have fresh baked cookies, brownies, and other treats, as well as delicious BLTs, quiches, bagels and *excellent* lattes. Though there are no tables to sit at, there are stools at a bar-like counter, plus benches situated along the cobblestone sidewalk. Nothing does the trick better when you're super hung-over—particularly their ham and cheese croissants, which are extraordinarily high on the grease factor. I highly recommend these, though there's nothing even remotely light or airy about them.

Coffee Heaven
Pařížská 1, Prague 1,
Staré Město
www.coffeeheaven.eu.com
TEL 222 311 967
HOURS Daily: 8:30–22:00
METRO Staroměstská ●
TRAM 17, 18 to Staroměstská

BALOUNKOVA CIKORKA A ŽITNÁ KÁVA zlepší Vaši snídani !

VINTAGE ADVERTISEMENT FOR SUGAR AND COFFEE, C. 1920

Missing your daily fix of Starbucks? Well, look no further than Coffee Heaven. This upscale chain of coffee shops will meet all your caffeine needs, from mocha to cappuccino, and everything in between. It's my personal guilty pleasure (especially their terrific bagel with smoked salmon). There's also another location downtown, at Na Příkopě 3-5, Prague 1, (Metro Můstek).

Country Life
Melantrichova 15, Prague 1,
Staré Město
TEL 224 213 366
HOURS Mon–Thu: 08:30–19:00; Fri: 08:30–17:00; Sun: 11:00–18:00
METRO Můstek ● ●

Should you find yourself hankering for a vegetarian meal or a certified organic peach, Country Life is where you'll want to head. Their canteen includes a small, very informal dining area with very cool tables carved from the trunks of trees both in the back and, during the warm months, out in the courtyard. The daily offerings include warm and cold food. While there, be sure to hop into their store across the courtyard, where they sell lots of soaps, lotions, oils and candles, some of which are from the Czech Republic, though many others are imported from France.

Cremeria Milano
Pařížská 20, Prague 1,
Staré Město
TEL 224 811 010
HOURS Daily: 09:00–23:30; Summer: 09:00–00:30
METRO Staroměstská ●
TRAM 17, 18 to Staroměstská

As something of an ice cream connoisseur, I can advise you with confidence that Cremeria Milano will satisfy even the most demanding customer. I usually get my cone or cup to go, or take it to one of the informal tables just outside. They also offer a wide selection of cakes and pastries, but I can assure you, ice cream is the way to go. There are three sizes available: 50 CZK; 90 CZK; and 120 CZK. They also have a smaller, and decidedly less decadent, second location at Husova 12, but unless you find yourself with a sudden and uncontrollable ice-cream craving around Husova and its immediate environs, the shop on Pařížská is the one you want—*total bliss*.

CukrKávaLimonáda
Lázeňská 7, Prague 1,
Malá Strana
TEL 257 530 628
HOURS Daily: 09:00–19:00
METRO Malostranská ●
TRAM 12, 20, 22, 23 to Malostranské náměstí

A charming place for breakfast, lunch or coffee, right in the heart of Malá Strana. Be sure to take note of the painted ceilings. The owner of this café also owns M. Material glass shop, and if you visit both, you'll quickly notice the similarity in interior design. CukrKávaLimonáda offers ciabatta sandwiches, frittata, pasta, salads, as well as both sweet and savory crepes—all at very reasonable prices. They also offer a continental breakfast, as well as

DINING

GRAND CAFÉ ORIENT: PERIOD PHOTOGRAPH
(BUT IT LOOKS JUST LIKE THIS TODAY)

eggs prepared in various ways, including the very bold and fabulous option of scrambled eggs with shrimp. My favorite is always the crepes, which are made with the very freshest ingredients.

CASH ONLY

■ ■ ■ ■ ■ ■ ■ ■ ■ ■ ■ ■ ■ ■
Culinaria
Skořepka 9, Prague 1, Nové Město
www.culinaria.cz
TEL 224 231 017
HOURS Mon–Fri: 08:30–20:00; Sat: 10:00–19:00; Sun: 12:00–17:00
METRO Národní třída ● or Můstek ● ●
TRAM 6, 9, 18, 21, 22, 23 to Národní třída

Culinaria is great for a quick lunch; they offer lots of salads, quiches, and pastas made daily and sold by weight. You can also get a made-to-order sandwich. Coffee and drinks, including smoothies, are on the other side of the

store. Should you have the sudden urge for a chocolate marshmallow pop-tart, I do believe this is the only place in town where you'll be able to satisfy it…

■ ■ ■ ■ ■ ■ ■ ■ ■ ■ ■ ■ ■ ■
Ebel Coffee House
Týn 2, Prague 1, Staré Město
www.ebelcoffee.cz
TEL 224 895 788
Daily: 09:00–22:00
METRO Můstek ● ● or Náměstí Republiky ●
TRAM 5, 8, 14 to Náměstí Republiky

If you want to sit down for a cup of coffee near Old Town Square but don't enjoy having your toes crushed by swarms of tourists passing by, Ebel Coffee House is a nice spot to keep in mind. The location is also great if you have kids, as it's tucked away in a courtyard where they'll be able to run around to their hyperactive little hearts' delight while you sip coffee (and try

to boost yourself back up to their energy level) without having to worry. Afterwards, pop into nearby Botanicus, a lovely shop filled with all sorts of scented soaps, potpourri and other fragrant goodies.

■ ■ ■ ■ ■ ■ ■ ■ ■ ■ ■ ■ ■ ■
Grand Café Orient at the Black Madonna Museum
Ovocný trh 19, Prague 1, Staré Město
www.grandcafeorient.cz
TEL 224 224 240
HOURS Daily: 09:00–22:00
METRO Můstek ● ● or Náměstí Republiky ●
TRAM 5, 8, 14 to Náměstí Republiky

The original Grand Café Orient opened in 1912 on the (European) first floor of the House of the Black Madonna department store, designed by the famous Cubist designer, Josef Gočár. Closed since 1925, it was just reopened

DINING

153

in 2005 after a painstaking renovation (guided by a few surviving plans and photos), and they have succeeded brilliantly in recreating the space. Replicas of the original café furniture and brass chandeliers, designed by Gočár, help to conjure up the original atmosphere, and it doesn't take a great deal of imagination or wishful thinking to step back in time. This café is more about the experience and echoes of history, however, than getting yourself a latte made to perfection. Not that this seems to be a problem for any of the locals who frequent it, along with some of the savvier tourists. Prices are inexpensive, so if architecture turns you on, I'd definitely put this on your hit list.

CASH ONLY

■ ■ ■ ■ ■ ■ ■ ■
Hotel Evropa
Václavské náměstí 25,
Prague 1, Nové Město
www.evropahotel.cz
TEL 224 228 117
HOURS Daily: 07:00–24:00
METRO Muzeum ● ●
or Můstek ● ●
TRAM 3, 9, 14, 24 to Václavské náměstí

If you love Art Nouveau style, then a coffee or pre-dinner drink here is a must for you. There's often a piano player in the late afternoon, and it's also a suitable rendezvous spot for a nightcap after a day spent strolling through the city. No matter the weather, sit inside and soak up the magical architecture and old-time ambience of the place.

CASH ONLY UP TO 500 CZK

■ ■ ■ ■ ■ ■ ■ ■ ■ ■
Kavárna Obecní dům
náměstí Republiky 5,
Prague 1, Staré Město
www.vysehrad2000.cz/
obecnidum
TEL 222 002 763
HOURS Daily: 07:30–23:00
METRO Náměstí Republiky ●
TRAM 5, 8, 14 to Náměstí Republiky

This café won't necessarily deliver the best cup of coffee the city has to offer or the tastiest piece of cake, but the setting is *over-the-top fabulous*. Simply put, this café is Art Nouveau at its most dazzling.

NOTE: There are two other restaurants in this building. The French one on the ground floor has a similarly fabulous interior (which, unfortunately, is too brightly lit much of the time) and serves food that is not only grossly overpriced but also fails to live up to the atmosphere. There's also a Czech pub in the basement where inspirations from Czech folklore abound by way of carved wooden booths, folk-art stenciling, and social realist murals. Utterly transporting, the pub is a good option if you're attending a performance in the concert hall later on and want to try some authentic Czech food beforehand.

■ ■ ■ ■ ■ ■ ■ ■ ■ ■
Kavárna Slavia
Smetanovo nábřeží 2,
Prague 1, Staré Město
www.cafeslavia.cz
TEL 224 218 493
HOURS Daily: 08:00–23:00
METRO Národní třída ●
TRAM 6, 9, 18, 21, 22, 23 to Národní divadlo

Perched on an incomparable river location just across from the National Theatre, Slavia is the oldest café in Prague, dating all the way back to 1881. The views across the river afforded from this historic Art Deco café are, in a word, *major*. The cake and coffee may not be the best in town, but, as with some of the other cafés I've mentioned in this section, Slavia is certainly worth a stop for the location alone. At the very least, you have to pop your head in just to see the space while you're in Prague.

■ ■ ■ ■ ■ ■ ■ ■ ■ ■ ■ ■
Lobkowicz Palace Café at the Prague Castle
Jiřská 3, Prague 1,
Malá Strana
www.lobkowiczevents.cz
TEL 602 595 998
HOURS Daily: 10:00–18:00
METRO Malostranská ●
TRAM 12, 18, 20, 22, 23 to Malostranské náměstí

Needless to say, the location of this café within the gates of the Prague Castle is outstanding, and there's probably no better place to take a break from your castle sightseeing. The restaurant features three terraces, each of which offers diners a sweeping view of Prague and is warmed up with heat lamps in the cooler months. There is indoor seating as well, but I wouldn't bother coming unless you plan to eat outdoors. Priced at a premium that reflects the location, the food is, frankly, less than extraordinary. That said, the view alone is worth it; so if the sun is shining, you should definitely stop by for goulash, a wrap sandwich, or soup.

■ ■ ■ ■ ■ ■ ■ ■ ■ ■ ■ ■
Lahůdky Zemark

Václavské náměstí 42, Prague 1, Nové Město
TEL 224 217 326
HOURS Mon–Fri: 07:00–19:30; Sat: 10:00–18:00
METRO Muzeum ● ● or Můstek ●
TRAM 3, 9, 14, 24 to Václavské náměstí

Although this vintage delicatessen in the heart of Václavské náměstí has been completely renovated, it remains faithful to Czech tradition, offering a wide range of *chlebíčky*, opened-faced sandwiches, and salads to be eaten while standing at the long metal tables. You can also get just about any Czech liqueur or chocolate at this fine, old-fashioned establishment.

■ ■ ■ ■ ■ ■ ■ ■ ■ ■ ■ ■
Paneria

Kaprova 3, Prague 1, Staré Město
www.paneria.cz
TEL 224 827 912
HOURS Daily: 08:00–21:00
METRO Staroměstská ●
TRAM 17, 18 to Staroměstská

Paneria is a bakery chain with locations throughout the city. You order at the register, making this ideal for a quick and informal breakfast or lunch. The Staré Město location is particularly good for breakfast if you plan to hit the Jewish sights in the morning, as it's just down the street from the Old-New Synagogue. They have a wide selection of pastries, both sweet and savory. My personal favorite is the *šnek* with raisins, and their

HAPPY WORKERS! INTERIOR OF DELICATESSEN, C. 1949 (SOURCE: ČTK / CZECH NEWS AGENCY)

butter croissant is also good. However, if starting your day off right requires a good cup of coffee, then it's best to go to another breakfast location, as their coffee is not exactly their strong point (in any sense!).
CASH ONLY

■ ■ ■ ■ ■ ■ ■ ■ ■ ■ ■ ■
T.Z. Cukrárna

Vítězná 14, Prague 5, Malá Strana
HOURS Mon–Fri: 10:00–18:00; Sat & Sun: 10:00–17:00
TRAM 6, 9, 12, 20, 22, 23 to Újezd

Step back in time as you walk through the doorway to this small *Cukrárna* (sweet shop) at the foot of Petřín hill. Be sure to order a selection of the classic and *very* affordable Czech baked goods, as well as a Turkish coffee (the way coffee was made under communism), which you can then enjoy at one of the small vintage gingham-covered tables. Now you're really in Prague...
CASH ONLY

■ ■ ■ ■ ■ ■ ■ ■ ■ ■ ■ ■
U Rozvařilů

Na Poříčí 26, Prague 1, Nové Město
HOURS Mon–Fri: 08:00–20:00; Sat: 09:00–19:00; Sun: 10:00–18:00
METRO Náměstí Republiky ●
TRAM 5,8,14 to Náměstí Republiky; 2, 24, 26 to Bílá labuť or Masarykovo nádraží

Now *this* is a dying breed. So if you really—and I mean *really*—want to eat where the locals eat, look no further than this old-time cafeteria. They offer both warm and cold options, but I would definitely recommend indulging in one of the three daily menu specials (for 60 CZK including soup). Last time I was there they offered *guláš*, *svíčková*, and *moravský vrabec* (all Czech classics) with bread dumplings. Gambrinus was on tap for 18.5 CZK for a .5 liter glass. After paying, take a seat at one of the many high metal tables and enjoy your breakfast, lunch or dinner without another tourist in sight.

CASH ONLY

■ ■ ■ ■ ■ ■ ■ ■ ■ ■ ■
U Zeleného čaje

Nerudova 19, Prague 1, Malá Strana
TEL 257 530 027
HOURS Daily: 10:00–22:00
METRO Malostranská ●
TRAM 12, 20, 22, 23 to Malostranské náměstí

This is a charming and cozy place to stop at for a tea, coffee or hot chocolate on your way either up to or down from the Prague Castle. The menu also includes various sandwiches and desserts. The apple strudel is good, but I highly recommend the *medovník*, a wonderful honey cake.

CASH ONLY

Further Afield
■ ■ ■ ■ ■ ■ ■ ■ ■ ■ ■
Štrúdl z taženého těsta

Jeseniova 29, Prague 3, Žižkov
TEL 222 590 912
MOBILE 732 543 799
HOURS Mon: 09:00–18:00; Tue–Thu: 08:00–18:00; Fri: 08:00–17:00; (Closed daily from 12:00-13:00)
Take a taxi and have it wait

Off-the-beaten-track is an understatement for this gem. Walk through a sea of nondescript *paneláky* (communist-era public housing), and you will *literally* stumble upon this hole-in-the-wall. Out of which comes the *best* strudel in town—maybe even better than your mom's (assuming you have a mother who bakes mouth-wateringly good traditional Czech strudels). This fabulous and

very focused enterprise sells only three items: apple strudel (*jablečný*), cheese strudel (*tvarohový*), and poppy seed strudel (*makový*)—all baked fresh daily onsite. With the most expensive one ringing in at 42 CZK, I encourage you to try all three, but poppyseed is definitely my personal favorite. Each strudel is about 12 inches in length, and the final step of powdered sugar dusting will be executed while you wait.

CASH ONLY

PUBS & BEER HALLS
■ ■ ■ ■ ■ ■ ■ ■ ■ ■ ■
U Černého vola
PUB

Loretánské náměstí. 1, Prague 1, Hradčany
TEL 220 513 481
HOURS Daily: 10:00–22:00
METRO Malostranská ●
TRAM 22, 23 to Pohořelec

This boisterous, smoky, old-fashioned pub with painted heraldic symbols covering its walls, right in the heart of the Prague castle district, is frequented mostly by locals and a few savvy tourists. Velkopopovický Kozel is the beer on tap, at 24.50 CZK for .5 liter. It's unlikely you'll find your own table, so if a space is free at a table, jump right in; it's absolutely normal to share. U Černého vola, or "the Black Bull," provides visitors with the perfect opportunity to try a variety of traditional Czech pub food; helpfully, they have a menu in English. Pickled hermelin cheese (*nakládaný hermelín*) and pickled sausages (*utopenec*) are an absolute must, as this is definitely what the locals will be noshing. And both are less than 50 CZK each, so you can afford to experiment! You'll be surprised to see how aptly these foods compliment the beer.

NOTE: Plan on coming early, as the pub tends to be full for the evening by 18:00.

CASH ONLY

BEER MEISTER, 1969
(SOURCE: ČTK / CZECH NEWS AGENCY)

DINING

A Beer Field Trip

Staropramen – Factory Tour

Staropramen Visitor's Centre; Nádražní 84, Prague 5, Smíchov (entrance from Pivovarská Street)
www.staropramen.cz
TEL 257 191 402, 296 (Reservation required)
ENTRANCE FEE 120 CZK
METRO Anděl ●
TRAM 4, 12, 14, 20 to Na Knížecí

Ahead of even ice hockey and mushroom-picking as a Czech national pastime is, of course, beer drinking. Czechs consume more beer per capita than any other country in the world, and, perhaps not surprisingly, take their beer brewing very seriously. If you're curious to find out just how it's made and taste a few along the way, I highly recommend that you reserve a spot on a tour of the Staropramen brewery, located just outside the city center. Tours must be booked in advance, but as they run daily, it should not be a problem getting on one. The duration is 60 minutes, including a beer tasting.

WINE BARS

Czech wines are not renowned for taking any blue ribbons, probably because they lack the edgy minerality one associates with excellent vintages. There are exceptions, but they are rare. Most local wines taste more like someone's grandfather made them at home in the family cellar, resulting in a very sour, *grapey* taste. White wines here tend to be the more interesting and successful, as the Czech Republic does not get enough annual sunshine to develop red grapes properly. That said, it's always fun to go local, so I've recommended the two best wine bars I know featuring Czech wines.

Many of the wines you see on bar or restaurant wine lists are not available at local shops, most of the Czech vineyards being very small, with a limited annual output. Should you want to own something you've tried, the wisest choice would be to ask the bar or restaurant if you can purchase a bottle or two, as this will often be the only way to acquire it.

▪ ▪ ▪ ▪ ▪ ▪ ▪ ▪ ▪ ▪ ▪ ▪ ▪ ▪

Bokovka
WINE BAR
Pštrossova 8, Prague 1, Nové Město
TEL 721 262 503
HOURS Sun–Thu: 16:00–01:00; Fri & Sat: 16:00–03:00
METRO Karlovo náměstí or Národní třída
TRAM 6, 9, 18, 21, 22, 23 to Karlovo náměstí or Národní třída

Bokovka is a small, *very* local wine bar, well off the beaten track. The atmosphere isn't particularly charming, but they offer wines from very small Czech vineyards that you won't find elsewhere. They only offer 5 wines by the glass, and the most interesting wines are by the bottle, so plan to settle in for the evening as the locals do (starting at 8 pm; if you go earlier, no one will be there), and try a few bottles. They also offer nibbles, including cheeses, meats and nuts. A recent evening there, including two bottles of wine, water and lots of nibbles came to 1,000 CZK, a real bargain. The menu is not in English, but the staff is always happy to assist.
CASH ONLY

▪ ▪ ▪ ▪ ▪ ▪ ▪ ▪ ▪ ▪ ▪ ▪ ▪ ▪

Dům vína U Závoje
WINE BAR AND RESTAURANT
Havelská 25, Prague 1, Staré Město
www.uzavoje.cz
TEL 226 006 120
HOURS Daily: 11:00–19:00
METRO Můstek ● ●

Dům vína U Závoje is perfectly charming, and it's obvious that the staff not only love wine, but are genuinely enthusiastic about working there. They even insist on serving wines in the appropriately shaped glass, a first for me in the Czech Republic! Dům vína U Závoje has an extensive list of wine by the glass—over 50 Czech wines—allowing for far greater experimentation than usual. An added bonus is that they have a wine store in the same complex, so should you fall in love, you can then purchase a bottle or two to take home with you.

See p. 128–129 for an interview on Czech wines with Bohuslav Uher, the assistant restaurant manager of Essensia restaurant at the Mandarin Oriental hotel.

DINING

The Ins and Outs of Czech Beer, from a Real Connoisseur

Evan Rail, a long-term expatriate, is the author of *The Good Beer Guide: Prague and the Czech Republic* (CAMRA [Campaign for Real Ale] Books, 2007), a comprehensive user's guide to all of the country's breweries and the beers they make, as well as dozens of places where one can sample them. Given his extensive knowledge, there could be no better person to turn to for a few insider tips to share with my readers:

Karen: Having written a book exclusively on Czech beer, what would you say is your all-time favorite Czech beer, and why?

Evan: Wow! That's a little like asking for a favorite wine, or a favorite color. Really, I like a lot of them, and it changes daily. But in general, I prefer to drink locally. So it depends on where I am. In Prague, I'm committed to Pivovarský dům's standard gold lager. It's one of the best beers of this type in the world, and I'm not the only one who thinks so.

Karen: In the Czech Republic, *where* one drinks his or her beer often seems at least as important as the beer itself; so what is *your* favorite "authentic" pub in Prague?

Evan: My favorite "real" place in Prague is U Černého vola (see p. 156). It's right in the middle of the tourist zone at Prague Castle, and yet it remains very much a locals' hangout: an authentic Prague pub serving great beer. I don't go very often, but I'm always very glad once I do.

Karen: For a true beer connoisseur, would you say it's worth it to seek out an unpasteurized beer during their visit to Prague? And, if so, where would you recommend?

Evan: It's worth it only if you care about how things taste! The difference in flavor is astronomical, and it also makes a difference in how you feel the next day. I usually take visitors to a Pilsner "tank" pub – Bredovský dvůr is my favorite; the beers are great and the ribs are fantastic – or to one of the city's great brewpubs: Richter Pub, Pivovarský dům, Pivovarský Klub, and the brewpub upstairs at U Medvídků.

Karen: Having lived in the Czech Republic for six years, what strikes you most about the beer culture in the Czech Republic versus that in the United States?

Evan: Contrary to the ads on TV, I've never seen people get in fights in Czech pubs, no matter how many beers they've drunk, whereas I couldn't imagine a beer garden like the one at Letna operating in my hometown in the U.S. without several fights breaking out. Here, the only fights I've seen were between dogs. It's just a different culture.

Karen: Are there any unusual and unique beers available in Prague that you recommend people try while they're here?

Evan: It's expensive, but the X-33 beer from U Medvídků might be interesting for people who don't normally like beer. They use traditional oak barrels for both fermentation and aging, and the beer comes out with 12.8% alcohol, much more like a dessert wine than a typical lager. It's actually quite similar to Sauterne: sweet and sticky, with notes of vanilla, leather and oak, and an incredibly long-lasting finish. It costs around 250 CZK per bottle, and it's worth every heller.

Karen: What's your favorite bar snack to compliment your beer?

Evan: Usually *topinky s česnekem* (fried bread with garlic). Though, if they have *škvarkové sádlo* (lard with cracklings), I'm all over it.

Pubs Recommended by Evan:

▪▪▪▪▪▪▪▪▪▪▪▪▪▪▪▪▪▪▪

Bredovský dvůr,
Politických vězňů 13, Praha 1, Nové Město
TEL 224 215 428
HOURS Mon–Sat: 11:00–24:00; Sun: 11:00–23:00
METRO Muzeum ⓘ ●
or Můstek ⓘ ●

Pivovarský dům
Lipová 15, Prague 2, Nové Město
TEL 296 216 666
HOURS Daily: 11:00–23:30
METRO I. P. Pavlova ●
or Karlove náměstí ●

Tram 4, 6, 10, 16, 22, 23 to
Štepánská

Pivovarský Klub
Křížíkova 17, Prague 8, Karlín
TEL 222 315 777
HOURS Daily: 11:30–23:30
METRO Florenc ● ●

U Černého vola
Loretánské náměstí. 1,
Prague 1, Hradčany
TEL 220 513 481
HOURS Daily: 10:00–22:00
METRO Malostranská
Tram 22, 23 to Pohořelec

U Medvídků
Na Perštýně 7, Prague 1,
Staré Město
TEL 224 211 916
HOURS Mon–Sat: 11:00–
23:00; Sun: 11:30–22:00
METRO Národní třída ●
Tram 6, 9, 18, 21, 22, 23 to
Národní třída

Further Afield
■ ■ ■ ■ ■ ■ ■ ■ ■ ■ ■ ■ ■ ■ ■

Richter Brewery
Pivovar U Bulovky
Bulovka 17, Prague 8, Libeň
TEL 284 840 650
HOURS Mon-Fri: 11:00–23:00;
Sat & Sun: 11:00–24:00
METRO Palmovka ● then
tram 10, 15, 25, 24 to Bulovka
Tram 10, 15, 25, 24

Czech Pub Culture, According to Czechs

Curious to learn more about Czech pub culture,
I turned to my co-worker Kristýna for some insights
to pass on, as she goes to pubs several times
a week and seems to be an avid beer consumer.
Kristyná was kind enough to answer my few
questions below.

Karen: What time do
Czechs typically head to
the pub?

Kristýna: Six or seven; we
go out much earlier than
Americans.

Karen: How do you choose
which pub you will go to?

Kristýna: *Beer* makes the
decision; I will always
choose the pub that has
the freshest beer!

Karen: So atmosphere
doesn't really play a role in
your decision-making?

Kristýna: No, it's all about
the beer.

Karen: What is your
favorite Czech beer and
why?

Kristýna: Pilsner, because
it tastes the best, but I also
like Gambrinus if I feel like
having a lighter beer.

Karen: How many beers do
you consume in a typical
evening?

Kristýna: Five or six, and
my boyfriend usually has
nine or ten.

Karen: Good lord, that's
a lot! How many hours do
you typically *stay* at the
pub?

Kristýna: Five or six,
because, lets face it, you
have nothing *else* to do,
and this is more fun than
staying at home...

Karen: What are your
favorite bar snacks
to accompany your beer?

Kristýna: *Nakládaný
hermelín* (pickled
hermelin) and *utopenec*
(pickled sausages).

Karen: I know it's not
unusual to indulge in a shot
or two during the course
of a beer-drinking evening;
what's your shot of choice?

Kristýna: I know you're
hoping I'll say *Slivovice*, but
that's only for old men in
the village; I like Jameson
whiskey myself.

DINING

BARMAN AND WAITER SERVE THE
THIRSTY MASSES, C. 1957
(SOURCE: ČTK / CZECH NEWS
AGENCY)

Entertainment

CONCERT VENUES

Worth Stopping At, For A Performance Or Just A Tour

Opera & Ballet

All three theatres listed below offer performances of opera and ballet, with nightly performances (usually starting at 19:00) and weekend matinees. The schedules vary, so check their websites for details.

▪ ▪ ▪ ▪ ▪ ▪ ▪ ▪ ▪ ▪ ▪ ▪ ▪

National Theatre
Národní divadlo

Národní třída, Prague 1, Nové Město
www.nationaltheatre.cz
TEL 224 901 111
HOURS Daily: 10:00–18:00; (July & August closed)
TICKETS 450–1,000 CZK
METRO Národní třída
TRAM 6, 9, 17,18, 21, 22, 23 to Národní divadlo

Majestically overlooking the Vltava River, the National Theatre was inaugurated in June of 1881, and ever since then has remained a true symbol of national pride. Indeed, Czechs both rich and poor voluntarily dug into their own pockets to pay for this magnificent building after the Hapsburg Empire refused to fund it. Then, on August 12 of the same year, the building was ravaged by fire. All that remained were the outside walls. Remarkably, within 47 days of the catastrophe, enough money was collected to rebuild the theatre, and work was completed in less than two years. The theatre was re-inaugurated on November 18, 1883 with a performance of Smetana's opera, *Libuše*, he composed especially for the occasion.

To Tour the National Theatre: Tours of the building are available on Sat & Sun: 08:30–11:00
ENTRANCE FEE 50 CZK
TEL 221 714 152
For a private tour outside the times listed above, contact Mrs. Ševčíková (TEL 224 901 570; m.sevcikova@narodni-divadlo.cz)

▪ ▪ ▪ ▪ ▪ ▪ ▪ ▪ ▪ ▪ ▪ ▪ ▪

State Opera
Státní opera

Legerova 75, Prague 2, Nové Město
www.opera.cz
TEL 296 117 111
HOURS Daily: Mon–Fri: 10:00–17:30; Sat & Sun: 10:00–12:00 & 13:00–15:30
TICKETS 550 CZK–1,200 CZK
METRO Muzeum ● ●
TRAM 11 to Muzeum

Built in 1888, the State Opera house suffers from a rather unfortunate location, as it is immediately adjacent to the one major highway running through town. Not only is all the pavement and whizzing traffic less than picturesque, it makes the building quite difficult to access. As a result I would recommend a visit to one of the other two opera houses listed over this one. Should these be all booked, however, or should you find the State Opera's program simply of greater interest, you won't be sorry you made the effort, at least not once you're safely inside. The largest theatre in Prague, it's graced by an opulent Neo-Rococo interior, and the quality of the productions here is consistently high.

To Tour the State Opera House: To arrange a private tour, call Mrs. Strejčková
TEL 221 714 151
ENTRANCE FEE 150 CZK (Minimum of 10 people); you can come with fewer people, certainly, but the minimum charge for the entire group remains 1,500 CZK.

▪ ▪ ▪ ▪ ▪ ▪ ▪ ▪ ▪ ▪ ▪ ▪ ▪

Estates Theatre
Stavovské divadlo

Ovocný trh 1, Prague 1, Staré Město
www.estatestheatre.cz
TEL 224 902 322
HOURS Daily: 10:00–18:00
TICKETS 650 CZK–1,990 CZK
METRO Můstek ● ●
TRAM 5, 8,14 Náměstí Republiky

NATIONAL THEATRE, C. 1920

VIEW OF THE PRAGUE CASTLE FROM THE RUDOLFINUM, C. 1920

Built in the 1780's, the Estates Theatre is my favorite of the National Theatre's several venues, as it is by far the smallest and most intimate. I also happen to love the light blue velvet chairs. Mozart had many connections to this theatre, the most famous being that *Don Giovanni* premiered here in 1787. It also happens to be one of only two opera houses in Europe that remain preserved more or less as they would have been during the composer's time.

To Tour the Estates Theatre:
You Need To Be Rich!
To arrange a private tour, call Mrs. Pavlíčková
TEL 224 902 231
ENTRANCE FEE 4,100 CZK (Regardless of your group size, up to 50 people)

Concert Halls
■ ■ ■ ■ ■ ■ ■ ■ ■ ■ ■

Obecní dům
The Municipal House
Náměstí Republiky 5,
Prague 1, Nové Město
www.obecni-dum.cz
TEL 222 002 101
HOURS Mon–Fri: 10:00–21:30
TICKETS 250 CZK–1,300 CZK
METRO Náměsti Republiky
TRAM 5, 14, 26 to Náměstí Republiky

The Prague Symphony, founded in 1934, utilizes the main auditorium at Obecní dům, Smetana Hall, for their concerts. Obecní dům is the Art Nouveau architectural gem of the Czech Republic, and a visit to this exquisite building should be included on every person's visit to Prague. The building officially opened in 1912, with interior decoration by the most prominent Czech artists of the day. Definitely

leave enough time to look around the building, as all the public spaces are amazing, and if you want an authentic Czech meal, stop by the pub in the basement, either before or after your concert.

■ ■ ■ ■ ■ ■ ■ ■ ■ ■ ■ ■ ■
Rudolfinum
Alšovo nábřeží 12, Prague 1, Staré Město
www.czechphilharmonic.cz/en
www.rudolfinum.cz
TEL 227 059 227–Concert Tickets
TEL 227 059 309–Exhibitions
HOURS Daily: Mon–Fri: 10:00–18:00; Sat: 10:00–15:00; Sun: 14:00–17:00
TICKETS 80 CZK–900 CZK
METRO Staroměstská ●
TRAM 17, 18 to Staroměstská

This Neo-Renaissance masterpiece was completed from 1876–1884 and is surely one of the most striking and recognizable

163

buildings along the river embankment (even serving as the backdrop for the opening of Tom Cruise's first Mission: Impossible movie). The interior is equally fabulous. Home to the world-famous Prague Philharmonic (its first concert here was directed by none other than Antonín Dvořák), it features a magnificent main hall, as well as a smaller space for chamber concerts, exhibition space featuring changing art exhibitions, and café.

NOTE: The box office is also open one hour before each concert, but will only sell tickets for performances on the same day.

Other

Church of St. Nicholas
Chrám sv. Mikuláše
Malostranské náměstí 25, Prague 1, Malá Strana
www.psalterium.cz
TEL 224 190 991
HOURS Daily: 2 hrs before performance
TICKETS 250–450 CZK
METRO Malostranská ●
TRAM 12, 20, 22, 23 to Malostranské náměstí

This is one of Prague's most celebrated churches, with a stunning Baroque interior and exceptional acoustics. Mozart played the organ here in 1787, which you can easily imagine while closing your eyes as you take in one of the many organ recitals they give here, as well as choral concerts—most days at 17:00.

CASH ONLY

Czech Films with English Subtitles on DVD

Three things to keep in mind, should you decide to purchase a DVD in Prague: **1.** Ask the store assistant to double-check that there are English subtitles. **2.** The DVD will only work in the U.S. if you have a "universal" system that plays both European and American DVDs, as the two are formatted differently. **3.** They are not cheap! The following recommended titles, for instance, range in price from 449 to 559 CZK.

Closely Watched Trains (Ostře sledované vlaky)
Jiří Menzel, 1966
(1967 Oscar for best Foreign Film)
Set at a village railway station in occupied Czechoslovakia, this movie concerns a bumbling young dispatcher who longs to lose his virginity. Utterly oblivious to the war unfolding around him, he embarks on a journey of sexual awakening at his sleepy depot. One of the most beloved films of the Czech New Wave.

Fireman's Ball (Hoří, má panenko)
Miloš Forman, 1967
Another Czech New Wave classic is this hilarious chronicle of a local fireman's ball held in a small town where nothing goes as planned, from lottery prizes being stolen to a less-than dazzling assemblage of Miss Fire-Department beauty pageant participants.

The Hop Pickers (Starci na chmelu)
Ladislav Rychman, 1964
The Czech equivalent of West-Side Story, this is a story of young love, set in the hop fields of Bohemia. One of my personal favorites.

Chapel of Mirrors
Zrcadlová kaple
Klementinum, Mariánské náměstí, Prague 1, Staré Město
TEL 221 663 111
HOURS Daily: 2 hrs before performance
TICKETS 400–600 CZK
METRO Staroměstská ●
TRAM 17, 18 to Staroměstská or Karlovy lázně

This pink marble (and marbleized wood!) chapel, decorated with frescoes illustrating passages from the Ave Marie prayer, features a vast early Baroque organ with exceptional sound, making it a wonderful venue for music. The only way to gain access to this over-the-top space is by buying a ticket to one of their concerts, but it's well worth it. Concerts usually start at 17:00 and 20:00.

CASH ONLY

Kolya (Kolja)
Jan Svěrák, 1996
(1997 Oscar & Golden Globe Best Foreign Film)
Set in Prague in 1988, just before the Velvet Revolution of 1989. The main character, previously a member of the Czech Philharmonic and now banned by the state from playing in his orchestra, finds himself playing at funerals for a living. But this hardened bachelor's world is soon turned upside down when a young Russian orphan unexpectedly comes into his life. The story is very true to the times and an enduring tale of music and love.

Limonádový Joe (Limonádový Joe aneb Koňská opera)
Oldřich Lipský, 1964
Central Europe has an odd fascination with the American west, and this 1964 musical send-up of Hollywood westerns pays homage to the "Spaghetti Western" style. Karel Gott ("The Golden Voice of Prague") is the singing voice of the lead character, Joe.

Little Otik (Otesánek)
Jan Švankmajer, 2000
Švankmajer is, without a doubt, the master of surrealist animation. Here he brings to life the classic folktale, Der Struwwelpeter, about a childless couple whose longing for a child transforms a tree root into a gnarly and insatiable baby.

Shop on Main Street (Obchod na korze)
Ján Kadár and Elmar Klos, 1965
(1965 Oscar for Best Foreign Film)
Set in Slovakia during World War II, this is the story of a peasant appointed by his Nazi bosses as the Aryan controller of a Jewish widow's button shop, and the movie explores his personal struggle between greed and guilt.

LUCERNA CINEMA INTERIOR: PERIOD PHOTO
(COURTESY OF LUCERNA)

CINEMAS

Thankfully, all movies are shown in their native language with subtitles in Czech. If a movie is dubbed, which is usually the case only for children's films, it will be clearly marked.

■ ■ ■ ■ ■ ■ ■ ■ ■ ■ ■ ■ ■ ■

Palace Cinemas Praha
Slovanský dům
Na Příkopě 22, Prague 1, Nové Město
www.palacecinemas.cz
TEL 257 181 212
TICKETS 159 CZK
METRO Náměstí Republiky or Můstek ●

This multiplex is located in a downtown shopping arcade, very near the Obecní dům. They show all first-run features—generally a month or two after the U.S. release—and even offer ham-flavored popcorn… Need I say more?!

■ ■ ■ ■ ■ ■ ■ ■ ■ ■ ■ ■ ■ ■

Village Cinemas Anděl
Radlická 1E, Prague 5, Smíchov
www.goldclass.cz
TEL 251 115 111
TICKETS 299 CZK
METRO Anděl
TRAM 4, 6, 7, 9, 10, 12, 14 to Anděl

OK, let me paint the scene: first, imagine the most super-comfortable la-Z-Boy recliner you've ever lounged in, including a foot rest, of course; second, put a table by your side where the waiter delivers you your drinks, finger food or popcorn; last, you sit back and enjoy one of the better first-run features out there in the most deluxe setting ever. "Gold Class" brings movie viewing to a whole new level, I have to say, and I definitely encourage you to enjoy life on the other side, should you manage to fit in a movie during your visit to Prague. The setting and the price, at 299 CZK per ticket (less than double the cost of a regular movie ticket), make it very hard to go back to standard movie viewing! Reservations are recommended, as this theater only has 24 seats; should you wish, though, it's also possible to rent the entire theater!

Art House Cinemas
- - - - - - - - - - - - -

Kino Aero
Biskupcova 31, Prague 3, Žižkov
www.kinoaero.cz
TEL 271 771 349
TICKETS 95 CZK
TRAM 9, 10, 16, 19 to Biskupcova or 1, 19 to Ohrada

Definitely go early to this little cinema, located nowhere near the beaten path, and rejoice in the fact that they serve beer instead of popcorn! The theater itself is 1970's auditorium-style, and the crowd is a healthy mix of the young and the simply film-savvy. Be sure to check for English subtitles in Czech and foreign films. Art films and classics often appear on the menu.

- - - - - - - - - - - - -

Kino Světozor
Vodičkova 41, Prague 1, Nové Město
www.kinosvetozor.cz
TEL 224 946 824
TICKETS 100 CZK
METRO Můstek ● ●
TRAM 3, 9, 14, 24 Vodičkova

LUCERNA CINEMA FOYER
(COURTESY OF LUCERNA)

Conveniently located in the city center, this cinema boasts one Czech film with English subtitles every day. Seeing the Czech reality on the silver screen is a great way to experience the culture, since it's unlikely that you'll ever get invited into someone's wonderfully authentic *panelák* apartment. You can also pick up a Světozor T-shirt for a unique souvenir.

- - - - - - - - - - - - -

Lucerna Palace
Vodičkova 36, Prague 1, Nové Město

www.lucerna.cz
TEL 224 216 920
TICKETS 110 CZK
METRO Můstek ● ●
TRAM 3, 9, 14, 24 to Václavské náměstí

The oldest permanently operated movie theatre in Europe, the Lucerna Cinema opened in 1909. It was also here that the very first "talkie" premiered in Europe. With its glamorous velvet curtain, gilt chandeliers and balcony, this auditorium will absolutely take you back to the golden age of cinema.

BOATING

As I'm not a fan of organized tours—especially ones that don't allow for easy escape—I always prefer to be the captain of my own vessel. And one wonderfully relaxing alternative way to see Prague is by your own privately rented boat on the Vltava. Here are a few ways to do just that:

■ ■ ■ ■ ■ ■ ■ ■ ■ ■ ■ ■ ■
Prague Inspirations, s. r. o.

Senovážné náměstí 23, Prague 1, Nové Město
www.cruise-prague.cz
TEL 774 278 473
TRAM 5, 9, 14, 24 to Jindřišská

This company allows you to rent boats of various sizes for private cruises along the river. My two favorites are:

The Chroust: If what you're envisioning is something like Ron Perelman's mega-yacht, then move on to choice two below (you will still be disappointed, but less so!). This tugboat, built in Dresden in 1896, is small, quirky and perfect for a picnic, as the seating onboard is around a table. So be sure to stop at Bakeshop Praha (see p. 151) to pick up some goodies on your way to the dock. The maximum is 10 passengers, and they offer hot and cold beverages.

COST: 2,500 CZK per hour, not including beverages, minimum of 1 hour (but I recommend 3).
CASH ONLY

The Elbis: A 19th century Australian steamboat replica built in 2002, this boat has a cabin that can accommodate up to 25,

and a sun deck for 20. Your experience on *The Elbis* will certainly be a bit more deluxe, as they offer hors d'oeuvres, a bar with hot and cold drinks, and a WC with full plumbing (as opposed to the *Chroust's* dry chemical toilet).

COST: 760 CZK per person for 2 hours, minimum charge of 11,400 CZK.
CASH ONLY

■ ■ ■ ■ ■ ■ ■ ■ ■ ■ ■ ■ ■
Rowboats & Paddle boats

Slovanský Island, Prague 1, Staré Město
HOURS Daily: Mar–Oct: 10:00–18:00
COST 80–120 CZK per hour
METRO Národní třída
TRAM 6, 9, 17,18, 21, 22, 23 to Národní divadlo

If *The Chroust* and *The Elbis* sound like too much of a commitment, or if you prefer to be not just the captain of your own ship, but also the source of *horsepower*, then manning a rowboat or paddle boat for an hour or two on the Vltava might be just the

ticket. On a sunny spring or summer afternoon, I have to say, it's one of my favorite pastimes. I prefer the paddleboats.
CASH ONLY

■ ■ ■ ■ ■ ■ ■ ■ ■ ■ ■ ■ ■
Boat to Troja Chateau and Zoo

Rašínovo nábřeží, Prague 2, Nové Město (Between Palackého and Železniční Bridge)
www.paroplavba.cz
TEL 224 930 017
HOURS Daily: May–Oct
TICKETS 100 CZK Adults; 60 CZK Children; 3 and under Free
METRO Karlovo Náměstí
TRAM 3, 4, 7, 10, 14, 16, 17, 21 to Palackého náměstí

If you're planning on visiting the Troja Chateau or the Prague Zoo, one very scenic and fun way to get there is a 75-minute boat ride on the Vltava. It's approximately a five-minute walk from the dock to either site (they are directly adjacent to one another).

Departures: 09:30; 12:30; 15:30
Return: 11:00; 14:00; 17:00
CASH ONLY

BOATS ON THE VLTAVA RIVER, C. 1940

HELICOPTER RIDES

No time to spare, but still want to visit a castle in the countryside? Flying by helicopter is an ideal solution for traveling when you don't have hours to spare driving (or if you just have a hankering to wear that cool headset!). A fairy-tale visit to Český Krumlov or a round of golf and spa treatment in Karlovy Vary are just a few options.

■ ■ ■ ■ ■ ■ ■ ■ ■ ■ ■ ■ ■

V.I.P. Helicopter Czech
Mimoňská, Prague 9, Prosek
www.helicopter.cz
TEL 731 150 142
COST starts at 20,000 CZK
Helicopters for 1, 2, 3, 4 or 5 passengers

Reservations should be made 14 days in advance, including payment by bank transfer or cash. However, two days in advance is often possible based on availability.

From Prague, helicopters depart from Ruzyně Airport or Letňany.

Prague—Český Krumlov—Prague: 55 min one-way, including a two hour visit 93,700 CZK

Prague—Karlovy Vary—Prague: 37 min one-way, including a four hour visit 86,500 CZK

Prague—Karlštejn Castle—Prague: 8 min one-way, including a two hour visit 46,600 CZK

Prague—Chateau Mcely: 22 min one-way drop-off 25,000 CZK

Prague—Chateau Mcely: 22 min one-way, including a 2-hour visit 45,000 CZK

Prague: 20 min sightseeing 118,400 CZK

All prices include VAT.

The cost for the flight over Prague is more expensive because a special heavy helicopter must be used.

All helicopters are insured and have the necessary certificates. The company also charters airplanes within the Czech Republic and Europe. Visit their website to see a complete list of their fleet.

Also Worth Noting: V.I.P. Helicopter is very flexible and happy to organize trips that meet each individual customer's needs. The examples listed above are just a sample itinerary to give you an idea of the time and cost.

CONTACT Marek Krátký, director; his English is excellent.
E-MAIL vip@helicopter.cz

HOT AIR BALLOONING

Are you dying to see the oh-so picturesque Czech countryside? Well, I can think of no better and more relaxing means of doing so than by hot air balloon. Here is how you do it:

■ ■ ■ ■ ■ ■ ■ ■ ■ ■ ■ ■ ■

Ballooning CZ
Hotel Treatrino
Bořivojova 53, Praha 3
www.ballooning.cz
TEL 607 517 535
HOURS Daily: Nonstop
COST 4,700 CZK per person weekdays; 5,200 CZK per person weekends & holidays (prices subject to change) Maximum Number of People: 7 (10% discount given)

The balloon departs from Konopiště, very close to the castle, and the flight will slowly float over this beautiful area of southern Bohemia for roughly one hour, though preparation takes an additional 30 minutes. If the balloon is booked for a single group, other launch sites are possible. Flights are available year round, but only in favorable weather (dry with 5km of visibility and little wind). Morning launches must take place no later then two hours after sunrise and evening launches must take place no later than two hours before sunset. Flights over the city of Prague are not possible.

NOTE: reservations must be made 14 days in advance, including payment by bank transfer or cash.

Directions, By Car, To Launch Site: Take highway D1 south towards Brno, then take exit 21 to join the E55 towards České Budějovice and Benešov. Alternatively you can take the train to Benešov, which takes about one hour, but I highly recommend either driving or being driven.

LOCAL SPORTS TEAMS

Of the two national pastimes in the Czech Republic—mushroom-picking and hockey, the latter is unquestionably the more riveting; so taking in a local game with the fans in their element could be great fun. While not as popular as hockey, soccer (or, football, as they call it here) also has a very strong following. Here's all what you need to know to get into the game:

Ice Hockey

HC Slavia

Sazka Arena, Prague 8,
Vysočany
www.hc-slavia.cz
TEL 266 121 122
TICKETS 100–200 CZK
METRO Českomoravská

Slavia plays in the largest
indoor rink in the Czech
Republic, built for the
2004 World Ice Hockey
Championships.

HC Sparta

T-Mobile Arena, Výstaviště
Exhibitions Grounds,
Prague 7, Holešovice
www.hcsparta.cz
TEL 266 727 443
TICKETS 40–130 CZK
METRO Nádraží Holešovice ●
TRAM 5, 12, 14, 17 to
Výstaviště

The local rival of HC Slavia.

Football (Soccer)

SK Slavia

Diskařská 100, Prague 6,
Strahov
www.slavia.cz
TEL 233 081 751
TICKETS 80–200 CZK
METRO Anděl , then bus
217 to Stadium Strahov

The local underdog.

AC Sparta

Milady Horákové 98,
Prague 7, Bubeneč
www.sparta.cz
TEL 220 570 323
TICKETS 50–200 CZK
METRO Hradčanská ●
TRAM 1, 8, 15 to Sparta

The defending champs, AC
Sparta is the team with the
largest following.

Who Better to Ask About Czech Hockey than a Former Slavia Praha Player?

Jiří Fiala
STATS
AGE 49
TEAM Slavia Praha Klub,
1974–1977
POSITION Defense
HOBBY Mushroom-picking

Karen: What makes Czech
hockey different from
North America's NHL?

Jiří: The Czech leagues
play excellent hockey, but
they're not at the same
level of play as the NHL.
There's more emphasis on
passing, positioning and
setting up plays
to score than in the NHL,
where such fancy play
will often be stopped
short by thundering body
checks. Czech hockey is
played on an international
size rink—the kind used
throughout Europe—
that's wider and longer
than an NHL ice rink, and
as a result, NHL hockey is
much faster. Czech hockey
leagues earn much more
money from sponsorship
than ticket sales or TV
broadcasts, so the players'
uniforms, the ice surface,
the boards surrounding
the ice, and even the
team names often have
sponsor's names and logos
plastered all over them—
but the players' salary
is peanuts compared to
what the NHL pays. In
short, Czech hockey is very
good and some of the best
you're likely to see outside
the NHL, but for a fraction
of the price.

Karen: Sports teams
always have personalities.
How would you describe
HC Slavia versus HC
Sparta?

Jiří: Under communism,
HC Sparta was owned
by one of the biggest
companies in the country,
and this allowed the
team to have far greater
benefits, including salary,
travel and even better
uniforms. However,

POND HOCKEY, 1972 (JIŘÍ FIALA IS SECOND FROM LEFT)

CONTINUED >

JIŘÍ FIALA AT HIS CHATA, C. 1980

■ ■ ■ ■ ■ ■ ■ ■ ■ ■

Monday After Easter
Velikonoce

MARCH / APRIL

Although Easter is certainly observed as a religious holiday, you'll find very few Czechs at church services. Instead they generally participate in a bizarre pagan ritual called *pomlázka*, in which Czech men beat women with willow sticks decorated with colorful ribbons in order to keep them fertile during the year to come. The women retaliate by throwing cold water over their male tormentors. Peace is finally restored when the women present the men with hand-painted eggs and shots of homemade brandy. Called *kraslice*, these eggs are decorated using various techniques, including the application of straw, thread, crochet work, wax, grass pulp, batik, and dyes applied with onionskins, to achieve a precise decorative motif. Small masterpieces, all of them.

See p. 98 for Manufaktura, the best source for painted eggs.

EASTER GREETINGS, 1919
(SOURCE: J. WENIGA)

they also had a lot more pressure on them due to this management structure. As a result, in general, I would describe the players as tougher...

HC Slavia, during this period, was a club team; the players played as a hobby, just for the love of the game. As a result, the team was much more laid-back. There was no management and no money. Today, I'm certain it's very different, as they are now owned by a large company, just like HC Sparta is.

Karen: Crazy fans always make a game much more fun. So which Prague team has the most intense fans?

Jiří: HC Sparta, no question!

Karen: What's your favorite Prague arena to see a game at?

Jiří: SAZKA. This is where the Hockey World Championship was played in 2004. In fact, it was built for the occasion, and it's far more deluxe than all of the other arenas.

Karen: What is your favorite team in the Czech Republic and why?

Jiří: HC Slavia, silly! Gotta stay loyal to my team.

ENTERTAINMENT

MAY DAY AT LETNÁ PARK, MAY 1, 1986
(SOURCE: ČTK / CZECH NEWS AGENCY)

Burning of the Witches
Pálení čarodějnic
APRIL 30

Marking the death of winter and the birth of spring, bonfires are lit throughout the countryside and occasionally in Prague, to purge the land of evil winter spirits and keep the witches at bay. Although it's illegal to light fires within Prague's city limits, an unofficial (though sanctioned) celebration is held on Petřín hill.

May Day / Labor Day
Svátek Práce
MAY 1

While this celebration may not be what it once was, you'll find plenty of communists out in Letná Park making a valiant effort to keep the party alive—the Communist party, that is, which is currently supported by 12% of the Czech population. The celebration is still going strong in the countryside; in 2006 I drove by a gathering with a float featuring an enormous head of Lenin made from papier-mâché, and teenage girls with pom-poms leading the way.

See p. 64 for a complete description of Letná Park.

Prague Spring
Pražské jaro
MAY 12 TO JUNE 2
Hellichova 18, Prague 1, Malá Strana (Box Office)
www.festival.cz
TEL 257 312 547–Information about the program
METRO Malostranská ●
TRAM 12, 20, 22, 23 to Hellichova

This internationally prestigious music festival is, bar none, the biggest arts event of the year in the Czech Republic. The event dates back to 1946 and traditionally begins on May 12, the anniversary of Smetana's death, with a procession from his grave in Vyšehrad all the way to the Obecní dům (Municipal House), where the composer's *Má vlast* (My Country) is performed in the presence of the president. The festival finishes on June 2 with a performance of Beethoven's Ninth Symphony. Tickets sell out fast, so if you're planning a trip during this time, you'll want to purchase tickets in advance, either online or through your hotel. Tickets go on sale December 12.

Prague International Marathon
LATE MAY
www.pim.cz

Runners from all over the world come to brave the

ENTERTAINMENT

cobblestones and traverse the Charles Bridge. If you'd like to join in, or simply observe, check their website for exact dates.

- - - - - - - - - - - - - -

Fringe Festival Prague

LATE MAY / EARLY JUNE
www.praguefringe.com

This weeklong festival, which celebrated their fifth anniversary in 2006, offers the best in theatre, cabaret, music, comedy and dance from around the world. This year, 38 companies from nine countries will present productions. The participating venues lean toward the intimate, and most performances run about 1 hour.

- - - - - - - - - - - - - -

World Festival of Puppet Art

LATE MAY / EARLY JUNE
www.puppetart.com

The World Festival of Puppet Art is a weeklong international festival organized by the puppeteer's world body, UNIMA, which is based in Prague and celebrated its 10th anniversary in 2006. Last year's festival had participants from 26 counties, including China, India, Russia and South Africa. The competition is juried, providing participants and audiences an opportunity to see great performances, both traditional and innovative, of this unique craft.

- - - - - - - - - - - - - -

Dance Festival

Tanec
JUNE
www.tanecpha.cz

Tanec is an international festival of modern dance

EVE OF ST. NICHOLAS, 1947
(SOURCE: ČTK / CZECH NEWS AGENCY)

CHRISTMAS GREETINGS, 1917
(SOURCE: J. WENIGA)

are lit and flowers are laid, but overall it tends to be pretty understated.

Eve of St. Nicholas
Mikuláš
DECEMBER 5

Should you happen to pass a trio dressed respectively as an Angel, a Devil and St. Nicholas on this night, fear not; you're not crazy, but simply happen to be in Prague on the eve of St. Nicholas—one of my personal favorite holidays. The costumed trio visits small children (and large ones, like me), with the angel handing out sweets to children who have been good, and the devil handing out coal and potatoes to those who have been bad—giving children a useful indication of what is to come on Christmas day! Should you happen to be in Prague with children during this time, ask you hotel concierge to arrange a visit for your children. Yes, the trios are actually available for hire, and the hotel should be able to take care of this.

Christmas
Vánoce
DECEMBER 24

Czechs celebrate Christmas on the night of the 24th. Festivities include a meal of fish soup, fried carp, potato salad, and *vánočka* (sweet cabled bread similar to challah) and cookies. Only after the meal are children allowed to open their presents beneath the tree… which, *pssst*, have been delivered by Baby Jesus (*Ježíšek*) not Santa Claus. Just to keep it clear.

that takes place over a period of three weeks at venues throughout the city. Past festivals have introduced Bill T. Jones and Merce Cunningham to Czech audiences. The event is often used as a platform for world premieres, and has attracted participants from all over the world, including Finland, Israel, Mexico and Taiwan.

Prague Autumn Festival
Pražský podzim
SEPTEMBER
www.pragueautumn.cz

Although not as prestigious as Prague Spring, this music festival is still mighty impressive. Held at the Rudolfinum, there are always plenty of top-notch performances to choose from.

Anniversary of the Velvet Revolution
Sametová Revoluce
NOVEMBER 17
Václavské náměstí, Prague 1, Nové Město

Commemorates the demonstrations that began the Velvet Revolution. Candles

173

HIPSTER GUIDE

Not for the faint of heart, easily offended, or even remotely square.

I asked a good friend of mine, Sarah Morris, to help me with this section. A mod little social butterfly, this chick flits around all the hippest, "Prague-est" bars and clubs for the under-30 set, so there's much we can learn from her...

Bars

■ ■ ■ ■ ■ ■ ■ ■ ■ ■ ■ ■ ■

Blind Eye

Vlkova 26, Prague 3, Žižkov
www.blindeye.cz
TEL N/A
HOURS Daily: 17:00–05:00
TRAM 5, 9 and 26 to Husinecká

Not usually as punk rock as the website may lead you to believe, Blind Eye features just the right amount of hardcore, and there's always a good mix of cultures. Service is slow, but just chill out and listen to the tunes of Johnny Cash, The Misfits, Judy Garland, Tom Waits, etc. The bartenders are usually down for a friendly chat, but they *really* don't care to hear about how you're from small-town, Iowa—remember, travelers are a dime a dozen in this joint. Open till 5 am, this is a good late-night stop.

■ ■ ■ ■ ■ ■ ■ ■ ■ ■ ■ ■ ■

Fraktal

Šmeralova 1, 170 00 Prague 7, Bubeneč
www.fraktalbar.cz
TEL 777 794 094
HOURS Mon–Fri: 12:00–

01:00; Saturday & Sunday: 11:30–01:00
METRO Hradčanská ●
TRAM 1, 8, 15, 25, 26 to Letenské náměstí

Sandwiched between two of Prague's most fabulous parks (Stromovka and Letná), this neighborhood joint is very cool. Czechs and expats alike enjoy the slightly gritty atmosphere and interesting design of this popular restaurant and bar. The food is delish— try the hamburger, quite possibly the best in Prague. Don't bring your mom.

NOTE: Fraktal is also known as a restaurant during non-hipster hours with burgers, nachos, weekend brunch and lots of good vegetarian options.

■ ■ ■ ■ ■ ■ ■ ■ ■ ■ ■ ■ ■

U Sudu

Vodičkova 10, Prague 1, Nové Město
TEL 222 232 207
HOURS Mon–Thurs: 08:00–03:00; Fri & Sat: 08:00–04:00; Sun: 08:00–02:00
METRO Karlovo Náměstí ○ or Národní třída ○
TRAM 3, 9, 14, 24 to Lazarská

Holy fire hazard, batman! This wine bar (which recently also started serving beer) spirals deep into the bowels of the earth. Stride confidently into the deceptively small first chamber, make a right, and then keep going downstairs—there's a bar on almost every level. The youngish, rather 'alternative' crowd here drinks, chats, and smokes way into the wee hours...

■ ■ ■ ■ ■ ■ ■ ■ ■ ■ ■ ■ ■

Ultramarin

Ostrovní 32, Prague 1, Nové Město
www.ultramarin.cz
TEL 224 932 249
HOURS Daily: 11:00–04:00 (Serves food until 1am)
METRO Národní třída ○
TRAM 6, 9, 18, 21, 22 and 23 to Národní třída

Also a restaurant with pretty good food and a surprisingly large Thai selection, Ultramarin serves cocktails that are outstanding. Best Bloody Mary I've had in this country, and mixed with theatrical flair. Go downstairs to the cellar bar, complete with DJ and foosball table.

Cafes

■ ■ ■ ■ ■ ■ ■ ■ ■ ■ ■ ■ ■

Duende

Karolíny Světlé 30, Prague 1, Staré Město
www.duende.cz
TEL 775 186 077
HOURS Mon–Sat: 11:00–01:00; Sun: 17:00–01:00
TRAM 17, 18 to Karlovy lázně

Great "Dadaist" café ambience with surprisingly friendly and charming service. A great stop during the day for coffee or tea, or beer or wine in the evening. Hip Czechs and foreigners alike grace the intimate tables.

■ ■ ■ ■ ■ ■ ■ ■ ■ ■ ■ ■ ■

Medúza

Belgická 17, Prague 2, Vinohrady
www.meduza.cz
TEL 222 515 107
HOURS Mon–Fri: 10:00–01:00; Sat & Sun: 12:00–01:00
METRO Náměstí Míru ●
TRAM 4, 10, 16, 22, 23 Náměstí Míru

This is *the* quintessential

Czech Music Scene

I turned to my friend Vladan Sir for some insight and recommendations on the Czech music scene to pass on to my readers. Vladan, who is a former editor for *Umělec* (see p. 88), also happens to be the hippest Czech I know. He always seems to be tuned in to the pulse of what's happening in music, both on a local and international level. In any case, Vladan was kind enough to answer my few questions below:

Karen: Which Czech band do you think an English speaker would be apt to get the biggest kick out of?

Vladan: Bruno Ferrari—for his decadence, style, and Iraqi descent. Check him out at www.brunoferrari.cz

Karen: What would be your favorite album recommendation?

Vladan: Silver Surfer by the Sebastians. It's early 90's music and one of the few Czech albums I can listen to anytime. Recently, I've been obsessed with a band called Jižní Pionýři and their first album. Their second album, Punk Is Dead, just came out under the band name Pio Squad. Other recommendations would include Monika Načeva's Možnosti tu sou.

Karen: If you were to equate Bruno Ferrari or the Sebastians to a singer or band on the global market, which would it be?

Vladan: Bruno Ferrari is incomparable, maybe Nick Cave on mushrooms? The Sebastians play very happy poppy guitar tunes, British-style.

Karen: What are your faves in the following categories: Rock, Funk, Rap and Dance?

Vladan: ROCK: I'm really not fond of Czech rock music. Maybe Monika Načeva, though. FUNK: Monkey Business—and they're best live. RAP: Pio Squad is my ultimate Czech hip-hop favorite. DANCE: Juanita Juarez

Plus don't forget about the particular Czech specialty: cover bands. There are a million bands like Velvet Revival, the Cure Revival, the Pearl Jam Revival, and the What-not Revival... I even SAW with my own eyes a Roxette Revival!!!

KAREL GOTT, "THE GOLDEN VOICE OF PRAGUE," SPORTING A FAB BOHEMIAN GET-UP, C. 1972 (SOURCE: WWW.KARELGOTT.NET)

---

old European café. The soups and little nibbles are good, and the ambience is perfectly old-school with furniture, rugs, and sugar bowls plucked from local antique stores. All of which is made even more authentic by the Bohemian mix of young and old patrons. Slightly off-the-tourist-track in a "real neighborhood," Medúza makes for a great stop during the day, or for a chill-out glass of wine in the evening.

Night Clubs

▪ ▪ ▪ ▪ ▪ ▪ ▪ ▪ ▪ ▪ ▪ ▪ ▪

Cross Club

Plynární 23, Prague 7, Holešovice
www.crossclub.cz
HOURS Mon–Fri: 14:00–Late; Sat & Sun: 16:00–Late
METRO Nádraží Holešovice ●
TRAM 5, 12, 15 to Nádraží Holešovice

Huge blinking robotic sculptures adorn the walls and ceilings—need I say more? In an industrial part of town (easily accessible

by metro), this club is pretty damn gritty. Expect throbbing techno, drum & bass, maybe even punk or experimental. Try your best not to look like a tourist.

▪ ▪ ▪ ▪ ▪ ▪ ▪ ▪ ▪ ▪ ▪ ▪ ▪

Lucerna Music Bar

Vodičkova 36, Prague 1, Nové Město
www.musicbar.cz
TEL 224 217 108
HOURS Daily: 20:00–3:00
METRO Můstek ● ●
TRAM 3, 9, 14, 24 to Vodičkova

Czech Jazz Scene

Glenn Spicker, the owner of U Malého Glena, has lived in Prague for 14 years. He's been booking jazz and blues shows for purists seven nights a week for the past 11 years, so he seemed like the perfect person to make Jazz recommendations for my readers.

Karen: When not taking in a show at your own venue, what's your favorite alternative jazz joint in town and why?

Glenn: U Staré paní. The owners are nice and definitely have class, several of the other well-known clubs are owned by stodgy functionaries, so the atmosphere ends up being very stale. U Staré paní, on the other hand, has a good bar, interesting design, and a friendly staff. Most other places are real downers—the clubs simply aren't interesting, the music isn't interesting—so they're not great places to hang out and listen to music. But, of course, you always have to check who's playing first.

Karen: Is there anything that makes the Prague Jazz scene unique?

Glenn: The fact that there are quite a few clubs, with prices that tend to be very reasonable, has certainly been beneficial in terms of creating a scene. Plus, just the aura of jazz in the former communist block has always been exciting. It developed (to some extent) as dissident music in Prague.

Karen: What Czech Jazz band or vocalist do you think an English speaker would be apt to get the biggest kick out of?

Glenn: Myriam Bayle is awesome. She is originally from Slovakia, but now lives in Prague. Olga Škrancová is great, too, but you don't see her in clubs or with good bands these days. For non-vocal jazz, the Robert Balcar Trio is usually a good call. But there are several young guys who can really play as well. Too many to name...

Karen: What is your favorite album recommendation?

Glenn: Dexter Gordon's Go—except he isn't Czech, so if you want a Czech Jazz musician, listen to George Mraz. Najponk's CDs are good, too!

Karen: Who are your favorites in following categories: Musician, Vocalist, and Overall?

Glenn: For a musician, I'd say David Dorůžka. For a vocalist, Myriam Bayle—though she's actually a musician too! Overall, I like Jiří Slavíček on drums, but his singing needs work, so I guess my overall favorite player would be Petr Dvorský on bass.

Jazz Club Recommended by Glenn:

■ ■ ■ ■ ■ ■ ■ ■ ■ ■ ■ ■

U Staré paní
Michalská 9, Prague 1, Staré Město
TEL 603 551 680
HOURS Daily: 19:00–02:00; Live Jazz: 21:00–24:00
METRO Můstek ● ●

Featuring 80's and 90's music on the weekends, this is where people go to dance. They also project music videos above the very stage you're allowed to dance on, so there are many levels of entertainment. Just keep those moves hot and the drinks coming. Lucerna also hosts bands and events, so check the website to see what's going on.

■ ■ ■ ■ ■ ■ ■ ■ ■ ■ ■ ■ ■

Palác Akropolis
Kubelíkova 27, Prague 3, Žižkov
www.palacakropolis.cz
TEL 296 330 911
HOURS Daily: 19:00–03:00
METRO Jiřího z Poděbrad ●
TRAM 11 to Jiřího z Poděbrad

This place has it all—café, gallery and main stage (a smattering of big name bands play here), as well as both medium and small DJ rooms. Every night you can find at least one of these open, and quite often all three are in full effect—each with a different danceable vibe. The understatedly trippy décor is not to be missed. Definitely one of the best-known (and loved) spots in the gritty neighborhood of Žižkov.

Nebe

Křemencova 10, Prague 1,
Nové Město
www.nebepraha.cz
TEL 224 930 343
HOURS Daily: 19:00–06:00
METRO Karlovo Náměstí or
Národní třída
TRAM 3, 6, 14, 18, 22, 23, 24
to Karlovo náměstí

Full of hipster study-abroad students, this joint is fully international. DJ's spin tracks of Indie, 80's or techno, depending on the night. Lots of comfy couches for maximum schmoozability. This bar's ambience will even impress those from LA and NYC. You'll find young boys experimenting with their sexuality and chicks with brand new asymmetrical "Euro Haircuts." Kitschy (yet beautiful) oil paintings of the Virgin and Child adorn the walls as a nod to the name *Nebe*—meaning "heaven" in Czech. Stays open late.

Radost FX

Bělehradská 120, Prague 2,
Vinohrady
www.radostfx.cz
TEL 603 193 711
HOURS Daily: 12:00–Late
METRO I. P. Pavlova ●
TRAM 4, 6, 10, 11, 16, 22, 23
to I. P. Pavlova

This is where the beautiful people go clubbing, so it can be a bit of a meat market—which is ironic, since it also happens to be a delicious vegetarian restaurant. Fabulously upholstered couches and an opulent theme prevail. Yummy nachos and other meals are served till 4 am in the upstairs lounge.

See p. 150 for additional information on Radost FX

NOTE: Also known as a restaurant serving entirely vegetarian interpretations of Mexican, Italian, and Mediterranean cuisines, including a great weekend brunch.

Roxy and Roxy NOD

Dlouhá 33, Prague 1,
Staré Město
www.roxy.cz
TEL 224 826 296
HOURS Daily: 20:00–Late
METRO Náměstí Republiky ●
TRAM 5, 8, 14 Dlouhá třída

A decrepit old theater turned all-night techno dance-party, Roxy also hosts touring live bands of all sorts (rock, ska, punk, reggae—you name it). The chill-out room, located downstairs in the club, comes complete with a large polar bear sculpture, as well as ice cubes to sit on.

You can also take the staircase from the entrance on the left up to *Roxy NOD* (daily: 12:00–Late) where you'll find an ever-changing art gallery, featuring contemporary young artists and perhaps a theatrical or musical performance. The café is rumored to have the only "real absinthe" in Prague, and they serve it in the French fashion—mixed with cold water. Free Wi-Fi, too.

Zlaté časy

Vladislavova 1, Prague 1,
Nové Město
www.zlatecasy.cz
TEL 224 948 170

HOURS Mon–Wed: 11:00–24:00; Thur: 11:00–02:00; Fri: 11:00–04:00; Sat: 16:00–04:00
METRO Karlovo Náměstí or Národní třída
TRAM 3, 9, 14, 24 to Lazarská

Fair warning: aptly named "Golden Times," Zlaté časy is nothing less than a Czech Disco. Don't expect the barmen to speak English, but *do* expect a scantily costumed professional dancer or two on the weekends. At some point the DJ will probably break into a medley of Czech hits that you've never heard, as the locals go wild on the dance floor. It's awesome.

Jazz Joints

U Malého Glena

Karmelitská 23, Prague 1,
Malá Strana
www.malyglen.cz
TEL 257 531 717
HOURS Mon–Fri: 10:00–02:00; Sat & Sun: 10:00–02:30
METRO Malostranská ●
TRAM 12, 20, 22, 23 to Malostranské náměstí

This jazz joint is tiny, so definitely make a reservation—and definitely don't chat too loud during the performance. The quality of acoustics produced within this small arched stone venue has been compared to the great clubs of New Orleans. Great place for an intimate handholding date, but equally appropriate to bring your mom.

NOTE: Music starts at 21:00 (you must be there by 20:45 to claim a reservation).

ENTERTAINMENT

Summer Beer Gardens

Two of the best beer gardens are in Letenské sady up on Letná Hill and in Riegerovy sady in the Vinohrady neighborhood. These parks are perfectly safe at night; just use your head.

■ ■ ■ ■ ■ ■ ■ ■ ■ ■ ■ ■ ■ ■

Letenské sady

Letenské sady 341, Prague 7, Bubeneč

TEL 233 378 200

HOURS Daily: May–Sept: 11:00–23:00

METRO Hradčanská ●

TRAM 1, 8, 15, 25, 26 to Letenské náměstí

Go up to Letná in the daytime to catch the amazing view of the river, bridges, and spires of the city. People will be spilling over from the picnic tables onto nearby grassy

Recommended Hopping

Žižkov

In summer, start at the Riegerovy Sady Beer Garden. Next move on to either Palác Akropolis or Blind Eye. These are close to each other, and both get "interesting" late, so while it doesn't really matter which one you try first, it's worth checking out both while you're in the neighborhood. Also, definitely make it a point to stumble over to the Žižkov TV Tower while you're here.

Nové Město

See a Czech film with English subtitles at Světozor to get a handle on the nation's black humor and their crazy way of rolling r's. Then, cross the street to check out Lucerna. Even if you don't want to party at the Music Club, you must see the horse sculpture hanging upside-down in the foyer by the same artist, David Černý, who created the alien babies in Žižkov. Stroll down or hop on the tram and have a few drinks at U Sudu to prepare yourself for the kitschy-ness of super-Czech Zlaté časy, or perhaps the ever-so-hipness of Nebe.

ENTERTAINMENT

GARDEN CITY: LOST IN TRANSLATION?

lawns, hanging out and drinking beer every day (and evening) of the week when the weather is nice. Just behind the beer garden is a slightly fancier place (meaning glass glasses), where you can get a real meal (pasta, salads, etc.).

NOTE: The beer garden is in Letná Park, between the National Technical Museum and the river. On the map, Štefánikův Bridge dead-ends into it—that's 3 bridges north of the Charles Bridge.

Riegerovy sady
Riegerovy sady, Prague 2, Vinohrady
TEL N/A
HOURS Daily: May–Sept: 11:00–23:00
METRO Jiřího z Poděbrad ●
TRAM 11 to Vinohradská tržnice

This park also has a nice sweeping view of the city, but not from the beer garden. It's just a low-key spot where you can grab a nice juicy *klobása* sausage, a cold beer and a game of foosball against the locals. Complete with a big screen projector, it's also a cool place to be during televised sports games. Bring your dog along and you'll fit right in.

NOTE: The beer garden is found in the northeast corner of the park.

GAY PRAGUE

"Prague is definitely the best place to come in Eastern or Central Europe, without a doubt" noted my friend Paul Coogles, who owns Prague Saints, a bar and full-service tour company for gay

visitors. I turned to him and his tour manager, Marek Nováček, for a bit of insight on the gay scene, as I'm not very clued in. One thing I learned is that their well organized and very informative website is the ideal starting point for planning your trip and/or information resource once you're already here.

Prague Saints
Polská 32, Prague 2, Vinohrady
www.praguesaints.cz
info@praguesaints.cz
TEL 222 250 326
HOURS Daily: 19:00–04:00
METRO Jiřího z Poděbrad ●
TRAM 11 to Jiřího z Poděbrad

They offer one-stop shopping for organizing and enjoying your (gay) stay in Prague. In fact, the only things they don't take care of are your flights. Through their organization, you can book an apartment or hotel, organize transfers from the airport or train station, and even book a private tour of Prague by day or night. "Gay Prague by Night" is my personal favorite tour, and Marek will serve as your personal tour guide, tailored to your specific interests, or he can simply take you to all the hot spots in the ever-evolving gay scene of Prague. Nothing better then hanging with a local!

If you do have the opportunity to meet Marek in person, you might ask him about his "sister"—which ought to win him over immediately. And, if you're lucky enough, you might even have a chance to meet her...

KIDS

As I'm really a kid a heart, I've listed a few of my favorite things to do which are, more often than not, thought of as kids' activities.

Entertainment

■ ■ ■ ■ ■ ■ ■ ■ ■ ■ ■ ■ ■
Cirkus Berousek
OLD FASHIONED ONE
RING CIRCUS
Letenská pláň, Prague 7, Holešovice
www.berousek.cz/program.php
TEL N/A
ENTRANCE FEE 160 CZK; 180 CZK; 250 CZK
METRO Hradčanská ●

BEROUSEK CIRCUS, 2006

TRAM 1, 8, 15, 15, 26 to Letenské náměstí

Have your concierge find out if this wonderful circus happens to be in town during your visit. It's a one-ring show that is bound to charm young and old alike, as it includes lots of acrobatics, animals and clowns. The highlight during my last visit was the bears riding motorcycles. Without even reserving tickets in advance, I was able to get front row seats at 250 CZK a pop. Needless to say, the horses, elephants and camels were perhaps closer than some would like, but the 4 year old next to me and I were both *definitely* in our element! You'll want to bring plenty of cash, as you're certain to be cajoled by your child into buying them popcorn, cotton candy and those very cool multi-color circus lights that play an annoyingly addictive tune. During intermission, you can take a ride on a camel in the ring, where, for a small fee you can have your Polaroid picture taken as a keepsake.
CASH ONLY

NOTE: It's possible to order tickets online, and I would recommend having your concierge take care of this to ensure that you get the best possible seats.

■ ■ ■ ■ ■ ■ ■ ■ ■ ■ ■ ■ ■
Zoo
LION & TIGERS & FLYING CHAIRS: OH MY!
U Trojského zámku 3, Prague 7, Trója
www.zoopraha.cz
TEL 257 315 212
HOURS Daily: March: 09:00–17:00; Apr, May, Sept, Oct: 09:00–18:00; Jun–Aug: 09:00–19:00; Nov–Feb: 09:00–16:00
ENTRANCE FEE 90 CZK Adult; 60 CZK children; 3 and under Free
Map 5 CZK, get it!
METRO Nádraží Holešovice ● then bus 112 to Zoologická zahrada

Not having been to the zoo since 1995, I wanted to be sure to revisit it before writing my book. Before heading over, I called my friend Constantino, age 4, to ask for general recommendations. "The flying chairs," I was told, are what he likes best, closely followed by the petting zoo and the bats in the Indonesian jungle. Clearly, Constantino is wise beyond his years, as these three things proved to be my own favorites as well.

The Flying Chairs, at 15 CZK per ride (and free for children under 6), are tranquil on the way up, and picturesque on the way down, with a stunning panoramic view of Prague. I was completely bewitched and went on it three times.

BOOK COVER, C. 1930

R. MCQUILKIN, 2005

The petting zoo provides the little ones a chance to pet and feed the goats and sheep. For 5 CZK, you can get a handful of nibbles from the dispensers on hand. They also offer pony rides at 20 CZK a pop, as well as a miniature tram ride for 10 CZK. This looked fun! There's a kiddy pool too, so if your little ones love the water, you'll want to bring a change of clothes.

The zoo is big enough that it'll be difficult to fit it all in during one visit; be certain to get a map when you buy your tickets, so you can be sure to and hit the exhibitions that interest you most.

The zoo is remarkably well run and they definitely understand their audience. There are lots of gift shops, with items that are not exclusively Czech but lots of fun, and plenty of food stands and bathrooms as well.

I had a great day there, and I'm certain you will, too. Enjoy!

NOTE: Bring coins if possible to pay for the flying chairs and other activities; should you forget, they do have machines that make change at the flying chair entry, as well as at the petting zoo.

AND ALSO NOTE: Instead of taking the metro and bus, recommend taking either a taxi or a boat (see p. 167 for boat information).

Troja Chateau and the Botanical Gardens are also at the same metro stop.

Parks And Playground

■ ■ ■ ■ ■ ■ ■ ■ ■ ■ ■ ■ ■ ■ ■ ■

Dětský ostrov
PLAYGROUND
Vltava River, Prague 1, Malá Strana; Entrance on Janáčkovo nábřeží
TRAM 6, 9, 22 to Zborovská

A wonderful little oasis where your little ones can run around Dětský ostrov ("Children's Island") that also includes an enclosed playground. Thankfully, there are lots of benches where you can relax as you take in the exceptional location.

■ ■ ■ ■ ■ ■ ■ ■ ■ ■ ■ ■ ■ ■ ■ ■

Petřín Hill
MIRROR MAZE (BLUDIŠTĚ) & VIEWING TOWER (ROZHLEDNA)
Petřín Hill, Petřínské sady, Prague 1, Malá Strana
TEL 257 315 212
HOURS Daily: May–Aug: 10:00–22:00; Apr & Sep: 10:00–19:00; Nov–Mar: 10:00–17:00
ENTRANCE FEE 50 CZK Adult; 40 CZK Children; 6 and under Free
TRAM 12, 20, 22, 23 to Újezd, then take the funicular (lanovka) railway

Wonderfully tourist-free, the mirror maze is housed in a mock-Gothic castle built for the 1891 Prague Jubilee. This hall of distorting mirrors is an opportunity for great hilarity among both young and old. You can take a funicular up using standard tram tickets, and the view is excellent. If you're up for it, you can also climb up the mini Eiffel Tower, also built for the Jubilee, which has a viewing gallery 53 meters

PETŘÍN TOWER, C. 1940

TRANSPORT HALL, NATIONAL TECHNICAL MUSEUM
(PHOTO COURTESY OF NTM)

(170 ft.) off the ground. The park at Petřín, in general, is very peaceful, so if your wee ones enjoy walking, this is a wonderful place to spend a few hours.

CASH ONLY

Museums

The National Museum
Národní museum
Václavské náměstí 68, Prague 1, Nové Město
www.nm.cz
TEL 222 497 111
HOURS Daily: May–Sept: 10:00–18:00; Oct–Apr: 09:00–17:00
ENTRANCE FEE 110 CZK Adult; 50 CZK Children; 6 and under Free
METRO Muzeum ● ●
TRAM 11 to Muzeum

At the National Museum, it's most likely the zoological collection that children will find most mesmerizing. Highlights include an elephant head, an entire giraffe, as well as various bats, squirrels and rats. And a *very* cute little baby penguin. Closed the 1st Tuesday of every month.

See p. 51 for a complete for a complete description.

National Technical Museum
Národní techniché museum
Kostelní 42, Prague 7, Holešovice
www.ntm.cz
TEL 220 399 111
HOURS Tue–Fri: 09:00 -17:00; Sat & Sun: 10:00 -18:00
ENTRANCE FEE 70 CZK Adult; 30 CZK Children; 6 and under Free
METRO Hradčanská ● or Vltavská ●
TRAM 8, 25, 26 to Letenské náměstí
Closed as of Sept. 12, 2006 due to reconstruction; re-opening planned for July 2008

This museum is tons of fun. The transport hall, a great Functionalist space, is filled to the brim with Czech-made vehicles, including vintage steam engines, cars, trucks, motorcycles (some with mud still on the tires), and bicycles, as well as airplanes suspended from the ceiling (this is my favorite room). Another attraction, by guided tour

MLADÝ TECHNÍK MAGAZINE COVER, 1952

only, is the mock coalmine in the basement, certain to be a real hit if you have any budding engineers in the family

Public Transport Museum
Muzeum městské hromadné dopravy
Patočkova 4, Prague 6, Střešovice
TEL 296 124 900
HOURS Apr 3–Nov 11: Sat & Sun: 09:00–17:00;
(other times by appointment)
ENTRANCE FEE 25 CZK Adult; 10 CZK Children; 6 and under Free
METRO Hradčanská ●
TRAM 1, 2, 15, 18, 25 to Vozovna Střešovice

This museum is a wonderful hands-on experience for young and old alike, featuring a wide selection of historic trams and buses, several of which you can even climb into and explore. The oldest is a horse-drawn tram that dates back to 1886. Located in an historic Prague tram depot built in 1909, the facility was used up until 1992. The museum provides a delightful window into Prague's past. A number of unusual items are for sale by the ticket booth; my favorite find is a puzzle of the Prague Metro.
CASH ONLY

Toy Museum
Muzeum hraček
Prague Castle, Jiřská 6, Prague 1, Hradčany
www.muzeumhracek.cz
TEL 224 372 294
HOURS Daily: 09:30–17:30
ENTRANCE FEE 60 CZK Adult; 30 CZK Children; 6 and under Free
METRO Malostranská ●

Baby Sitters

Agentura Pohoda
Za Třebešínem 14, Prague 10, Strašnice
www.agenturapohoda.cz
TEL 274 772 201, 602 252 873
RATES 130–150 CZK per hour; 1,500 CZK for 24 hours

This agency offers baby-sitting, with a minimum of two hours. Their services have been utilized by any number of international film stars, embassies and multinational corporations, so you can feel confident that your little tyke will be in good hands.
CASH ONLY
NOTE: prices listed are based on one child, review their excellent website for a complete price list.

Nanny Active Childcare
1nanny@seznam.cz
TEL 721 187 246, 721 307 311
(Contacts: Hana and Jana)
RATES 150–170 CZK per hour; Sundays & holidays: 170 CZK per hour

Your little ones will love Nanny Active Childcare; they are great at creating unique activities for your child and come prepared with a suitcase full of crafts and games. My friend Jack, age 4, is a loyal client, and each time I visit I'm impressed with the fabulous masterpieces he's created while spending time with them, including kites, animals in a variety of media, paper houses, holiday decorations, cool collages and cards. If your wee ones love glue and glitter, I'm confident you can't go wrong with this choice.
CASH ONLY

If, like me, you love toys, definitely put this on your to-do list. The collection dates back over 150 years, and runs the gamut from Markin toy trains and stations to turn-of-the-century kitchen dioramas, teddy bears, dolls, tin toys, and even Barbie who gets an entire floor all to herself (even though the only remotely Czech thing about her is her rather impossible measurements).
CASH ONLY

SPEED RACER
(PHOTO BY STUART ISETT, 2006)

Resources

POLICE STATIONS

STARÉ MĚSTO
Bartolomějská 14, Prague 1,
Staré Město
TEL 974 851 700
HOURS 24 hours
METRO Národní třída
TRAM 6, 9, 18, 21, 22, 23 to
Národní třída

MALÁ STRANA
Vlašská 3, Prague 1,
Malá Strana
TEL 974 851 730
METRO Malostranská ●
TRAM 12, 20, 22, 23 to
Malostranské náměstí

NOVÉ MĚSTO
Jungmannovo náměstí 9,
Prague 1, Nové Město
TEL 974 851 750
HOURS 24 hours
METRO Můstek ● ○

VINOHRADY
Šafaříkova 12, Prague 2,
Vinohrady
TEL 974 852 720
METRO Náměstí Míru ●
TRAM 10, 16, 22, 23 to
Náměstí Míru

LOST AND FOUND

Karolíny Světlé 5, Prague 1,
Staré Město
TEL 224 235 085
METRO Národní třída ○
TRAM 6, 9, 18, 21, 22, 23 to
Národní divadlo

EMBASSIES

Australian Consulate
Klimentská 10, Prague 1,
Staré Město
TEL 296 578 350
Mon–Fri: 09:00–13:00
METRO Náměstí Republiky ○
TRAM 5, 8, 14 to Dlouhá třída

British Embassy
Thunovská 14, Prague 1,
Malá Strana
TEL 257 530 278
(emergencies 602 217 700)
HOURS Mon–Fri: 08:30–12:00
METRO Malostranská ●
TRAM 12, 20, 22, 23 to
Malostranské náměstí

Canadian Embassy
Muchova 6, Prague 6, Dejvice
TEL 272 101 800
HOURS Mon–Fri: 08:30–12:30
METRO Hradčanská ●

Irish Embassy
Tržiště 13, Prague 1,
Malá Strana
TEL 257 530 061
HOURS Mon–Fri: 09:30–12:30
& 14:30–16:30
METRO Malostranská ●
TRAM 12, 20, 22, 23 to
Malostranské náměstí

U.S. Embassy
Tržiště 15, Prague 1,
Malá Strana
www.usembassy.cz
TEL 257 530 663
(emergencies 257 532 716)
HOURS Mon–Fri: 08:00–12:00
METRO Malostranská ●
TRAM 12, 20, 22, 23 to
Malostranské náměstí

TRAVEL ADVERTISEMENT, C. 1930

WEBSITES

AIRLINES
www.csa.cz
This is Czech Airlines'
website, and, whether
you're just planning your
trip or thinking about
a side trip once you're
already here, it could
prove extremely useful.

www.easyjet.com
Budget airline

www.skyeurope.com
Budget airline

www.smartwings.net
Budget airline

ČSA AIRLINE CABIN, 1940
(COURTESY OF CZECH AIRLINES)

BACKGROUND INFORMATION ON THE CZECH REPUBLIC

www.czech.cz

This is the official foreign ministry site for the Czech Republic. It includes general information about the country, but most importantly, it includes entry requirements. Definitely double-check this site before traveling to the Czech Republic, as requirements vary within the European Union.

CULTURAL INFORMATION

www.ngprague.cz

The National Gallery website, should you be curious to see what temporary exhibitions will be up during your visit.

EXPATRIATE-ORIENTED SITES

(With General Information that May Prove Useful to Temporary Visitors as Well)

www.expats.cz

This site is the Holy Grail for local expats, and you'll find information on anything and everything here, including: a date, job, movie listing, or restaurant. Expats is just an all-around excellent resource.

www.prague.tv

This site also primarily serves the expatriate community. For cultural listings, including cinema, I find this site easier to use than www.expats.cz.

GENERAL INFORMATION FOR VISITORS

www.czechtourism.com

This site covers not only Prague but also the entire Czech Republic. It's not as easy to navigate as the *Prague-info* site listed next, but it can also be a very helpful resource.

www.prague-info.cz/en

If you're traveling to Prague, this is the best site to utilize as a resource, as it's easiest to navigate. It offers excellent information on Prague, particularly concerning cultural events.

www.praguecard.biz

If you're a die-hard sightseer, the 4-day card that this site offers could be an excellent investment: It provides free admission to over 50 museums and attractions, including the Prague Castle. Visit their website to see what destinations are included and where the card can be purchased.

COST 790 CZK Adults; 490 CZK Students

JEWISH INTEREST

www.kehilaprag.cz

Everything you wanted to know about the current Jewish community in Prague.

NEWS

www.praguepost.com

The Prague Post is the major English language newspaper in Prague, and their website is a helpful tool for cultural listings, as well as real estate (should you fall in love with the city and decide to stay a while).

www.praguemonitor.com

A daily summary of the Czech news in English.

POST OFFICE

www.cpost.cz

This site from the Czech Post Office might come in handy if you've been extraordinarily indulgent and purchased far too much to carry home.

TICKET PURCHASING FOR CULTURAL AND SPORTING EVENTS

www.ticketpro.cz

One-stop shopping for any cultural or sporting event ticket in town, including theatre, ballet, sports, music, and even social events.

www.czechopera.cz

An excellent website that allows you to see what performances will be offered at all the major venues in town; it also lets you order tickets online.

TRANSPORTATION

www.dp-praha.cz/en/index.htm

If you're a municipal transport junkie—and I know some of you out there are—this site tells you everything you ever wanted to know about the Prague municipal transport system, including its history.

www.vlak.cz

If you'll be traveling by train, this is a great resource for all kinds of useful information.

www.metroweb.cz

For a bit of fun, check out this site that includes maps, historical images, future development, and even MP3s of all your favorite metro announcements.

WEATHER

www.prague.ic.cz/prague-weather.htm

Get your 12-day weather forecast here.

www.myczechrepublic.com/weather/prague-weather.html

General information on climate, including detailed weather forecasts for Prague.

VAT Refund TAXFREE Program

Added to the price of all merchandise that you see in stores is a Value Added Tax (VAT) of 19%. If you spend over 2,000 CZK on the same day in one store that participates in the VAT refund program, however, you will be entitled to get most, though not all, of the tax back (GlobalRefund, the executor of this program, subtracts 4% as their fee for processing).

Lots of people will advise you that it's not worth your time and effort; however if you're a spender like I am, it is indeed worth your time and effort, as 19% on enough crystal, fur or wooden toys can begin to add up...

WHAT YOU NEED TO DO
1. Request a TAXFREE form from the merchant. They may ask to see your passport in filling out the form. From my experience, however, Czech stores are very lenient about this; I have yet to know anyone who has absolutely had to show their passport, as one must in, say, Paris, where it really *is* a requirement.

2. You will need to fill out the following on the document: Name, Home Address, Country, Passport Number, and Signature.

Fill in this information *before* you get to the airport, as it will save time in executing your claim.

3. At the airport, before you check in, go to "Tax Free For Tourists," "Customs," and "Goods to Declare," to turn in your paperwork; these are right next to

"Oversize Luggage."

AT THIS TIME YOU WILL NEED TO:
1. Give the inspector your form, (*not* the envelope it came in)
2. Plane Ticket
3. Passport
The inspector will then review the paper and might ask to see a specific item as proof that the merchandise is actually being exported; this does not happen often, but better safe than sorry, and this is why I recommend you stop here *before* checking in. The inspector will then stamp your document, after which you can proceed to check in.

4. If the Czech Republic is your last stop in the EU, then once you've checked in and passed through passport control, you can then proceed to the GlobalRefund booth to collect your refund. Be sure to advise them what currency you want to receive the refund in as you hand them the papers.

NOTE: I strongly recommend that you take the cash refund versus having it sent to your credit card.

5. If the Czech Republic is *not* your last stop in the EU, then you will not be able to get your refund at the Prague airport. Instead, you will need to hand the papers in at your *last* stop in the EU before heading home.

EXCEPTIONS YOU SHOULD BE AWARE OF
• Paperwork must be turned in within 90 days of purchase.
• You must be over 15 years

of age to file a claim.
• Antiques do not have VAT on them.
• You cannot claim a VAT refund on food, alcohol or cigarettes.
• VAT on books varies (it can be either 5% or 19%); in either case, however, a claim can be made.

HEALTH CARE

Dentist
See Canadian Medical Center listed below.

Doctors And Clinics
■ ■ ■ ■ ■ ■ ■ ■ ■ ■ ■ ■ ■ ■ ■
Canadian Medical Clinic
Veleslavínská 1, Prague 6, Veleslavín
www.cmc.praha.cz
TEL 235 360 133 (After hours & weekends: 724 300 301)
HOURS Mon–Fri: 08:00–18:00
METRO Dejvická ●
TRAM 20, 26 to Nádraží Veleslavín

■ ■ ■ ■ ■ ■ ■ ■ ■ ■ ■ ■ ■ ■ ■
Poliklinika Na Národní
Národní 9, 3rd Floor, Prague 1, Staré Město
www.poliklinika.narodni.cz
TEL 222 075 120 (Emergency: 720 427 634)
HOURS Mon–Fri: 08:30–17:00
METRO Národní třída ○
TRAM 17, 18, 22, 23 to Národní divadlo

Specialist
■ ■ ■ ■ ■ ■ ■ ■ ■ ■ ■ ■ ■ ■ ■
Elena Figurová, MD
OBSTETRICS & GYNECOLOGY
Vodičkova 28/30, 2nd Floor, Prague 1, Nové Město
www.gynecology.cz
TEL 224 220 037
HOURS Mon, Thu, Fri: 08:00–

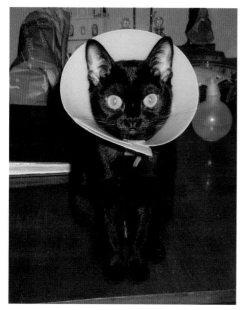

MAISIE (THE AUTHOR'S CAT) IN HER ELIZABETHAN COLLAR, AFTER A SUCCESSFUL VISIT TO PANDA VETERINÁRNÍ KLINIKA.

Pharmacy U Palackého

Palackého 5, Prague 1,
Nové Město
Tel.: 224 946 982
METRO Můstek ● ○
CASH ONLY

Opticians

GrandOptical

Myslbek
Na Příkopě 19/21, Prague 1,
Staré Město
TEL 224 238 371
HOURS Mon–Fri: 09:30–
20:00; Sat: 10:00–19:00;
Sun: 10:00–18:00
Metro Můstek ● ○
or Náměstí Republiky ○

Should you happen to lose or break your glasses while in Prague, you'll be happy to have this address. They'll give you new glasses in one hour.

12:00 & 13:00–17:00; Tue & Wed: 13:00–19:00
METRO Můstek ● ○
TRAM 3, 9, 14, 24 to Václavské náměstí

Hospitals

Motol Hospital

V Úvalu 84, Prague 5,
Smíchov
TEL 224 433 681 emergencies
TEL 224 436 107 / 108
HOURS Daily: 24 hours
METRO Hradčanská ●
then Bus 108, 174

Emergency treatment, plus a hospital dedicated to the treatment of foreigners. Take a taxi.

Na Homolce Hospital

Roentgenova 2, Prague 5,
Smíchov
www.homolka.cz

TEL 257 271 111 switchboard
TEL 257 212 191 adult internal medicine emergency
TEL 257 272 043 pediatric emergency
HOURS Daily: 24 hours
METRO Anděl ○ (exit Na Knížecí), then Bus 167, (or take a taxi)
TRAM 4, 7, 9, 10 to Anděl

For emergency treatment, take a taxi.

24-hour Pharmacies

Pharmacy U sv. Ludmily

Belgická 37, Prague 2,
Vinohrady
TEL 222 519 731
METRO Náměstí Míru ●
TRAM 4, 6, 16, 22, 23 to Náměstí Míru
CASH ONLY

Veterinarian

Panda Vetrinární klinika

Krkonošská 8, Prague 2,
Vinohrady
TEL 222 725 345
HOURS Mon–Fri: 08:30–
21:00; Sat: 09:00–13:00;
Sun: 16:00–19:00
METRO Jiřího z Poděbrad ●
TRAM 11 to Jiřího z Poděbrad

As it seems the majority of the hotels I listed accept pets, I figured I'd list my personal vet, just in case your little munchkin is traveling with you and happens to be a bit under the weather. My personal vet is Pavla, and she is excellent, but regardless of whom you get, I'm confident your baby will be in good and caring hands. Best of all, they speak enough English that you will know what is going on.

NOTE: I recommend taking a taxi, although it's very close to public transport.

OTHER

Computer Repair

- - - - - - - - - - - -
Kinetik

Bělehradská 68, Prague 2, Vinohrady

www.kinetik.cz

TEL 221 501 511

HOURS Mon–Fri: 09:00–18:00

METRO Náměstí Míru ●
or I.P. Pavlova, then tram 6, 11
from I.P. Pavlova to Bruselská

If panic is beginning to set in, and you can already feel your heart palpitating quicker than it ever has, relax, take a deep breath and call this firm—you will be in good hands. My friend Raul needed to pay them a visit when his Apple laptop went on the blink during his visit here. We found this place after the Apple store proved completely incapable of doing anything but tying to sell him new products. Kinetiks works on both PCs and Macs, and are the authorized repair firm for Leveno (formerly IBM). I recommend that you take a taxi and have it wait until you know how long you might be.

Private Tour Guides

If you're traveling alone or in a small group, there's no better way to see the city and learn its lures and legends than with a private tour guide. I find it very cumbersome to travel with groups, as they never seem to travel at the right pace for me—I always feel guilty if I'm holding everyone up by wanting to pop into a store to check out a few items. But with a private tour, you will be the master!

The two guides listed below will customize unique tours to meet your specifications. Payment in cash is required, whether CZK or EUR.

400 CZK per hour is the starting price for both guides; however, the price increases with the number of people on your tour, so you'll want to confirm the exact price once you finalize your itinerary.

NOTE: this fee does not include entry fees to museums and exhibitions!

- - - - - - - - - - - -
Šárka Pelantová

www.prague-guide.info

saraguide@volny.cz

TEL 777 225 205

Šárka has a terrific website that clearly outlines the various tours and services she can provide for you. In addition to various Prague tours, she offers several to the countryside as well.

CASH ONLY

- - - - - - - - - - - -
Kateřina Svobodová

www.praguewalker.com

katerina@praguewalker.com

TEL 603 181 300

Kateřina's website is also helpful, showing the various tours to consider taking during your visit. Jewish burial customs were the subject of her senior thesis at Charles University, and

YOUNG PIONEER, C. 1955

her entire final year was spent focusing on Judaic customs. If this is an area of interest to you, she's an excellent choice for a guide. Kateřina also offers several tours to the countryside as well.

CASH ONLY

Private Driver

- - - - - - - - - - - -
Mike's Chauffeur Service

www.mike-chauffeur.cz

info@mike-chauffeur.cz

TEL 241 768 231

MOBILE 602 224 893

If you decide to take a day trip to Český Krumlov, Karlovy Vary, Telč, or even a short trip to Nelahozeves (see p. 49), this might prove to be a useful contact. Mike can also take you to your next destination outside the Czech Republic, be it Budapest, Dresden, Salzburg, or Vienna, with stops along the way.

Mike's site is easy to use and includes standard pricing, though he's also able to quote a price for unique itineraries. A list of his fleet and the number of passengers each vehicle can accommodate is also on the site.

While his fleet is not as current, chic, or comfortable as cars available at any of the hotels I've suggested, using his services instead of your hotel's for a day trip will save a bundle of crowns, I can assure you.

CASH ONLY
(CZK, EUR OR USD)

Artěl Style Consulting

If you enjoyed this book, let Artěl Style create a personalized agenda for your trip to Prague.

We are here to assist you in...
• Finding just the right accommodations
• Selecting restaurant and bar choices to suit your mood and desires
• Revealing the best that Prague has to offer in both luxury goods and one-of-a-kind finds

Artěl Style Consultants can:
• Help you choose hotels, restaurants, and other services in advance of your stay or while you're in town.
• Advise you on a shopping agenda tailored to your specific taste and interests, and/or prepare a customized list of must-hit stores (complete with opening hours, maps, and directions).
• Join and assist you for a morning, afternoon or day of fabulous finds (two hour minimum).

Please contact us at consulting@artelstyle.com for our fee schedule or for further information about Artěl Style consulting services.

www.artelstyle.com

SERVICE WORKER, C. 1971
(SOURCE: ČTK / CZECH NEWS AGENCY)

INDEX

Main entries are indicated in **bold** type.

Drinking & Nightlife Index

Restaurant & Café Index by Cuisine

RESOURCES

Sights Index

ROOSTER GONE ART NOUVEAU (POSTCARD), C. 1905
(ILLUSTRATION BY B. JARONĚK)

METRO & TRAM MAPS

PRAGUE METRO

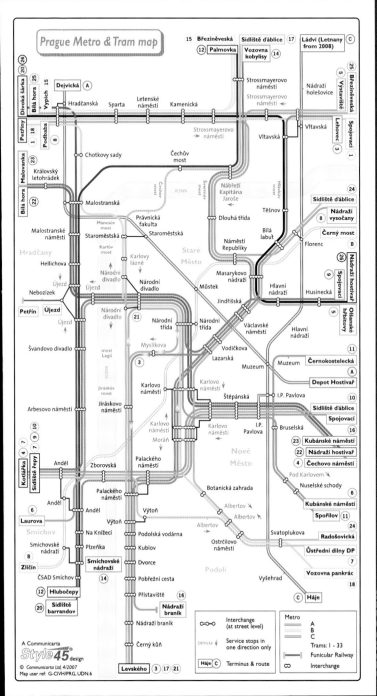

CONVERSION TABLES

Currency

$1 = 22.5 CZK €1 = 28 CZK

CZK	$	€
0,50 CZK	0.02	0.01
1 CZK	0.04	0.03
5	0.22	0.17
10	0.44	0.35
20	0.88	0.71
50	2.22	1.78
100	4.44	3.57
200	8.88	7.14
300	13.33	10.71
400	17.77	14.28
500	22.22	17.85
600	26.66	21.42
700	31.11	25.00
800	35.55	28.57
900	40.00	32.14
1,000	44.44	35.71
1,500	66.66	53.57
2,000	88.88	71.42
2,500	111.11	89.28
3,000	133.33	107.14
3,500	155.55	125.00
4,000	177.77	142.85
4,500	200.00	160.71
5,000	222.22	178.57
10,000	444.44	357.14
15,000	666.66	535.71
20,000	888.88	714.28

Temperature

32°F = 0°C

TO CONVERT F° TO C°
Subtract 32 and
multiply by 5/9 (.555)

TO CONVERT C° TO F°
Muliply by 1.8
and add 32

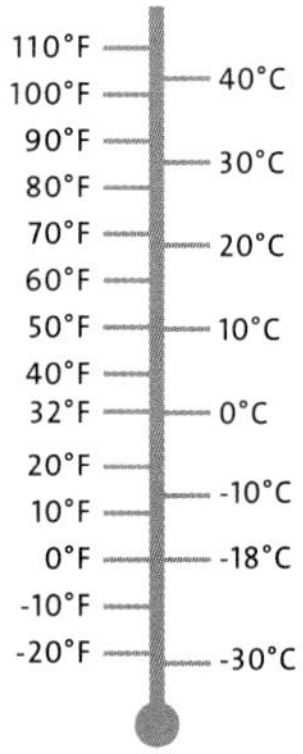

°F	°C
110°F	
100°F	40°C
90°F	30°C
80°F	
70°F	20°C
60°F	
50°F	10°C
40°F	
32°F	0°C
20°F	
10°F	-10°C
0°F	-18°C
-10°F	
-20°F	-30°C

Women's Clothes

CZ	UK	USA
32	4	2
34	6	4
36	8	6
38	10	8
40	12	10
42	14	12
44	16	14
46	18	16
48	20	18

Women's Shoe Sizes

CZ	UK	USA
35	2.5	5
36	3.5	6
37	4	6.5
38	5	7.5
39	6	8.5
40	6.5	9
41	7	9.5
42	7.5	10

Men's Shirts

CZ	UK	USA
35	14	14
36/37	14 ½	14 ½
38	15	15
39/40	15 ½	15 ½
41	16	16
42/43	16 ½	16 ½
44	17	17
45	17 ½	17 ½

Men's Shoe Sizes

CZ	UK	USA
38	5	5.5
39	6	6.5
40	6.5	7
41	7.5	8
42	8	8.5
43	9	9.5
44	9.5	10
45	10.5	11
46	11.5	12

ART NOUVEAU SKIER

KOH-I-NOOR PENCILS
(WWW.KOH-I-NOOR.CZ)

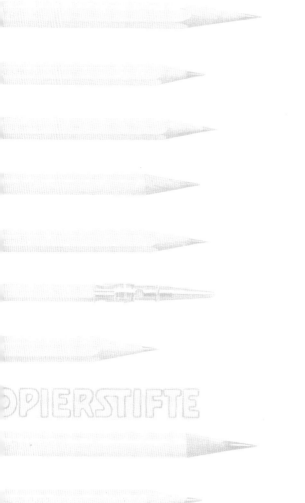

ARE YOU SATISFIED?

COMMENTS, OPINIONS, AND INPUT
Thank you for buying this book! Your comments, opinions, and input are extremely important to me, as they will help me to improve and update the guide for the next edition. If you can take a moment to fill out and submit the questionnaire below, I would be very grateful.

THE FORM CAN BE SUBMITTED EITHER BY:

Post
Send To: Artěl
164 Vinohradská
130 00 Prague 3
Czech Republic

Email
The form is located on our website,
www.artelstyle.com

▪▪▪▪▪▪▪▪▪▪▪▪▪▪▪▪▪▪▪▪▪

ABOUT YOU

NAME

STREET

CITY

POSTCODE

COUNTRY

E-MAIL

▪▪▪▪▪▪▪▪▪▪▪▪▪▪▪▪▪▪▪▪▪

Which age group are you in?
○ Under 25   ○ 26–35   ○ 36–45
○ 46–60   ○ 60+

Where did you buy this guidebook?

Why did you choose this guide?
○ Content   ○ Recommended by a friend
○ Price   ○ Recommended in a
○ Other   publication

Did you purchase any other guidebooks for your visit to Prague? ○ Yes ○ No

If yes, which ones and which was your favorite?

What did you think of the content and format of the book? Please check the most appropriate choice:

Size
○ EXCELLENT   ○ SATISFACTORY   ○ NEEDS IMPROVEMENT

Hotels
○ EXCELLENT   ○ SATISFACTORY   ○ NEEDS IMPROVEMENT

Shopping
○ EXCELLENT   ○ SATISFACTORY   ○ NEEDS IMPROVEMENT

Restaurants
○ EXCELLENT   ○ SATISFACTORY   ○ NEEDS IMPROVEMENT

Sights
○ EXCELLENT   ○ SATISFACTORY   ○ NEEDS IMPROVEMENT

Entertainment
○ EXCELLENT   ○ SATISFACTORY   ○ NEEDS IMPROVEMENT

Hipster
○ EXCELLENT   ○ SATISFACTORY   ○ NEEDS IMPROVEMENT

Layout
○ EXCELLENT   ○ SATISFACTORY   ○ NEEDS IMPROVEMENT

Maps
○ EXCELLENT   ○ SATISFACTORY   ○ NEEDS IMPROVEMENT

Practical Info
○ EXCELLENT   ○ SATISFACTORY   ○ NEEDS IMPROVEMEN

Visuals
○ EXCELLENT   ○ SATISFACTORY   ○ NEEDS IMPROVEMENT

What was your favorite listing in the guide?

NAME   PAGE

What made it your favorite?

While you were in Prague, did you find anything new and fabulous that you think should be included in the next edition?

NAME

DESCRIPTION

What could be changed or improved for the next edition?

Would you like to be on our mailing list for announcements about new publications and new editions? ○ Yes ○ No

COMMENTS

RESOURCES